A Guide to Negotiation and Mediation

Gary Goodpaster

Transnational Publishers, Inc.
Irvington-on-Hudson, New York

Published and distributed by Transnational Publishers, Inc.
Ardsley Park
Science and Technology Center
410 Saw Mill River Road
Ardsley, NY 10502

Phone: 914-693-5100
Fax: 914-693-4430
E-mail: info@transnationalpubs.com
Web: www.transnationalpubs.com

ISBN 1-57105-208-9

Manufactured in the United States of America

CONTENTS

PREFACE

Reflective negotiation practitioners, and those who aspire to that goal, need and want a clear explanation of overall negotiation processes, dynamics, and possibilities. They want to understand "what's really going on" in given negotiations and how to deal with that.

This book is about understanding what goes on in negotiations, about knowing how to think and talk about negotiation and conflict resolution, and about knowing how to negotiate and resolve conflicts. It is intended for the practical study of negotiation, and it summarizes the important ideas and insights of negotiation theorists and successful practitioners. It aims to teach interested parties how to "read" situations of conflict, dispute, or potential cooperation or collaboration and to provide them with the awareness, sensitivities, skills, and techniques useful in resolving conflicts.

This book is different from other negotiation books. Those range from the highly academic and theoretical to the practical or anecdotal. The academic books, while offering many useful insights, do not systematically teach how to negotiate, at least not in ways readily accessible or understandable. These books, from academic disciplines such as economics, game theory, social psychology, international relations, and management science, are predominantly theory-seeking books. The know-how they may offer is a by-product of the laboratory, logical deduction, and some reflection on negotiation simulations, not an expression of actual experience. They are useful in helping a student think more broadly about negotiation processes, but less useful as guiding models for how to negotiate and resolve disputes.

The more easily read practical books, with a few notable and worthy exceptions, advocate or promote some narrow view of negotiating—generally what the author claimed worked in his or her negotiating practice. Readers seeking to become better negotiators, while gaining a few tips, often find the advice and "teaching" so general, so personality-specific, or so tied to a particular view of the world as to be unuseful. Mantra advice, such as "Don't be discouraged," "Don't be intimidated," or "Listen to what the other side is saying," may provide a psychological buck-up, but does not enhance understanding. Such mental tools, if they are tools, neither engage the aspiring negotiator's intelligence nor fit his purposes to shape results. Generally, the anecdotal books amount to little more than entertainment.

Specialized books and courses also provide substantive information about negotiations in particular fields. Knowledge of a substantive area is quite important, but in itself is not enough. If you are negotiating a real estate development contract, a computer services and software contract, or a film contract, knowledge of the industry or field is essential. That may tell you *what* to negotiate about, and perhaps what constitutes a good deal—or at least help you decide those matters—and give you useful information regarding standard practices and expectations. It will not, however, provide an understanding of the negotiating process.

While this book seeks to provide what others do not, book-learning alone does not make accomplished negotiators, mediators, or conflict specialists. This book offers negotiation and dispute resolution models and tools, but those have real value—lead to a working understanding—only in use. Experience in negotiating and attempting to resolve disputes, experience in trying techniques and skills, experience in dealing with others in negotiation and conflict situations, is essential.

Fortunately, this kind of experience is not too difficult to gain. All of us negotiate all the time whenever we deal with others in an attempt to get something that we want, and so there are ample opportunities to practice and try out new ideas. Furthermore, the kind of experience that's necessary to acquire a new skill or to practice a new way of doing things need not even be "real world" experience. Negotiation and dispute simulations are a great way to learn about negotiating and also provide opportunities, without downside risks of real world loss, to try new ideas and techniques and to get useful skill practice. Consequently, while this book provides core knowledge essential to understanding negotiation and dispute resolution generally, it is also useful for practice and workshop courses on negotiation and conflict resolution. In such courses, participants actually engage in simulated negotiations to develop the behavioral or practical skills, the understandings through action, that result in skillful and successful negotiation.

There is more, however. All teaching texts simplify, often using models that convey some important features of reality, but not all. A model is a kind of map, and a map, if you know how to use it, will help you navigate the terrain. The map, however, is not the territory it represents. Negotiating models attempt to describe how parties may actually bargain, yet those who use models to design and effect their negotiations perpetuate the models and thereby create negotiation and conflict resolution norms. Negotiation and conflict resolution literature, particularly works aimed at providing readers and students with knowledge of specific strategies, tactics, and skills, create and perpetuate the very behaviors they seek to describe and explain. At some point, the only answer to the question of the innocent observer, "Why do you negotiate or resolve conflicts this way?" is "Because that's the way we do it."

This is not a satisfactory answer, for it disregards the moral, social, and personal costs and consequences of a given way of bargaining. In other words, in the literature and teaching of negotiation, description tends to become prescription, ignoring the larger moral and policy questions about the desirability of given ways of negotiating. We should ask, and answer, serious questions about the consequences of ways of bargaining.

Negotiators should seek not only to find agreeable ways of bargaining that get the job done, but should also consider what they may be creating, furthering, or perpetuating by the way they choose to bargain. We are, and should think ourselves, responsible for what we do. If we embrace a way of doing things simply because it appears to fit and bring a kind of success, perhaps we need to consider it more deeply.

In this book, description is not always prescription. To prepare anyone to bargain or resolve disputes and conflicts effectively, my aim is to describe as well as possible what can actually occur in bargaining. I do not, of course, recommend all that I describe. Specifically, although I detail it at length, I do not advocate "tricky" or deceptive bargaining. Everyone who negotiates should be aware of what this sort of bargaining entails—that's a matter of intelligent self-protection and self-defense.

Rather, I advocate that parties, while protecting and furthering their legitimate interests, should seek to bargain honestly and with integrity, and should attempt to fashion fair, just, and even wise agreements. Still, there is a great difference between intelligent, knowledgeable, and honest dealing in situations understood for what they actually are, and innocent or naive groping and hoping for the best. Only those who understand how people *may* behave in negotiations, disputes, and conflicts can deal with them effectively over a wide range of possibilities. Perhaps, with a wise humility that arises from seeing situations as they are, they can also aspire to realize their best aims and highest purposes, for themselves and others.

In closing these introductory remarks, I would like to recognize some special individuals who helped me complete this work. I wish to acknowledge and thank Andrew Fogg, 2L, University of California, Davis, School of Law, for his excellent assistance in helping me extend, revise, edit, and improve the text; and Saralee Buck, Rena Contreras, and Ann Graham, my long-time, cheerful, helpful, extraordinary secretaries. My editors and publishers at Transnational Publishers, Inc., have been superb. Finally, I wish to note that earlier versions of parts of this text initially appeared as articles in several different negotiation and dispute resolution journals. These articles are *A Primer on Competitive Bargaining,* J. of Dispute Resolution; *Coalitions and Representative Bargaining,* 9 Ohio St. J. of Dispute Resolution 243 (1994); *Rational Decision-Making in Problem-Solving Bargaining,* 8 Ohio St. J. of Dispute Resolution 299 (1993); and *Lawsuits as Negotiations,* 8 Negotiation Journal 221 (1992).

CHAPTER 1
BASIC NEGOTIATION DYNAMICS

Negotiating is the process of working to come to an agreement with other parties, an interaction and communication process as dynamic and varied, and as subtle and nuanced, as humans themselves are or can be. People negotiate in countless situations in which they need or want something that another party can provide or withhold; when they desire to gain the cooperation, assistance, or approval of another; or wish to resolve or lessen disputes or conflicts. These situations range from simple and friendly cooperative efforts to arm's-length, perhaps mutually profitable business transactions, to antagonistic competitions, and even to complicated instances of severe and apparently intractable conflict between extremely hostile parties. These negotiations can involve just two people, many parties, or shifting alliances or coalitions. They can involve a single issue or many issues, and can be one-time, repetitive, or ongoing.

Indeed, we all negotiate all the time in our business, personal, public, and private lives, with family, friends, partners, colleagues, employers, employees, officials, salespeople, strangers, competitors, opponents, and enemies. We often negotiate without consciously realizing that we are doing so. In most of our ordinary daily negotiations, it does not matter a lot that we haven't thought much about how to negotiate or approach our interactions with others as "negotiations." In working out our accommodations with others, "live and let live" and "go along to get along" philosophies of daily living serve well enough.

Yet there are those "big" or important negotiations that we worry about and want to succeed in: buying or selling a house or a business, seeking a new position, working out the terms of a contract, and so on. Further, many of us have positions or roles that require us to negotiate all the time: we are in business as entrepreneurs, executives, managers, administrators, lawyers, officials, or have other responsible positions. In all these cases, we need to know what we're doing when we negotiate and to do it as well as possible.

Most of us haven't trained in negotiation nor, aside from perhaps reading a book or two, studied it in any intensive way. What we know comes primarily from on-the-job experience. While we may think we're good at what we do, we're still not quite sure we completely understand what's going on in all our negotiations, nor how to improve our ways of negotiating.

Negotiating, bargaining, and resolving disputes and conflicts—all related processes—sometimes seem to be complex, even mysterious activities. We may feel we have trouble getting what we want in our dealings with others. We may think that if only we were more skilled, or more knowledgeable, we could be more successful. Sometimes after negotiation with others we may feel that we've been taken, although we're not sure and can say neither quite what happened nor how. At other times we hear of others' successes or realize they've "done better" than we feel we've done, and we wonder how they managed. We also occasionally read about skilled negotiators or mediators who seem to work a kind of magic to get the results they did, but usually the reports don't tell us how they did it.

Yes, it seems as if negotiating might be an arcane art, too complicated to learn readily. The study of negotiation and conflict resolution involves examining human behaviors and communications aimed at securing agreement of some kind in a myriad of arenas and contexts. A study that includes such diverse, complex activities as union-management bargaining, lawsuit settlements, business deals, negotiation between nations, bargaining within bureaucracies and organizations, simple and complex sales transactions, as well as situations of interpersonal and group conflict, is ambitiously wide-ranging and comprehensive. Indeed, the ways of bargaining range over so great a variety of human behaviors in such manifold contexts that it all seems too complicated even to consider.

Fortunately, for practical purposes, it isn't that difficult. When we examine many negotiation case studies and the ways in which the parties interact to reach—or not reach, as the case may be—agreement, we find *patterns* in the ways the parties interact and negotiate. Studying and learning negotiation involves learning these patterns and how to work with them. In your study you will find that although there are specific strategies or ways of bargaining and negotiating, there are no unvarying rules about how to negotiate.[1] Learning how to negotiate, consequently, is not a matter of acquiring rules as much as it is one of appreciating and "reading" negotiation situations, tactics, and possibilities. It also involves knowing how and when to use particular techniques of proven value in furthering particular negotiation aims. This kind of learning, rather than limiting you to a formula, allows you to focus your own intelligence, perceptions, and skills on the right problems. This understanding helps you get what

[1] Indeed, even though parties may sometimes act as if there were prescribed rules, there are no invariant rules governing the ways in which parties arrive at agreements—except perhaps in highly formalized or ritualized contexts where well-known rules regulate the moves that one can make.

you want by enabling you to know "what's really going on," and to adapt your approach to that.

In studying negotiation, we also discover that some ways of moving toward and reaching agreement are better than others. What we mean by "better," of course, depends on what criteria we use to assess negotiation processes and results. If we judge negotiation success by examining which party got the most immediate gain from a negotiation and how it managed to get that gain, we could look at the specific ways that party got its results. If we judge success in a different way—say, how well *all* the parties did—we find that other techniques and processes lead to those results. Introducing yet other criteria—such as long-range gains, positive change in the parties' relationships, or benefits to third parties or to the larger community—gives us other ways to assess negotiation processes and results. Depending on the parties' purposes, we learn that there are a variety of ways of negotiating successfully. We also discover that each way of negotiating entails certain consequences that the parties may, or may not, take into account, and which may be desirable or undesirable.

To get a better understanding of all this—to begin to see and feel how it all works—it's most useful to consider the basic interactive dynamic that frames negotiations. Negotiation is not a static process, but an interactive, dynamic process. The way we interact with others shapes the way they interact with us, and their reactions and responses to us affect our further interactions with them. It's like a game: I make a move; the other player responds with a move; and I respond in turn.

The game metaphor is useful because it captures the fluid, unscripted, contingent character of negotiating. Not only is negotiation like an interactive game, it is like a game of strategy and tactics, a game such as chess or football. Such games operate on several levels simultaneously. There is what you are actually doing, what the other player or players think you are doing, what you think the other players are doing, and what they are actually doing. There is also your effort to think through what the other players will think you are doing. "If Sam thinks I am doing Y, Sam will do A. If Sam does A, then I will do Z, because Z will help me reach my goal. So I will attempt to get Sam to think I am doing Y." Of course, Sam may be engaging in a similar kind of thinking process. You may therefore have to try to figure out whether Sam is trying to get you to think he is doing one thing while his aim is actually otherwise. If you conclude he is engaging in such behavior, you may want him to think that you think he thinks that you think—and so on.

Negotiations can be game-like, but are not necessarily games. Negotiators can treat negotiations as games, but need not. They can, but may choose not to, engage in strategic and tactical calculations. The point to emphasize, however, is that negotiation is, or can be, a multilevel process, and that the parties' *perceptions* or appraisals of what's going on are deeply important. This is because the parties base their decisions regarding what moves to make and where to settle on their idea of what the other wants or is willing to do.

I. SIMPLE BARGAINING

In simple negotiations the parties establish the field of negotiation play by staking out initial positions. For example, in the Oriental Rug Bazaar, Mustafa offers to sell me the intricately patterned and colorful Kurdish woven silk rug I've admired for $2400. I really like the rug, but that's far more money than I want to spend for it. I respond therefore that I wouldn't pay more than $1000. If each of us is agreeable to further dealing on this particular rug, our initial figures establish the range within which we will bargain.

Now Mustafa and I each are likely to have some figure in mind that we're not willing to go beyond in our bargaining with one another over the rug, our "bottom lines" or "reservation points." Let's say I'm not willing to pay more than $1800 for the rug and Mustafa isn't willing to sell it for less than $1600. Of course, at the beginning of our bargaining, neither of us knows how far the other is willing to go. Likely, each of us is trying to do as well as he can—I to buy the rug as cheaply as possible; he to get as much profit as he can.

Because our initial offers are so far apart, yet we each remain interested in making a deal over the rug, we must make moves to close the gap. If we are each trying to do as well as we can, we will make attempts to see how far the other is willing to go or concede. In doing so, we will provide each other with information about our willingness to move. Although initially far apart, the fact that we continue to talk shows that we each remain interested and that there may be some possibility of closing the gap. Once I offer $1600 or the dealer offers $1800, we have narrowed our differences to our actual or realistic bargaining range. As our bottom lines overlap, we can make a deal and it will be somewhere between $1600 and $1800.

In simple negotiations, each party has some figure or settlement point at which he or she would like to arrive. These will likely differ as between the parties. The difference between them sets the actual range of possible settlement between the parties. In other words, the respective desired settlement points of the parties set the upper and lower bounds to possible settlement. Within this range, if the parties' actual reservation points overlap, and they continue to bargain by trading offers, they can find some mutually acceptable settlement point.

Now, let's take a somewhat more complicated example to see how negotiating parties could manipulate one another's perceptions of their respective willingness to settle at given points. Assume someone is selling a house and has decided she will not take less than $425,000 for it. Of course, she would like to get more, and therefore offers the house at a higher selling price, say, $450,000. Suppose an interested buyer would pay as much as $440,000 for it if satisfied, but would like to pay less. On these assumptions, these parties could settle on a price anywhere in their actual bargaining range, a price between $425,000 and $440,000. This situation is illustrated in Figure 1–1.

Figure 1–1

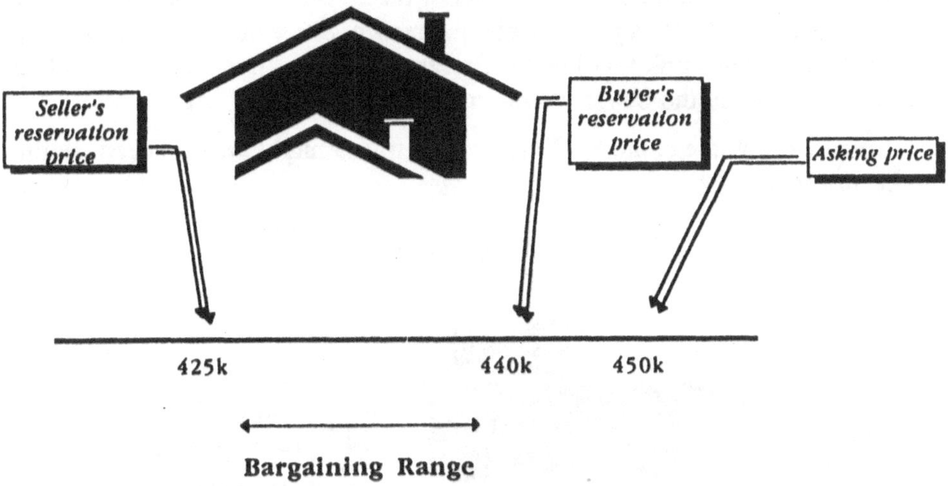

Typically in negotiations, neither party has full information about what the other party is willing to do. Consequently, neither can accurately determine the real bargaining range, at least not without getting information from the other side. In other words, as in the previous example, neither party is likely to tell the other what his or her bottom line is. If a party did know, or could somehow figure out, the other side's bottom line, however, she would be at an advantage in any effort to maximize her gain at the expense of the other. If the buyer knows the seller would take $425,000, then the buyer would offer only $425,000 and stick firmly to that offer. The buyer would realize that at some point—and assuming there is no better offer coming from somewhere else—the seller would accept his offer. Similarly, if the seller knows that the buyer will pay as much as $440,000, but no more—and really wants this house—the seller could refuse to go below $440,000 as the asking price.[2]

[2]Theoretically, if the parties were completely open and forthcoming about providing information, each of them could determine the other side's bottom line. If these figures were disparate, as in the example, say $425,000 and $440,000, neither party might be willing to give, but prefer instead to attempt to reach the other side's bottom line, which is better than its own. This might then be a case where full information hindered the reaching of an agreement, but that is because, hypothetically, each party is equally firm in seeking to realize all the gain possible. This suggests that in some situations in competitive bargaining, a negotiator's

Let's assume that the negotiators in this transaction each want to maximize their own gains. They could do this by treating the negotiation as an information game in which the parties trade information that each side can use to infer the other's reservation price. In an information game of this sort, the person who gets the most accurate information about the other side's reservation price, while providing the least about his own, will win. With such knowledge or good guessing, he can make his offers at or near the other side's reservation price and persist until the other side agrees. Consequently, the seller would seek to get as much information as possible about the buyer's actual reservation price while revealing as little as possible about her own. She would also likely attempt to get the buyer to think that her own reservation point is other than it actually is. In this example, the buyer would engage in a similar effort.

Consider how the contest of information trades might now proceed, as illustrated in Figure 1–2.

Figure 1–2

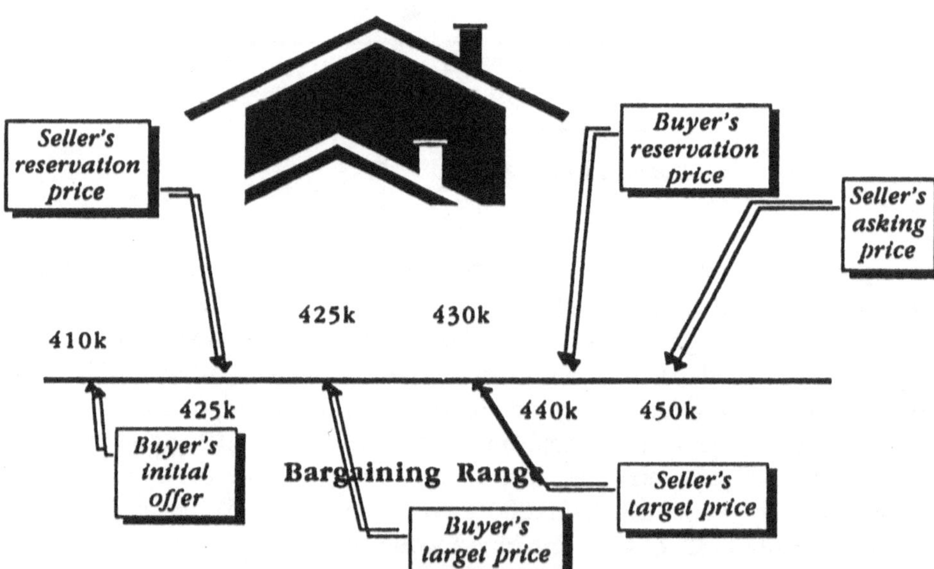

Seller has made the first move in the information game by presenting an asking price of $450,000. This figure is beyond buyer's reservation price, and the buyer will not agree to it. Buyer could offer $440,000, his reservation price. However, if seller's reservation price is below that, which buyer presently has no way of knowing, seller may accept and buyer will have to pay the excess—in

uncertainty about the other side's bottom line is what leads to agreement. The negotiator's conclusion or guess that he's gotten about as much as he can get is what prompts him to settle.

this case, an additional $15,000. In order to test the firmness of seller's asking price, buyer makes a counteroffer of $410,000, which is below his own reservation price. Seller could interpret the counteroffer as providing information about how high buyer will go. If she were not firm in her own reservation price of $425,000 and really believed she could get no more from buyer, she might accept. But she really doesn't believe buyer is at his limit, so she counteroffers $440,000. This drop indicates that the original asking price of $450,000 wasn't her bottom line. It also gives buyer an opportunity to counteroffer and provide more information about his own bottom line.

Assume the counteroffers continue. As long as they do, each party knows the other side hasn't yet reached its reservation price. Further assume that seller realizes that buyer is trying to determine her reservation price, but knows that all he has to go on is the information provided by her counteroffers. If, in responding to each of buyer's counteroffers, she reduces the asking price in increasingly smaller increments, she will give the appearance of coming close to her reservation price. This is so even if she hasn't.

Suppose that once buyer offers $425,000, seller counteroffers $439,000 and thereafter lowers her asking price in even smaller increments. Buyer may, as she hopes, read seller's counteroffers as progressively declining concessions, cumulatively pointing to a figure which must be her bottom line. In other words, her concession behavior suggests she is becoming more firm or rigid, and that signals she won't move much farther. This, of course, could be true. In the example, however, her real bottom line is $425,000. She is, however, attempting to signal that her bottom line is $435,000. This is actually her target price or "aspiration point"—that is, the amount she ideally would like to get—rather than her reservation price or the least amount she would take. Treating the negotiation as an information game, she is giving buyer information that will shape his perception or appraisal of her actual position. This "information " is "misleading"—misleading, not because it is false, but because buyer has read it incorrectly, albeit seller took action to make it likely that he would do so. In other words, seller has successfully, from the point of view of maximizing her gain, caused buyer to infer that her bottom line is $435,000.

In a typical, arm's-length negotiation, each party tries to determine what the other is willing to do. Because each party is uncertain about the other, perhaps even initially somewhat mistrustful, the parties disclose information about what they are willing to do selectively and incrementally. The parties trade information through counteroffers, concessions, and through arguments and reasons they give for their offers, counteroffers, and concessions. They use supporting arguments and reasons to show that a particular position taken is firm, that is, to persuade the other side that the party is at her bottom line. As the parties gain this information, they incrementally evaluate it and incrementally reassess their own positions in light of it. In other words, the overall process is one of progressive disclosure and closure.

In the interactive and communicative process of negotiation, negotiators constantly make ongoing evaluations and assessments of one another and make responsive moves or choices based on these. These evaluations and assessments are interpretations of the ''evidence'' at any given moment. The ''evidence'' is often ambiguous or unclear, and interpreting it, to draw a conclusion, sometimes involves filling the gaps.

CHAPTER 2
NEGOTIATION VARIABLES

The major factors or variables that shape, and finally fix, party perceptions during negotiations are *information, power, strategy,* and *style,* all of which are interrelated. For example, the information a party has about the other side's needs may give it some relative bargaining power. Similarly, party A can adopt a particular bargaining strategy in order to shape party B's perception of party A's position. Another way of considering this is to say that A, by adopting a particular strategy, gives B certain information, from which B may draw certain conclusions about A. The conclusions B draws will affect its perceptions of A's power.

I. POWER AND INFORMATION

A. Bargaining needs and bargaining

Parties enter bargaining relationships because they think they need one another to get something they want. The level of neediness, of course, varies from situation to situation. It ranges from the simplest of wants or desires that many parties could satisfy to serious needs or necessities that only one party, or a few parties, could satisfy. If you want to buy a new shirt, but don't really need one and don't have anything particular in mind, you can browse many stores, yet not buy one. If, however, your business employees are going to strike and you can't replace them, your options are more limited, and you pretty well have to deal with them.

These simple examples clarify that a party's need to deal with another confers a kind of power or leverage on the other. Much of negotiating comprises the parties' efforts to determine just how much, and in what respects, they each need the other to get what they want. This is much of what negotiation information trades convey. Through the information the parties have, and that which they hope to obtain over time, they try to evaluate their relative dependence on one another and what the eventual costs will be to get what they want. This is a question of the relative balance of "power" as between them.

The term "power" has unfortunate connotations of force or domination—a party's unilateral ability to have its way. As used in negotiation analysis, however, it's a shorthand term referring to the dependency relationships between the negotiating parties. In negotiation, a party's power is a relational matter. It arises from the parties' dependence on one another to obtain something they want or need from that particular relationship.[1] A's power depends on B's need of A to obtain something that B wants and on A's need of B to get something it wants.

If Sally doesn't need what Harry controls or can provide her, or if she needs or wants it but has other ways of getting it, she need not negotiate with Harry. She is independent, rather than dependent. Her independence, assuming that Harry does not have a similar capability of satisfying his wants outside of negotiating with Sally, confers bargaining power on her. Harry's neediness to obtain particular results from Sally increases his dependence on her. This decreases his power with respect to her, at least regarding those particular outcomes he desires to reach by dealing with her.[2] Sally has power in her negotiation with Harry if she has at least one reasonably good alternative way to get what she wants outside of settling with him. She also has power over Harry if he does not have a good alternative way of getting what he wants without settling with her.

On the other hand, if Sally is unable to obtain what she wants other than by bargaining with Harry, she is dependent on Harry and has relatively less bargaining power. Similarly, the more specific the items Sally needs to get from Harry, the less her relative bargaining power over him. The greater her need to obtain specific things or particular outcomes for herself from a particular negotiation, the less power she has.[3] She not only lacks alternatives to doing without Harry, but also lacks alternatives for dealing with Harry.

If Sally needs to sell her house because she has purchased a new one, and Harry is the only prospective buyer she has, she has no alternative to dealing with him. If Harry has no particular need for Sally's house, as compared to other houses on the market, he does have alternatives to dealing with her. If Sally has to sell her house immediately, her freedom not to deal with Harry is even more restricted.

---

[1] SAMUEL B. BACHARACH & EDWARD J. LAWLER, BARGAINING: POWER, TACTICS, AND OUTCOMES 56 (1981).

[2] Somewhat paradoxically, however, Harry's neediness could turn out to be a source of power for him. Because he needs to obtain particular results, he may expend great effort to achieve them. In other words, neediness motivates and may generate impression management moves that persuade Sally to do what Harry wants, even though in some absolute, objective sense, Sally has greater "real" power. *Id.* at 64.

[3] *Id.* at 60.

In these circumstances, if Sally wants to increase her bargaining power, she needs to find alternative ways to get what she wants without Harry. Otherwise, she must reassess what she needs to get from negotiating with him, or she must act to increase Harry's dependence on her. She needs either to find other prospective buyers, come up with a way to relieve the pressure for immediate sale, or induce Harry to want her house above all others available to him.

Bargaining power in negotiation is thus a relational, relative, and changeable matter. It's not possible to say how much bargaining power a negotiator has without considering how much the other negotiator has, for it's a question of their relative dependency on one another to realize particular outcomes. Furthermore, the parties' dependencies on one another are not necessarily fixed or static, for the parties often can act to change them.

B. Using agreement alternatives

Working with alternatives to a possible agreement is an important way to enhance bargaining power and negotiation outcomes. Sally could seek to lessen her dependency on Harry by developing alternative ways of getting what she wants outside of her particular bargaining relationship with him. If she finds another buyer, she may not have to deal with him at all. Similarly, she could reduce her commitment to a particular outcome from the bargaining and thereby increase her power. If she decides she doesn't have to sell her house immediately, she gives herself more time. Finally, although there is no apparent way for her to do so in the house-sale example, she could in theory also seek to worsen Harry's alternatives to dealing without her.

C. Impression management: shaping perceptions to enhance bargaining power

In many negotiations, the parties have only partial or incomplete information, if any, about the alternatives the other side has, outside their particular bargaining relationship, to satisfy its wants. Similarly, the parties do not know exactly what the other side's commitment to other alternatives may be nor what costs the other side may experience in resorting to other alternatives. Finally, the parties may not know what standards, criteria, or values the other side uses to assess possible alternatives.

Consequently, negotiating parties usually do not actually know just how dependent they are on one another. The exact character of their dependence is unclear or ambiguous. In other words, the bargaining parties may not know how much respective or relative bargaining power they have. A significant part of negotiation discussion involves party efforts to obtain information that, when added to what they already know, will enable them to assess their relative dependence on each other.

In the world of human relationships, a person has power if others perceive that he has. The perception of power is as important, perhaps more important, than actual, measurable advantage. Having real advantage—in the sense that the other party truly needs you to get what it wants—of course confers power. Lacking that, however, getting the other party to *think* that it needs you or that you *don't* need it may also confer bargaining power. Consequently, negotiators often attempt to shape the other side's perceptions of the relative power between the parties.

Indeed, much of the communication process in many negotiations involves perception or impression management, each side working to shape the other side's perceptions of its relative dependence on the other. Such impression management can be honest, sincere, or forthright, as when a party simply tries to inform the other side of its actual power position. It can be merely interpretive, as when the parties are unclear or uncertain about their dependencies and their situation is subject to interpretation and persuasion based on interpretation. Finally, it can be consciously manipulative, as when a party actively tries to mislead the other side about their respective dependencies.

D. Bargaining power and bargaining arguments

Specific arguments negotiators use to advance their positions and persuade others vary depending on particular bargaining issues and contexts. There are, however, some characteristic patterns of argument that revolve around, or implicate, the power relationships between the parties. Since the perception of relative power may be as important as actual power, the parties are likely to attempt to persuade one another about their relative power positions.

Suppose I am negotiating with you over some matter. In order to maximize my gains, I will try to shape your perceptions about what I want and about your need of me to get what you want. I am likely to argue that I have other alternatives to dealing with you. Or I may say that while I have some interest in what you have to offer, it is not as great as you had supposed. I may disclose that my priorities are not as you think them to be. Similarly, I might try to persuade you that you don't have good alternatives to dealing with me, or that if you think that you do, they're not as good as you thought they were.

My arguments may be "true," in the sense that I really believe them or that they are in fact so. Alternatively, my arguments may be advocacy, in the sense that I interpret everything in my favor and I attempt to persuade you to view matters the same way. After all, the "reality" of a situation is often what we agree that it is or mutually decide it to be. So-called "facts" are often disputable and we may need to settle them by agreeing as to what they are. Even where the facts are clear, their meaning, as they bear on decisions about what to do, may not be clear, but are matters of human valuation, judgment, and decision, open to persuasive efforts.

Finally, I could know that the situation is other than I claim it to be. Yet if I realize, or believe, that you don't know that, I can try to persuade you that it is as I say it is. This argumentation intends to persuade you by shaping your perception of your relative bargaining power. Hopefully, if I am trying to "win" the negotiation, I would convince you that I am in the stronger position, and, if we are to settle, you must concede more than me. If, instead, I am simply trying to ensure that an agreement with you serves my interests, hopefully I will persuade you that what is in my interest is in yours as well. Of course, depending on what you are trying to achieve, you can and will make similar arguments to me. We will influence each other, to varying degrees, given the understanding we bring to the situation and the "learning" we experience through discussion, and draw our own conclusions about where we need to settle.

E. Information and negotiation transaction costs[4]

While negotiation bargaining power is a question of relative dependency, it's useful to specify in greater detail the elements or variables on which it depends. The apparent variables, already discussed, are a party's needs or wants and its alternative ways of satisfying them. In relation to these, we must also consider the information a party has, a party's negotiation transaction costs, and its belief in the other party's ability to meet its needs.

A party has some relative bargaining strength if it has an alternative way of satisfying its needs other than through negotiation with a particular party. Nonetheless, if the party doesn't know that, it is effectively without bargaining power. So we need to factor into the bargaining power equation the state of a party's information about its alternatives. If a party is clear and certain about its alternatives, it can readily test the value of possible settlements by comparing them with its alternatives. Where it is uncertain or insecure about its alternatives, it will have to discount them accordingly. Furthermore, discovering what effective alternatives it has may impose time, expense, and other costs on a party. To the degree that a party fails to gather the information it needs to specify its alternatives realistically, it weakens its relative bargaining position.

There are also other costs associated with negotiating that may factor into the bargaining power equation. The first of these is investment costs, that is, all

---

[4] For a more detailed and sophisticated discussion of the points made in this section and for a comprehensively stated bargaining power model, see ALVIN GOLDMAN, SETTLING FOR MORE 27–52 (1991).

those costs associated with initiating the negotiation and carrying it to its current stage. These will include research and time costs, expenses related to setting up the meeting, and any lost opportunity costs the actual negotiation may occasion. All other things being equal, the more a party has invested in a given negotiation, the more likely it is to settle. It will still need to compare any proffered settlement with its alternatives, but the costs it has experienced in negotiating may change its view of its alternatives. If it refuses to settle, it loses whatever it has invested in the negotiation. In that sense, the negotiation has made it more costly for the party to resort to its alternatives. In brief, the costs of negotiating may discount the value of the alternatives the party has. Thus, increasing a party's investment in the negotiation tends to decrease that party's bargaining power.

The other important negotiation transaction cost is the anticipated cost of going forward with negotiations. The greater this is, the more attractive alternatives to negotiation may become. It follows that one enhances her bargaining power by reducing the *other side's* anticipated negotiation costs. If the cost of continuing negotiation is low, there is less incentive to resort to alternatives to negotiation, and the party likely will continue.

A final variable is a party's belief in the other party's ability to meet its needs or wants. Suppose you wish to remodel your house and you contact contractors for bids. Before you settle on a contractor, you will want assurance that he is capable of doing the work you want, of a quality and at a price you desire, and that he is dependable. If a particular contractor does not persuade you that he meets these conditions, you will not hire him. Consequently, where a party's performance is important in a negotiation, the other party's belief in its capability, trustworthiness, and reliability is a critical variable. Therefore, when performance is important, the performing party can increase its bargaining power by enhancing the other side's belief in the existence of these qualities. On the other hand, one can possibly weaken the performing party's bargaining position by questioning its ability to perform.

Negotiating parties base their negotiating decisions on their perceptions of the negotiating situation. Consequently, it is the parties' perceptions of their alternatives, the certainty and quality of their information, their costs, and their respective abilities to perform which determine their relative bargaining power. This means that a negotiating party can increase its bargaining power by bettering its alternatives, improving its information, reducing its negotiation transaction costs, and improving the impression it gives of its ability to perform. It can also increase its relative bargaining power by acting to decrease the other party's bargaining power. It can do this by worsening the other party's alternatives or its *perceptions* of its alternatives. It can undermine the other party's confidence in the information on which it bases its bargaining position. It can work to increase the other party's negotiation investment cost and it can seek to convince the other party that further negotiation transaction costs will be low.

Finally, it can also increase its bargaining power by attempting to persuade the other party that it can meet its needs better than any alternative ways the other party has of meeting them.[5]

F. Bargaining power and arguments of principle

In addition to perception-shaping moves, which are an inevitable part of any negotiation, the perceived power relationships between bargaining parties also elicit characteristic negotiating arguments. Three common types of normative arguments—appeals to equity, equality, and responsibility or need—are particularly revealing.[6] Equity arguments claim that parties should receive benefits in proportion to their contributions. Equality arguments contend that parties should receive equal payoffs regardless of their contributions or inputs. Responsibility arguments assert that need should be the basis of distributing benefits.

Assuming that bargaining parties choose those arguments that best advance their interests as they see them, the normative arguments they choose to make reveal their perceptions of their bargaining power. Thus, a bargaining party that believes it is in the stronger position is likely to compete and seek gains through domination. It will most likely advance "take it or leave it" and equity arguments to distribute bargaining gains. It will get more this way and believes it can command the results it wants. Where a party views itself of roughly equal power to the other party, it is more likely to bargain cooperatively and engage in compromise. It will likely make the equality claim that gains should be distributed equally or will propose trades of roughly equivalent value. Finally, where a party perceives itself in a significantly inferior power position, that is, where it views itself as highly dependent on the other, it is likely to make general fairness or moral obligation appeals. Of course, in the same situation, the party with the greater power is likely to make a demand or equity argument.

The normative arguments a party makes reveal its power perception of itself. Therefore, examining a party's choice of arguments is a useful tool to

---

[5] Obviously, there are many variables that affect bargaining power. Further, negotiating parties can manipulate or shape one another's perceptions of these variables. Clearly, negotiation can be a complex, fluid, dynamic, interactive process:

> In more complex and realistic bargains, when interests, knowledge, and resources are neither certain nor stable, the bargaining range is specified and respecified by each player's changing valuations of his changing perceptions of agreements and alternatives to agreement. Players simultaneously try to resolve uncertainties about technology, references, and outcomes, try to defend against factual, normative, and alternative-based manipulation, and try to control the knowledge, norms and resources of opponents.

Arthur Isak Applbaum, *Knowledge and Negotiation: Learning Under Conflict, Bargaining Under Uncertainty* 5 (1987) (Unpublished Ph.D. dissertation, Harvard University).

[6] BACHARACH & LAWLER, *supra* note 1, at 175.

determine how it perceives the power relationship and what kind of concessions it may claim or give. Note further that a shrewd party might choose its normative arguments as a part of an impression management scheme to shape the other side's perceptions of the power relationship between the parties.[7] Finally, a shift in normative arguments over time may also be meaningful. For example, if a party shifts from an equity argument to one of equality, the shift may signal either that it has changed its view of its power or has given up an unsuccessful pose.

G. Bargaining informational moves

Our mutual efforts to shape one another's perceptions of our relative bargaining strength determine more than just the character and direction of some of our bargaining arguments. They also determine what information we seek and what we are willing to disclose. For example, I may try to persuade you that I am not very dependent on you or that you are more dependent on me than you think. I would not disclose to you any information that reveals I am more needy than I claim. Similarly, I would likely seek from you information that tells me exactly how much you think you need me to get what you want. If you are an inexperienced or naive negotiator, or for some other reason do not realize this is the strategy I am using, you may be fully revealing. If you are more sophisticated, or are playing the same negotiation game I am playing, then you will likely selectively disclose and withhold information in the same manner as I.

Bluffing in a game like poker is a good example of this. The rules of poker confer no special advantages on any player, although chance in the shuffle and deal may. The poker players have some information, usually inconclusive, about other players' hands, and cannot draw strong conclusions about how good another's hand or relative power is. The bluffer uses appearances, and subtle signals or messages of confidence, to convince other players he has an unbeatable hand. Essentially, the bluffer in poker negotiates a win by manipulating the information he knows the other players have and by providing additional, misleading information. In this, the bluffer may cannily play off the other players' personalities and the revelations their prior play has provided about how they play the game.

---

[7] "Responsibility norms are the only hope for bargainers in a highly disadvantaged position because equality norms require more concessions from the opponent than a very weak party can reasonably expect. The only way for a lower-power party to receive more concessions than implied by equity . . . is to appeal to the opponent's responsibility for its plight. . . . In a bargaining relationship, responsibility appeals cast the opponent in the role of helper and portray the needy as unfortunate and desperately needing more concessions from the opponent." *Id.* at 177.

He will feed them messages he calculates will cause them to draw the conclusion he wants them to draw.[8]

Not only do negotiators shape one another's perceptions of the situation, it is also important to note that the focal negotiator[9] herself may shape her own self-perceptions disadvantageously. Unskilled or innocent negotiators, for example, often make the common mistake of focusing on and internalizing weaknesses in their own bargaining position rather than focusing on objective information. Entering negotiations aware that they do not have good alternatives to settlement causes them to bargain needily. Their self-perception of weakness often entails a conclusion that the other side is stronger and more able to dictate terms. In fact, the other side may be as badly, or worse, off. A more skilled negotiator would not assume that her own side's weakness meant corresponding strength on the other side. She might even suspect, at least to the point of testing the hypothesis, that the other side's appearance of strength might mask real weakness. She would seek information that would permit her to assess the other side's real strength objectively. She would also seek to give the appearance of relative strength. She could do this either through a confident and unyielding demeanor or through tactics aimed at masking her own weakness. This would mislead the other side, and negatively shape its assessment of its own strength.

II. NEGOTIATION STRATEGIES

Negotiation strategies are basic ways of managing power relations, information exchanges, and interactions between the negotiating parties. Although often complex and varied, negotiation and bargaining behaviors generally fit into essentially three basic negotiating strategies: *competing, compromising,* or *collaborating in joint problem solving.*[10] There are variations on these strategies, of course, and negotiators' personal styles, or ways of playing their strategies, can also complicate matters. Nonetheless, understanding the three basic negotiation strategies or models, their characteristic tactics and techniques, and the ways to package and combine them, prepares anyone for most negotiations.[11]

---

[8] Bluffing is an interesting tactic, involving a certain degree of risk. A bluff may be just a "feeler" thrown out to obtain information, but it could backfire if called. Bluffing is least risky when the bluffing side has substantial information about the other side's strengths and weaknesses while the other side has little information about the bluffer's situation. The bluffer can then tailor the bluff in such a way that it's unlikely to be called. *Id.* at 173.

[9] A "focal negotiator" is a negotiator, mediator, or other consensus-seeking facilitator involved in multiparty negotiations where coalition-building activity is likely. *See* Chapter 10, Coalitions and Representative Bargaining.

[10] DEAN G. PRUITT & JEFFREY Z. RUBIN, SOCIAL CONFLICT 29 (1986).

[11] It is helpful to look upon different kinds of negotiations as related, but different, kinds of games, playable, as most games are, at different levels. If you understand which negotiation game you are playing and know how to make the moves appropriate to that game and its level, you basically know how to negotiate.

Other than avoiding or withdrawing from others, or accommodating them completely, these strategies represent the three basic ways of dealing with other people in situations involving some possibility of deal-making. Most negotiators adopt one or more of these behaviors in an effort to reach agreement. As a negotiation strategy, each of these ways of dealing with others has a different substantive aim, and rests on different, but usually unarticulated, premises or assumptions about human behavior. Each uses certain characteristic techniques and tactics to move toward settlement or agreement or to resolve disputes or conflicts.

A. Competing

Bargaining competitively, sometimes also called *hard-bargaining, distributive, positional, zero-sum bargaining* or *win-lose bargaining,* has as its purpose maximizing the competitive bargainer's gain over that of those with whom he negotiates. He is trying to come out "ahead of," or "do better than," any other party in the negotiation. For this reason, we sometimes also refer to the competitive bargaining strategy as a *domination* strategy. This means that the competitive bargainer tends to treat negotiations as a kind of contest that he or she seeks to win.

The competitive negotiator tends to define success in negotiation rather narrowly. It is simply getting as much as possible for himself: the cheapest price, the most profit, the least cost, better terms than others could get, and the like. At its simplest, this strategy focuses on immediate gain, and does not concern itself with questions of the relationship between the negotiating parties. A more complex version of this strategy focuses on long-run gain. This usually requires some effort to maintain or further a relationship and moderates the competitive, often aggressive, behavior that jeopardizes a relationship and possibilities of long-term gain.

B. Compromising

A second negotiation strategy is *cooperative–compromise bargaining,* sometimes called *soft-bargaining* or *win-some–lose-some,* or *give-and-take bargaining.* Compromise bargainers believe they must trade off some of what they want in order to get at least something. This means that, in some sense, they concern themselves not only with their own gain, but with that of the parties with whom they are dealing. They may do this out of genuine concern for others' well-being or because they conclude they must give up something to

---

If you know how to transform the particular negotiation game the other side seems to be playing into one you prefer to play, then you know how to negotiate well.

reach any agreement at all. In this sort of bargaining, for whatever reason, the negotiator doesn't get all that she wants, but only some of it.

For cooperators, success in a negotiation is often a combination of how the negotiation feels and what they get. They want to be reasonable, and for them this means accommodating to a certain degree. If the negotiation involves roughly equivalent compromises on both sides and the final deal is satisfactory or "fair," then the cooperator thinks the negotiation has been a good one. This view of success implies some concern for the relationship between the parties. When the parties compromise equally—or at least appear to each other to have done so—they feel they have been treated equally. Results within an acceptable range satisfy them. Such equal and fair treatment can reflect a concern for maintaining good relationships and, in any case, does not damage them.

A person can cooperate or compromise as a matter of principle or a matter of necessity. In the simplified, typecast image presented here as an introductory sketch, the cooperative bargainer compromises as a matter of principle. By contrast, a competitive bargainer compromises because he has to—there will be no deal if he does not. Consequently, although both cooperative and competitive bargainers may compromise, there are nonetheless differences in why they do so, how they go about it, and how much they are willing to compromise.

C. Collaborating or problem solving

Another important negotiation strategy is that of collaborating or working together with others to further all parties' interests and aims. Negotiators refer to this kind of bargaining as *integrative* or *problem-solving bargaining.*[12] It is also sometimes called *interest bargaining* or *positive-sum,* or *win-win bargaining*. In integrative or problem-solving bargaining, the parties aim to satisfy their own interests and those of the other negotiating parties as well. Another way to say this is that they seek to maximize their own gain *and* the gain of the other parties. To do this, the parties must collaborate to solve the problem of discovering what mutual action they can take to satisfy their respective interests.

Integrative bargaining is also a form of cooperative bargaining—how could one cooperate more than by engaging in joint problem-solving with another? The integrative bargainer defines ideal negotiating success as satisfaction of both parties' interests, *without compromise*, if at all possible. The interests the parties seek to satisfy in the negotiation are as many and as broad as they wish to define them. This model therefore conceives of negotiation success more broadly than

---

[12] Roger Fisher & William Ury, Getting to Yes: Negotiating Agreement Without Giving In (1981); David A. Lax & James K. Sebenius, The Manager as Negotiator (1986); Carrie Menkel-Meadow, *Toward Another View of Legal Negotiation: The Structure of Problems-Solving*, 31 UCLA L. Rev. 754 (1984).

does competitive bargaining, which focuses primarily on acquiring the most of anything in contention between the parties. The integrator is not trying to get "the most" or outdo the other side competitively, but simply seeks to further or realize her aims. Unlike compromise bargaining, integrative bargaining treats negotiations as creative opportunities for problem solving which the parties can exploit to serve each of their interests fully so that each benefits as much as possible from the negotiation.

D. Choice among bargaining strategies

Nothing, excepting perhaps local culture, custom, or practice in a particular industry or negotiating arena, requires negotiating parties to negotiate in any particular way. None of these ways of bargaining is *necessarily* "better" than any other way, although most sophisticated practitioners would probably acknowledge that integrative bargaining is the most economically productive and efficient way to bargain.[13]

The way a party chooses to bargain—assuming she makes a choice rather than just jumping in and doing what seems natural or what prior experience suggests—depends very much on her particular aims in a given negotiation. Her aims will, to a certain degree, depend on the aims of the party negotiating on the other side. Context, circumstances, parties' expectations and personalities, the nature of the parties' interests and the issues between them, and the parties' relative knowledge of bargaining methods deeply shape their choice of bargaining strategy. Nonetheless, negotiators either consciously or unconsciously adopt negotiation aims and methods that conform to one of the foregoing basic forms or some combination of them. Anyone who does much negotiating should be familiar with each strategy, know how to recognize it, how to use it, and how to deal with it.

Some issues, the way the parties define them, or the circumstances of the situation appear to dictate particular kinds of bargaining. For example, when each party wants the same indivisible thing, but each cannot have it, or when what one wants apparently conflicts with what the other wants, they are quite likely to bargain competitively. Where the matter in dispute is divisible and the parties anticipate a future relationship and neither need nor desire to dominate, each party may simply compromise. Where the parties have common or complementary interests such that mutual action will satisfy or enhance their respective interests, they are likely to bargain integratively. These examples, however, do not exhaust the possibilities, and negotiators can transform one kind of bargaining into another.

---

[13] LAX & SEBENIUS, *supra* note 12, at 245–246; HOWARD RAIFFA, THE ART AND SCIENCE OF NEGOTIATION 148–165 (1982).

III. NEGOTIATING STYLE

Negotiators' personalities and their own characteristic ways of dealing with others also inevitably affect negotiations. Some people are naturally disposed to be competitive or cooperative, or are pragmatic and inclined to take a problem-solving approach in dealing with issues. Others acquire one disposition or another through training or experience. Further, individuals often react differently in different contexts or respond differently to different persons. Finally, some persons are self-aware, have some control over their basic dispositions, and can adapt themselves effectively in interactions with different people. Others seem always to be pretty much what they are and act much the same way with everyone.

These simple observations imply that a negotiator's basic bargaining strategy can be, but is not necessarily, a simple reflection of his or her basic personality. One who tries to "win" a negotiation by doing better than the other side, by extracting more gain than the other side, may also have a competitive personality and bargain competitively for that reason. Alternatively, the same negotiator could, if aware and in conscious control of his own behavior, bargain competitively on substance yet maintain a cooperative, "reasonable," or nonaggressive bargaining manner. Similarly, one who has a competitive nature can decide that it is in his best interests to be cooperative or collaborative, either in a particular situation or in general. There will also be occasions when persons who view themselves as compromisers or problem-solvers will take a hard line and bargain competitively.

Consequently, while there are three basic ways of negotiating substance, a negotiator's behavioral style can mask or otherwise affect the strategy in actual use. Thus, a competitive negotiator who acts agreeably and gives the appearance of cooperation may be mistaken as a cooperator even though he is a hard bargainer on matters of substance. Obviously, one shouldn't mistake style for substance. Although style could reflect strategy, a person's attitude and demeanor in a negotiation are not sure guides to the basic bargaining strategy.

During the course of a negotiation, any given negotiator may both change demeanor and mix or combine different ways of negotiating. A negotiator can compete, compromise, or seek to integrate interests or problem-solve, and also use tactics and techniques appropriate to any of these ways of dealing with others. Negotiations also become more complex as the number of issues and parties involved increase. Adding issues and parties increases the interaction and trade-off possibilities and affects the psychological dynamics of the negotiating process.

What this all means is that while there are three models of basic ways of negotiating which we can use to organize our analysis, thinking, planning, and negotiating, there are many permutations and combinations among them. The issues, the parties' personal interactions and the dynamics among them, their sophistication, as well as contextual and cultural factors, shape and shade every negotiation.

CHAPTER 3
COMPETITIVE NEGOTIATION

People bargain competitively essentially for three, often overlapping, reasons. First, by inclination or calculation, they view the negotiation as a kind of competition, and they wish to win, or gain, as much as they can. Second, they do not trust the other side. Where parties are untrusting, they are nondisclosing, and withhold, rather than give, information. Withholding information leads to further distrust and defensive or self-protective moves. Parties may be untrusting because they are unfamiliar with the other side, or because they are generally or situationally untrusting. Finally, a party may bargain competitively as a reaction to, defense to, or retaliation for competitive moves directed at it. Indeed, one effective way of dealing with a competitive bargainer is to compete back,[1] a case where mutual competition between parties may ultimately lead to cooperation.

I. COMPETITIVE NEGOTIATION STRATEGY

In competitive negotiation or distributive bargaining the parties' respective aims or goals conflict, or the parties at least perceive them to conflict, and each negotiator sees his aim as maximizing the realization of his side's goals. Since his goals conflict, in fact or supposition, with the other side's, his side's gains are the other side's losses. His aim therefore is to win by gaining as much value as possible from the other party. The basic idea is that the negotiation is about a fixed good or sum that must be divided between the parties. One party's gain is the other party's loss; the competitive negotiator is out to gain as much as he or she can, and will take risks—even the risk of nonagreement—to secure a significant gain.

The competitive negotiator seeks to gain through a strategy that involves the taking of firm, almost extreme, positions, making few and small concessions,

[1] ROBERT AXELROD, THE EVOLUTION OF COOPERATION 21 (1984).

and withholding information that may be useful to the other side. The intention behind, and general effect of, this basic strategy is to persuade the other side that it must concede in the direction of the competitor's expressed positions if it is to get an agreement. Some competitors in some circumstances also use various ploys or tactics aimed at pressuring, unsettling, unbalancing, or even misleading the other side to get it to agree to their demands.

In an important sense, a competitor plays negotiation as an information game, hoping to get as much information from the other side as possible while disclosing little. Alternatively, a competitor sometimes provides misleading information causing the other side to draw wrong conclusions which benefit the competitor.

The competitive negotiator seeks to find what the other side's bottom line is, such as just how much or what the other side will maximally give or minimally want to make a deal. On the other hand, the competitive negotiator wants to persuade the other side about the firmness of its own *asserted* bottom line. It works to convince the other side that it will settle only at some point that is higher (or lower, as the case may be) than its *actual* bottom line.

> In skillful hands the bargaining position performs a double function. It conceals, and it reveals. The bargaining position is used to indicate—to unfold gradually, step by step—the maximum expectation of the negotiator, while at the same time concealing, for as long as necessary, his minimum expectation. By indirect means, such as the manner and timing of the changes in your bargaining position, you, as a negotiator, try to convince the other side that your maximum expectation is really your minimum breaking-off point. . . . Since you have taken an appropriate bargaining position at the start of negotiations, each change in your position should give ever-clearer indications of your maximum expectation. Also, each change should be designed to encourage or pressure the other side to reciprocate with at least as much information as you give them, if not more.[2]

Taking a firm position and conceding little will incline the other side to think the competitor has little to give. If there is to be a deal, the other side must give or concede more.

A. Pure bargaining, haggling, and just trading figures

When the parties are apart, and they have *no reason*, other than their mutual choice, to settle at any particular point between them, they are in a "pure bargaining" situation. It's easy to see how a simple negotiation, such as the rug purchase described in Chapter 1, can degenerate into a contest of haggling or just trading figures in this fashion. The parties' positions—the particular dollar

---

[2] Edward Peters, *Strategy and Tactics in Labor Negotiations* 122 (1955), *quoted in* Richard E. Walton & Robert B. McKersie, A Behavioral Theory of Labor Negotiations 86–87 (1965).

figures they're offering—are not connected to any reason or rationale. Basically, both buyer and seller are seeking to maximize gains, and each attempts to do so by seeing how far he can push the other side.

This happens often in competitive bargaining, particularly with unsophisticated competitive bargainers and usually in the latter and ending stages of a negotiation. When it occurs, the "take as much as you can" technique is transparent. It is a fairly dead giveaway that the parties, or at least one of them, is bargaining just to win as much as possible. Automobile dealers' sales practices exemplify the phenomenon. A new car dealer usually pegs an asking price to a manufacturer's suggested retail sticker price, plus the cost of items the dealer adds to the car. Once dealer and buyer leave those starting prices behind, however, they usually just trade dollar figures until they reach one they find comfortable. Similarly, travelers who visit native markets or bazaars, or those who visit flea markets or garage sales in this country, sometimes experience much the same kind of trading. Each side throws offers and counteroffers back and forth. Each side tests the other side's resolve to stick with a figure by refusing to budge further or threatening to walk away. In essence, bargaining in this fashion is really nothing but a contest of firmness or a game of chicken.

B. Focal points or mutually prominent alternatives[3]

It's revealing to analyze a pure bargaining situation where two equally competitive negotiators bargain with each other. Once the bargaining parties, having assured their bottom lines or reservation values, have staked out their respective positions on the bargaining range, nothing inherently seems to impel settlement at any particular point between the positions. Nothing, that is, except each side's expectations regarding what the other side will accept. This is problematic, however, for:

> [W]ith each guided by expectations and knowing that the other is too, expectations become compounded. A bargain is struck when somebody makes a final, sufficient concession. Why does he concede? Because he thinks the other will not. "I must concede because he won't. He won't because he thinks I will. He thinks I will because he thinks I think he thinks so. . . ." There is some range of alternative outcomes in which any point is better for both sides than no agreement at all. To insist on any such point is pure bargaining, since one always *would* take less rather than reach no agreement at all, and since one always *can* recede if retreat proves necessary to agreement. Yet if both parties are aware of the limits to this range, *any* outcome is a point from which at least one party would have been willing to retreat and the other knows it! There is no resting place.[4]

---

[3] THOMAS SCHELLING, THE STRATEGY OF CONFLICT 21 (1960); DEAN G. PRUITT, NEGOTIATION BEHAVIOR 57 (1981).

[4] SCHELLING, *supra* note 3, at 21–22.

Notwithstanding this apparent problem of infinite recursion, there is an operating "logic of indeterminate situations,"[5] and competitive bargainers do find and agree on a resting place. The logic is not that of one will dominating another in the struggle over gain. Instead, it is one of belief and congruent behavior. Each side believes it has gotten as much as possible, given the reasons offered, or each side moves naturally to a mutually acceptable resting place.

In bargaining, parties can settle at one of two points. They can settle at a position which one side has with some convincing reason persuaded the other side to accept. They can settle at a *focal point* or *mutually prominent alternative*, a salient point on the otherwise featureless negotiation landscape that seemingly and naturally draws the parties to it. Focal points are those outcomes having an "intrinsic magnetism,"[6] "especially those that enjoy prominence, uniqueness, simplicity, precedent, or some rationale that makes them qualitatively differentiable from the continuum of possible alternatives."[7] For example, the midpoint between final offers still some distance apart is a focal point and an attractive and obvious place to compromise. Similarly, a precedent, a bargaining point that makes the parties' positions symmetrical, round numbers, and the like, can all operate to set focal points. Focal points are simply situational clues giving the bargaining parties ideas for coordinating their behavior so that they can arrive at a common position.

In preparing for a negotiation, a shrewd negotiator would consider potential focal points and attempt to script the negotiation so that it converges on a focal point providing him the most gain. No one could generally list all possible focal points, for what may constitute a focal point in any given negotiation depends on the situation and circumstances at the time. It's possible, however, to see how this could work from an example. Suppose our automobile dealer and a customer are bargaining over the price of a new car. The manufacturer's retail suggested price (MRSP), plus dealer add-ons and charges for the car, is $31,500. The dealer's actual price is $27,500, but the customer doesn't know this. The car's price, without dealer charges, is $31,000, and without dealer add-ons as well is $30,500. Those figures are easy to determine because a sticker in the car window specifies those charges. In this example, there are two possible focal points in the range defined by the figures $27,500 to $31,500, and these are $30,500 and $31,000. It becomes apparent to the dealer, however, that the customer will not buy at either of those prices. The dealer knows he can make a profit if he sells the car for at least $28,000. But how, other than through just trading figures or haggling, can the dealer and customer find a suitable figure between $28,000 and $30,500 where they can agree? Now suppose that the

---

[5] *Id.* at 21.

[6] *Id.* at 70.

[7] *Id.*

MRSP for last year's model of the car was $29,000, and the dealer tells the customer he will sell him the car for last year's price of $29,000. The $29,000 figure becomes a new focal point, and it is quite possible the parties will settle there, *even though* last year's price has no real relevance to this deal. That figure stands out on the otherwise completely featureless negotiation landscape, and both parties will focus on it even though there's no particular reason to do so other than its having been mentioned. When nothing better exists, a focal point virtually declares itself as a potential place of agreement.

C. Reasons, rationales, and justifications

More sophisticated competitive bargainers know that simple haggling exposes the game for what it is, a contest for gain and a test of one's ability to read the other side. To avoid revealing her hand, the sophisticated competitor devises reasons for the positions she takes and the concessions she makes. Providing a rationale for a position makes it more credible and persuasive. The other side will have difficulty countering a good rationale without providing equally, or more, persuasive reasons for the positions it takes in turn. The new car dealer may, for example, say that his car price is just the manufacturer's suggested retail price. He means that the price reflects, as dealer profit, only such markup as the manufacturer thought fair. That might persuade some buyers, and, in any case, appears to treat all buyers the same way. Even if a savvy buyer responds that the manufacturer's suggested price is not dealer invoice, but considerably above it, and offers to buy for a figure lower than the former, the dealer has responses. He could either shift to haggling or, more shrewdly, make a price concession based on a rationale difficult to challenge, e.g., a sales price based on dealer invoice, plus overhead assignable to the car, plus a standard profit of 10 percent or some such figure. The offer sounds reasonable, but may not actually be. Such a price rationale, based in part as it is on an intangible and generally unverifiable "overhead" figure, hides much, but is quite difficult to challenge. Buyers unarmed with comparative price information to counter such a position may not be able to break through the strong facade of the dealer's position.

II. A COMPETITIVE NEGOTIATOR'S OPERATING ASSUMPTIONS

The competitive negotiator seeks to persuade the other side that she will not agree to settle above or below a certain point. In devising a negotiating strategy, the competitor uses some general approaches and rules of thumb. These are described below.

A. Negotiation is an information game

The competitor treats negotiation as a game in which the side with the most, and most accurate, information wins. The competitor thus seeks as much information as possible while giving little. The competitor may also give or manipulate information to lead the other side to draw conclusions the competitor wishes it to draw. Knowing that the other side will decide on the basis of what it thinks and believes, the competitor seeks to shape, manage, and manipulate the other side's perceptions of the situation and its available choices.

B. Take an opening position at the margin (high or low openers)

The negotiator who opens high or low and who makes few and small concessions generally has the most success in negotiation. As used here, "opens high" or "opens low" means at the extreme or far end of the potential bargaining range, but sufficiently within it to retain credibility. The competitive negotiator prepares her opening position by first estimating her best possible deal, and then staking out an initial position considerably beyond that, developing justifications for the latter.

C. Treat concessions as a way to gain and disclose information

Concessions convey information about what a party wants and values, about its preferences and intentions, and about its perception of the other side. The skillful negotiator "reads" concessions to infer this information and plans her own concessions to give the other side only those impressions she wants it to have. Concessions are thus not only, perhaps not even principally, a way to give something to the other side to narrow differences, but also a way to gain advantage. The skillful negotiator crafts concessions to shape the perceptions and expectations of the other side.

D. Hang tough on concessions

Concessions seem to beget concessions. There is a customary expectation in bargaining that when one side makes a concession, the other side will make a concession in return. Indeed, one side usually makes concessions *in order to* gain a concession. Notwithstanding this expectation, it is not *always* necessary to give a concession in exchange for receiving one. Indeed, failing to note a concession or to make a return concession may have the effect of causing the other side to make one or more additional concessions.

Furthermore, when making a concession in exchange for a concession from the other side, it also is not necessary to give something having a value equivalent to the value received. For example, take the typical case of someone negotiating to purchase a relatively expensive new car. The dealer says he wants $30,000 and the buyer says he wants to pay only $24,000. They negotiate awhile, and the buyer relents and offers $26,000. The dealer, rather than making an equivalent $2000 concession, counters with $29,000, effectively exchanging $1000 for $2000.

While this kind of exchange is common, what many do not realize is that *any* concession from the other side often satisfies the desire to get something back in exchange for a concession. In addition, in weighing a concession, the side receiving it may place on it the value that the conceder apparently gives it. Suppose side A in a negotiation concedes something having a value of, say, $100, and side B makes a return concession having a value of $50. Side A may conclude that B values $50 as much as A values $100. This could be true if B has fewer resources, is more needy, and so on, but need not be so, for B may simply wish it so to appear. In short, a negotiator need not respond to a concession by making a concession of equal value, and competitive negotiators often do not.

E. Make small, infrequent, and declining concessions

As a corollary to the foregoing, the competitive negotiator makes it a practice to make small concessions and force the other side to work very hard to gain any concession at all. The aim of this practice is to send the message that there is not much to give. If there is to be a bargain, the other party will have to move much farther than the competitor. The competitive negotiator also makes concessions in declining increments so as to suggest approach to his bottom line.

One effect of "hanging tough" and making small concessions is to shape or alter the other side's expectations or aspirations about what it can get out of the negotiation. Treating a negotiator's concessions as information about what it is possible to achieve, the other side is likely to alter its expectations in a way favorable to the negotiator.

F. Select opening positions by reference to the midpoint rule

Once two settlement offers are on the table, the natural settling point is the midpoint. This rule of thumb, while not always true, is true often enough that competitive negotiators can use it to good effect. Typically, the competitive negotiator will let—or more likely—*get* the other side to make the first offer.

This then allows the competitive negotiator to set her offer at the most advantageous point, given the likelihood that once both offers are out, the negotiators will settle in the middle. Alternatively, the competitive negotiator simply starts with an extreme offer, hoping that the other side is either innocent or will overvalue the item being negotiated and will open with an offer higher than originally intended. The competitor's high opener draws the other side's opener in her direction. If they then go on to bargain and end by settling in the middle, the competitor will have extracted additional gain.

G. Link positions and concessions to justifications

Experienced competitors know that they may not be able to persuade the other side to agree to settle at any particular point in the perceived bargaining range simply by hanging tough. Simple firmness is sometimes enough, but will not work with everyone. In bargaining situations, people want justifications for positions taken. Understanding this, in preparing for a negotiation, the competitive negotiator picks positions on the bargaining continuum that he can defend with some plausible justification. For example, the woman selling her house, described in Chapter 1, might say she priced her house at $450,000 because that's the price she bought it at, adjusted for inflation over the years she's had it. Alternatively she might say she compared prices for comparable houses and that while their prices were somewhat lower, her house has special features that justify the price differential. Note that these justifications have some persuasive value, but are certainly not without flaws or counters and may not be the reason she chose the figure. She may have chosen the figure because that's what she needs to buy a new condominium and still get the $125,000 one-time, over age-55, tax exclusion on profit from a home sale. The latter reason, however, is less likely to carry as much weight with the buyer as the former, and she would find it easier to maintain the former in the face of argued counterproposals. In short, giving reasons or justifications for positions taken is persuasive, even when they are not the real reasons.

The same reasoning applies to concessions. To convince the other side that a new position is a real bottom line, a concession made by moving from one position to another needs to make sense in terms of some plausible justification. For example, after bargaining for a while, the house seller might say, "Well, OK, you've convinced me the price is too high for you. The house may need a new roof in a few years, and I think that $10,000 would be a reasonable amount by which to reduce the asking price to reflect that." Note again that whether or not the reason given is true, it sounds reasonable.

Justifying positions taken not only hides the potential grab involved in competitive bargaining, it also permits planning a strategy for moving from position to position. Actually moving from one position to another or to several different, but understandable, positions may cause the other side to believe it has gained from bargaining and therefore feel satisfied with the deal struck.[8] Of course, had it known more, or pressed and probed further, it might have discovered there was more to gain.

Good competitive negotiators prepare for negotiations by developing plausible rationales for the positions they are going to take and the concessions they may make. They also attempt to anticipate what positions the other side may take and what rationales it may provide, and then develop counter-positions and arguments. While position and concession strategy and developing rationales are important, a competitive negotiator nonetheless does not limit himself to only these kinds of negotiation moves. Instead, he may also orchestrate negotiation strategy and a variety of informational and psychological tactics to manage, manipulate, pressure, cajole, or persuade the other side in ways useful to extracting as much gain as possible.

H. Deadlines help induce agreements

When both sides bargain competitively, but also want a deal, most concessions will likely occur toward the end of the negotiation, as the deadline for its end nears. In the initial stages of a competitive negotiation, the parties mutually explore positions and test one another's firmness and resolve. If both engage in competitive bargaining, they will both follow the firmness strategy. When they do, the negotiation becomes a contest of respective resolve, and neither party is likely to move much until it appears absolutely necessary. Deadlines can bring the parties to the brink of the consequences of nonagreement. This is particularly true of externally imposed deadlines that seriously inhibit further negotiations, for example, the beginning of a trial or a company's need for a certain product to meet its own manufacturing deadline or other contractual obligation. Indeed, it is as the deadline approaches that competitors are most likely to play the game of chicken, that is, to attempt to outwait the other side so that its need to settle and the time pressure cause it to concede.[9] The United States' trade disputes with China often display this pattern, and provide a good example of the phenomenon.[10]

---

[8] Jeffrey Rubin & Bert Brown, The Social Psychology of Bargaining 278 (1975).

[9] Interestingly, when both parties in a negotiation bargain competitively, there is a possibility they will end up bargaining cooperatively. If both parties are equally competitive and equally firm, and neither has a good alternative to settlement, then both may conclude they each must cooperate, by making concessions, in order to agree. The parties are not likely to arrive at this point without significant exploration and testing of one another's positions and firmness. Sometimes parties in this position even deadlock before they begin to cooperate.

[10] *See e.g.*, Rone Tempest, *China Averts U.S. Sanctions by Going After CD Pirates Trade*, L.A. Times, June 18, 1996, at A1.

CHAPTER 4
COMPETITIVE NEGOTIATION TACTICS

In addition to using basic hard-bargaining strategy, a competitive negotiator may also use ploys and tactics to persuade or induce the other side to settle at a point that favors him. Not all competitors use these devices. Some manage quite well with just the basic *high demand-small concession-firmness* strategy. Even those who use such devices do not use them all, nor do they use any standard set of them all the time. Nonetheless, some are in common use, and some are a part of standard practice in particular negotiating arenas.

Knowing these ploys and tactics gives a clearer and deeper understanding of how hard bargainers may operate. They may use these devices throughout an entire negotiation or just for some issues in a negotiation. Even in positive sum or win-win negotiations, a negotiator might resort to them when the parties seek to allocate shares of whatever gains they have managed to create.

More important, though, a large part of negotiating well involves understanding how the other side is negotiating and being able to respond appropriately. That can entail negotiating defensively, so as not to be taken. It may involve taking the initiative and trying to change the very character of the negotiation as a process—for example, transforming a competitive negotiation into a problem-solving one. To again use the game metaphor, except for lucky breaks, you usually can play a game well only if you understand the game you are playing. There are several different basic negotiation games, and more complicated negotiation games may involve elements of each. To negotiate well, you must understand the negotiation game the other side is attempting to play. Recognizing the other side's moves helps you figure out their game and game plan. You can then play that game, if you choose, or, at least, protect yourself and defend your interests. If you think you can better achieve your aims by negotiating in a different way, you can seek to change the negotiation game.

Furthermore, although you might not wish to use some of the competitive ploys and tactics—some of them are quite shady—you should nonetheless have others at your command. Although typically used by competitive bargainers, some of these devices are useful to cooperative bargainers as well. For example, one effective way of dealing with a hard-bargainer may be to hard-bargain back. This shows the other side you can play its game, and respond in kind to its tactics, which may be all that's necessary to induce some cooperation.

Most of the ploys and tactics a competitor may use involve informational or psychological manipulations. The informational tactics manage expectations, create doubt, misdirect, play off mistaken assumptions the other side may make, and sometimes even mislead. The psychological tactics create pressures or inclinations to settle.[1] Some of these tactics are ethically dubious, and some, depending on the duplicity involved, are downright immoral.[2]

I. COMPETITIVE NEGOTIATIONS

A. Tactics

1. Preconditions

Sometimes a party will refuse to negotiate prior to the satisfaction of some condition or demand. Actually, setting a *precondition* is a way of obtaining a concession without giving any in return—in effect, the price of admission, the price paid to get the other side to bargain. Demanding satisfaction of a precondition may not only gain a concession without cost, it may also reveal how eager the other side is to secure a deal. If the other side meets the demand, it signals that it is willing to give way, that its positions may be soft, and that one may possibly push it hard, with success, during the negotiation.

Simply understanding that precondition demands actually are, and should be, a part of the principal negotiation dictates the appropriate response. Essentially that response is simply to make clear that you consider the precondition

---

[1] Many of these tactics operate on psychological principles of reinforcement of behavior. Positive reinforcement is action which either elicits or rewards a particular behavior. Negative reinforcement is action which either inhibits or halts a behavior. Viewing a negotiation, in part, as a reinforcement session, the competitive negotiator focuses on behaviors of the other side that it wants to encourage or inhibit, and rewards or punishes them accordingly. For example, if the other side somehow discloses some doubt about the strength of its position, the competitor would encourage the doubt. If the other side makes a concession, the competitor will in some way reward the concession, often with a very minimal reward, e.g., a softening of demeanor or a small concession in return. Similarly, fractionating concessions—that is, dividing a concession into smaller concessions—and doling them out as rewards to the other side for its negotiation behaviors gives the competitive bargainer opportunities to reinforce on a variable schedule, a classic way to anchor certain desired behaviors, and to keep the other side at the bargaining table a long time.

[2] I discuss the ethics, as well as the practical advisability, of using such ploys and tactics in the next chapter.

issues to be a part of the negotiation. Then, you should either demand reciprocal concessions in return for any concessions you make, or put off consideration of the demands until the full negotiation takes place.

2. *"Your move" or "you first"*

If competitive negotiation is an information game, the party that has the most, and best, information regarding the underlying issues and the real desires of the other side positions itself to maximize its gains. Competitors thus seek to gain as much information as possible while disclosing as little as possible. One way to do this, often disguised as simple politeness, is to get the other side to make the first offer. That information, whatever it is, allows the negotiator to set her own first offer advantageously, adjusting it for maximum ultimate gain.

3. *First offer–large demand*

As a first offer, ideally made only after the other side has made an offer, the competitive negotiator states an extreme demand—beyond or at the far margin of the range of credible or reasonable offers. This has the effect of setting the perceived or apparent bargaining range. When combined with the tactic of splitting the difference,[3] it allows the user to manipulate the other side for maximum gain.

A variation on the first offer–large demand tactic is the *extreme demand–small demand* ploy. The negotiator first makes an extreme demand, one that she knows the other side is certain to refuse. On refusal, the negotiator then makes a "smaller" demand. The smaller demand looks reasonable by contrast, and the other side, "indebted" by withdrawal of the extreme demand, may more readily grant the smaller demand.

If the other side's initial demand is extreme or high in this fashion, it's a good indicator it is engaging in hard-bargaining. In dealing with such an opening, one can either ignore it, tactfully state that it's extreme and not a basis for bargaining, or counter with an equally extreme demand in the other direction. All of these moves have the effect of nullifying the initial claim.

4. *Anchoring*

Anchoring is fixing or establishing the focus of discussion around a certain point, whether it be a figure, a range, an issue, or the like, simply by asserting

[3] *See* Chapter 2, Part I.G., Bargaining Information Moves, *supra*.

it. As a technique, anchoring plays on human suggestibility, that is, on the human tendency to fix attention on, and be influenced by, what someone says.

Psychologists sometimes demonstrate the phenomenon of anchoring in the following way.[4] A psychologist will divide a group into two smaller groups, say groups A and B. She will then ask the members of group B to close their eyes while she asks a question and writes a number on a blackboard for the members of group A to see. She will then ask a question such as, "What is the population of Nepal?" and write a figure—say 4,000,000—on the blackboard so that group A can see it. She then erases the figure and has the groups switch roles, group A members now closing their eyes and group B members watching. She repeats the question and writes another number on the board—this time let's say the number is 30,000,000—and then erases that. After this, she tells the entire group that the figure she wrote on the board was not the correct number for the population of Nepal; the number she wrote was unrelated to that figure. She then asks everyone to estimate the correct number for the population of Nepal. When she tallies the results, she discovers that group A members estimated lower population numbers than group B members. Evidently, the figure the psychologist wrote on the board influenced the later estimates of those who saw it, notwithstanding its asserted irrelevance to the actual population figure. In other words, simple assertion of an item sets it as an anchor holding the hearer's mind in its vicinity.

5. False demand–false concession

In using the false issue or *false demand–false concession* tactic, a negotiator attempts to convince the other side that an issue, about which she actually cares little or not at all, is very important. The negotiator claims she will concede the issue only if the other side makes some particular concession. When the other side makes the concession, the negotiator "reluctantly" gives up or concedes the false demand. In effect, the negotiator obtains an important concession with an asserted, but not real, exchange of value.

A variation on false concession is *reverse false concession*. In this ploy, the negotiator inflates the significance of an issue that she actually considers minor, but which she knows is important to the other side. After intense bargaining, she then concedes the issue. Later, however, she demands a large concession, on an issue she truly deems important, in return for the earlier concession on the minor issue.

The false demand–false concession tactic is difficult to deal with because our ideas of what is important to the other side usually come from information

---

[4] ROBYN DAWES, RATIONAL CHOICE IN AN UNCERTAIN WORLD 121 (1988).

it provides. It is therefore difficult to discount its claims that some issue has great importance to it. Obtaining outside information, assessing probabilities, and probing questioning aimed at establishing convincing justifications for the other side's claims are the major defenses.

6. Escalation

Escalation involves raising demands, in some way, either before or during a negotiation. Escalation before a negotiation can take the form of adding conditions to be met before the negotiation takes place. During a negotiation, escalating demands is also a way of pushing to find the limits of what the other side is willing to give to effect an agreement. This is particularly effective when used against conciliatory or naively cooperative negotiators.

A negotiator can also escalate demands as the first move in a negotiation. Suppose, for example, that two parties are to meet to discuss a proposed contract of sale of real property where the offered price is $650,000. When the negotiation begins, the seller could say that he was sorry, but that he had to raise the asking price, for a variety of reasons, to $750,000. The buyer, who was originally prepared to try to whittle down the $650,000 figure, now has to struggle to reach it. The tactic makes $650,000 look awfully good.

One should deal with an escalation taking the form of precondition demands as such. First-move escalations change the parameters of the negotiation you prepared to enter. Such escalations also invite a countermove: as all your preparation was based on other assumptions, you are not willing to negotiate on the basis of the change. This may induce the other side to return to the original proposal.

One counters escalations during a negotiation by calling attention to them, by indicating counterescalations are possible, and by refusing to agree to any escalated terms.

7. Nibble or late hit

The *nibble* or *late hit* is a form of escalation that comes at the end of a negotiation after the parties have invested time and energy and have resolved major matters. The nibbler then raises a further item, relatively small, but yet undiscussed, indicating it is a "must have" or the negotiation may otherwise fail—in other words, a "deal-breaker."[5] Usually, both because of the large psychological investment in the potential agreement and the apparent risk of

[5] HERB COHEN, YOU CAN NEGOTIATE ANYTHING 37–39 (1980).

loss, the other side concedes. Note, however, that this kind of escalation can involve either significant or relatively small matters.

The nibble is really a test of firmness or resolve and plays on possible impatience and frustration, on concerns one may have about "sunk costs,"[6] and on deal momentum. In dealing with a nibble, it helps to recognize that both sides can play the game of threatening a final agreement. Expressing a willingness to see the deal fail and refusing to give in to the nibbler may cause him to retreat.

8. Low-balling[7]

A difficult point in many transactions and negotiations is getting a party to make a decision. Once a party makes a decision, however, and has committed himself to it in some way, it is unlikely he will back out. *Low-balling* is a ploy playing on this psychological phenomenon. In low-balling someone induces another party to make a decision, or a commitment to a particular choice, confirms that commitment, and then changes the original terms that induced it. Automobile salespersons, for example, often use low-balling. They offer an automobile on very favorable terms—more favorable than the prospective buyer imagined he could get—and induce him to buy on that basis. They have him sign papers, and perhaps even permit him to use the car prior to any money changing hands. They then claim there's a mistake or that the manager won't approve the original deal, and ask for more money. Since the buyer has committed himself to buying the car, he's likely—assuming he's unaware of the ploy—to accept the new demands and pay the additional money. Generalizing, it's easy to see that low-balling is a way of baiting a party and a different form of "nibble." The way to deal with this tactic is to protest the changed terms and express a willingness to walk away from the proposed deal if terms vary from those originally set.

9. Linkage

Negotiators sometimes attempt to expand the scope of a negotiation by bringing in issues which, while not clearly related, one can make a plausible case for considering. Successful *linkage* may have the effect of changing bargaining power, the focus and character of the dispute, or the set of gains the parties are trying to divide. A famous recent attempt to transform a dispute and gain bargaining power through linkage was Saddam Hussein's attempt to tie the

---

[6] DAWES, *supra* note 4, at 22.

[7] *See* ROBERT B. CIALDINI, INFLUENCE 102–105 (1984), for a good discussion of low-balling.

issue of Iraq's withdrawal from Kuwait to the Palestinian issue.[8] Hussein's effort was not only to introduce another, perhaps neither apparent nor evidently relevant, issue. It was rather to shift the alignments of the parties and even introduce new parties and new concerned "audiences." Had he succeeded, he would have thus not only changed the focus of the dispute from unjustified invasion of a sovereign state and possession and control of world oil supplies to include the Arab-Israeli conflict. The added issue would have been a "wedge" issue, for it offered Arab states reasons to break their alliance with the western nations.

Linkage of issues or parties can have a positive or negative effect in a negotiation.[9] Adding issues creates possibilities of trade-offs that may not have existed before. Adding parties may do that as well and also change the dynamic of the negotiation. On the other hand, adding issues or parties can sometimes complicate matters, particularly where the added issues or parties increase the potential for conflict. One should agree to, or resist—as the case may be—linkage, insofar as, after careful study, it appears either to enhance or inhibit possibilities of agreement. A party unprepared or unwilling to deal with added issues and the consequences that handling them may entail, as was the case with the United States regarding the Palestinian issue, should certainly resist efforts to add issues.

10. Salami

Eventually, as one slices thin rounds of salami, the salami disappears. The salami tactic involves making a series of small demands that add up to something considerable. Psychologically and practically speaking, small demands may be easier to tolerate and concede than large demands. *Salami* plays on this—and incredible wheedling persistence—to make significant gains from small, consecutive, and perhaps seemingly inconsequential requests. Note too that a negotiator could use salami as a concession tactic as well as a demand tactic, but the effect might be the reverse, that is, giving up less overall.

11. Boulewarism

Boulewarism is a single offer approach to coming to agreement, and is the antithesis of genuine bargaining to resolve issues. It involves making a single, firm offer—usually based on a unilateral idea of what is fair or right under the

---

[8] Dan Balz, *Bush Bars "Linkage" in Crisis*, WASH. POST, Dec. 5, 1990, at A19; William Claiborne, *Saddam Links New Crisis to Old Middle-East Disputes*, WASH. POST, Aug. 13, 1990, at A1.

[9] DAVID A. LAX & JAMES K. SEBENIUS, THE MANAGER AS NEGOTIATOR 138–139, 221–226 (1986).

circumstances—and, in effect, telling the other side to "take it or leave it."[10] The offeror may act quite sincerely and believe that it is making the most reasonable offer possible. There is a certain arrogance in this as the posture does not permit the other party's input, and therefore does not treat it as a bargaining equal. Apart from any question of the substantive position taken, this is likely to create resistance and anger.

If genuine, the Boulewarist posture tells the other side there is nothing to bargain, and is certainly a way to assert an upper hand or make clear where one quite firmly stands. Of course, a party can use this approach as a tactic to mislead the other side into thinking there is no give when there can be. While Boulewarism may be inimical to developing good relationships, it wears a cloak of righteousness and could be effective with weak or dependent parties. In this sense, it is a kind of authoritarian paternalism as much concerned with maintaining authority and future freedom of action for the offeror as it is with the substantive merits of a proposal.

12. Split the difference

Splitting the difference is a common phenomenon in negotiations. The parties reach a point where they are close to agreement, but still some distance apart. Each side lacks compelling reasons to convince the other side to accept its position, and each is unwilling to give up its position. In these circumstances, the parties often agree to settle by splitting the difference, which seems fair, appears to involve equal concessions, and saves face. Aware that parties close to agreement are likely to split the difference, one who may already have everything she wants in a negotiation can consciously use it as a tactic to exact a further gain. Negotiators often effectively combine this procedure with the large demand tactic.

Splitting the difference is not a bad thing to do—unless, of course, the other side has so manipulated the game that it gets an unwarranted gain after the split. What's important to remember is that while splitting the difference seems fair, it is not necessarily so—it depends on where the parties start. Splitting the difference is not the only "fair" formula to use to close the gap when the parties are some distance apart, and you should seek other formulas which might divide the difference more advantageously.

13. Other offer

To test the other side's willingness to agree or to extract concessions, a negotiator can state he has another offer or possibility and either specify what

---

[10] Harry T. Edwards & James J. White, The Lawyer as Negotiator 119 (1977).

it is, or deliberately leave it vague. If true, the other offer gives a baseline to judge the superiority of any pending agreement. If untrue, this is just a tactic used to gain information or secure an advantage from the other side. Direct lies in negotiations carry considerable risks, particularly when the parties will have future dealings. When there is this kind of risk, those using this tactic may merely hint or imply they have another offer. Vagueness allows them, if the other side discovers there was no other offer, to claim misunderstanding.

Never accept vague assertions of the existence of other offers. You can best deal with claims of other offers by demanding detailed information about them so that you can assess their reality and firmness, and can compare their terms concretely with your own offer.

14. False scarcity

Psychologically speaking, people generally tend to respond to the scarcity of some item or commodity by valuing it more highly. In addition, psychological reactance theory holds that when opportunities which were once open are limited, people react by wanting the opportunity *more* than when it was more openly available.[11] For example, there may be a scarcity of items or items on which some authority imposes restrictions on use. Negotiators sometimes use this psychology by trying to induce the other side into agreeing to certain positions or terms by suggesting that the opportunities to get those terms are somehow quite limited.

15. Induced competitiveness

There is a distinct form of *false scarcity* that combines aspects of the *other offer* ploy. *Induced competitiveness* involves converting what would ordinarily be a two-party negotiation into a multiparty negotiation where all the parties interested in a particular good must compete with one another for it. The effect of the competition is to make the item more desirable and drive up its price. Suppose, for example, that someone wishes to sell some item, but instead of dealing with prospective buyers one at a time invites them all to meet with him simultaneously. The appearance of a number of persons apparently interested

---

[11] The psychological dynamic involved here has been postulated as a theory—Brehm's theory of psychological reactance—well-described as follows:

> [W]hen [persons] are tightly constrained in their behaviors or choices, they will react against such constraints by becoming dissatisfied and attempting to remove the constraints. . . . [L]abeling a resource as scarce may cause reactance . . . and produce more vigorous action to obtain the resource and more dissatisfaction with its unavailability. JEFFREY PFEFFER, POWER IN ORGANIZATIONS 83 (1981).

in the item will likely make it appear more desirable and incline some to want it more. (A particularly duplicitous form of this ploy involves using confederates or shills to act as competitors.) An alternative way of inducing a similar effect is to create an auction for the item. In one reported case, when broadcasting companies attended an auction to bid on a Hollywood movie rather than engage in two-party bargaining, the movie went for more than $1 million more than the highest price ever previously paid for a similar broadcast showing.[12]

16. Final offer

Final offer is just a statement that the negotiator has reached her final position and will concede no further. This may be true or false. If false, a final offer is just a tactic used to mislead the other side into thinking the stated position is firm. In some ways, this is a risky tactic to use if one is not prepared to walk away on rejection of the final offer. To claim "final offer" and then concede is to disclose that the offer was not actually final and create a "cry wolf" reaction to subsequent final offer claims. One could evade this consequence by linking a retreat from the asserted final offer to receiving some significant concession. If consciously used this way, the final offer tactic is like a false demand.

17. Misleading concession pattern

In win-lose or distributive negotiations, each side, using all available information, tries to figure out the other side's bottom line in order to extract all possible gains. Reading the concession pattern is one way to do that. In theory at least, a party will make smaller and smaller concessions as the bargaining converges on his bottom line or reservation point. Knowing that this is a common view, a negotiator can mislead the other side by devising a concession pattern that appears to converge on a point above or below, as the case may be, his actual bottom line. The other side, "reading" the concession pattern, may then extrapolate it to that point, and mistakenly conclude the conceder has reached his bottom line.

18. Red herring

A *red herring* is essentially a false, yet highly distracting, issue that a party can use to bring pressure to bear on the other side in a negotiation. The use of

[12] As reported by one of the participants in the auction:

[After the bidding started,] ABC opened with two million. I came back with two point four. ABC

a red herring is prevalent in politics, where politicians, playing off easily manipulated public fears, attack opponents regarding their stands, or lack of them, on the red herrings. The American communist, or "red scare" in the late 1950s and the early 1960s is a good example. Red herrings may be most useful in negotiations where the parties represent outside constituencies which can be manipulated to bring pressure to bear on the recalcitrant party. Negotiators, however, also sometimes use them tactically in ordinary negotiations. The *false issue–false demand* tactic, for example, is one version of a red herring brought into ordinary negotiations.

19. Threats, anger, and aggression

The use of *threats, angry displays,* and *aggressive tactics* in a negotiation may evidence personality, frustration, or calculation. If the threat is real and the one making it can carry it out, the threat is an exercise of power and poses to the recipient the adverse consequences of a wrong choice. Negotiators, however, sometimes deliberately use such tactics simply to intimidate, disturb, and confuse the other side. Psychological assault can unnerve a party and incline it to seek to conciliate the tantrum-thrower. Negotiators who use such tactics, therefore, are attempting to create, and play on, vulnerability in order to induce appeasement and exact concessions.

20. Blaming or fault-finding

Perhaps most common in negotiations involving interpersonal issues, *blaming* or *assigning fault* is an aggressive tactic possibly having several aims. The tactic may invoke conciliatory behavior, either because of induced guilt feelings or a sensed need to mollify. It may be a distraction—an attempt to focus the negotiation on a substantively irrelevant, but psychologically volatile or conflictual, relationship issue. "Winning" the relationship issue may result in concessions on the substantive issue. Note, however, that a person can use the tactic even in arm's-length transactions where the parties do not have a psychologically invested relationship. For example, the department store claims adjuster could parry a customer claim by asking "Do you have a receipt?" If a receipt is not actually necessary—and it may not be—the question implies that a receipt is necessary, and that the customer is *at fault* for failing to have one. *For that reason,* the store cannot process the claim.

---

went to two point eight. And the fever of the thing caught us. Like a guy who had lost his mind, I kept bidding. Finally, I went to three point two; and there came a moment when I said to myself, "Good grief, if I get it, what the heck am I going to do with it?" When ABC finally topped me, my main feeling was relief. CIALDINI, *supra* note 7, at 254.

21. Sudden change of mood

Sometimes, a negotiator will shift radically from a reasonable and more or less friendly—albeit arm's-length—tone, to an angry, abusive, hostile tone, or vice-versa. Such a shift may reflect the conscious use of psychological tactics designed to confuse the other side, place it off-balance, and create vulnerability. One who is the target of another's anger often assumes, many times mistakenly, that he somehow caused it. There is then a natural human reaction to attempt to placate the angry person in order to smooth the situation and save the relationship. Response in kind, or *tit for tat*[13] is an effective way of dealing with such tactics.

22. Intransigence and entrenchment

Negotiators sometimes just dig in their heels and refuse to budge from a position. They may offer all sorts of reasons for not moving, and they may skillfully counter arguments offered to persuade them to move. The refusal to move can be a ploy aimed at testing the other side's firmness and discovering just how much concession room there is.

23. Sowing doubts; dismissals out-of-hand; put-downs

Sowing doubts about, or cursory *dismissals* of, offers, positions, and concessions are ways of shaping the other side's perceptions of its own bargaining position and its expectations of what it can get out of the negotiation. Unless the other side enters the negotiation reasonably well-prepared and hard-skinned, this kind of devaluation can undermine its confidence. It might then make faulty judgments about the relative merits of its bargaining position.

24. Playing to fears or assumptions

Negotiators can sometimes advantageously *manipulate the other side's fears or assumptions*. Suppose, for example, a buyer who wants an item badly and fears others may be interested volunteers the following to the seller: "I suppose there are a lot of people interested in that." The statement discloses the buyer has a concern about competition. The seller might respond, truthfully, "Well, you might say that," suggesting, without affirming, that the buyer's statement is true. The buyer might take the remark as confirming that others were interested

---

[13] Robert Axelrod, The Evolution of Cooperation 118–120 (1984).

in buying the same item and decide she should buy the item while she still has the opportunity.

Whenever a party discloses in some way that it has made an assumption favorable to the other side's bargaining position, the other side can use that knowledge to its advantage. It can do this even where the assumption is not true simply by failing to disconfirm it or disabuse the party of its mistake. In order to do this, however, a negotiator has to draw the other side out, getting a sense of its thought processes and how it approaches the negotiation.

25. Stalemate, deadlock, and walkout

A *stalemate* or *deadlock* occurs when the parties assert they are, or seem to be, hopelessly unable to agree. A *walkout* is a unilateral termination of negotiation, often in a righteous huff, usually expressed by actually walking out of the negotiating room. Negotiations sometimes stymie; the proceedings and lack of progress so upset the parties that they feel they must leave.

Deadlocking is risky behavior because it may mean there will be no negotiated settlement. Deadlocking is likely when a party fears what it may lose through a negotiation. Psychological prospect theory[14] is helpful in understanding this. This theory holds that persons will act to conserve current wealth. This means they have a risk-averse orientation toward seeking gains and a risk-accepting orientation toward preventing losses. In other words, persons will take risks rather than face a loss, but will not take equal risks in order to secure gains.[15] Consequently, parties who enter negotiations concerned with what they may lose are likely to engage in risky behavior, for example, escalation tactics that risk deadlock.

Whether or not they can articulate prospect theory, people understand it instinctively, that is, they take a party declaring a deadlock to mean that the negotiation proposals under discussion will impose an unbearable loss. Knowing that this is the likely conclusion, negotiators sometimes consciously use deadlock and walkout as tactics. Indeed, as former Secretary of State Henry Kissinger once said "stalemate is the most propitious condition for settlement."[16] When used as tactics, they are simply threatening pretenses designed to mislead the other side into thinking the deadlocking party is at its bottom line. They are also a way of testing resolve and of impelling the other side to make major concessions. Such risky and high-stakes tactics, however, make credible retreat

---

[14] Daniel Kahneman & Amos Tversky, *Prospect Theory: An Analysis of Decision under Risk*, 47 ECONOMETRICA 263, 264 (1979).

[15] Amos Tversky & Daniel Kahneman, *The Framing of Decisions and the Psychology of Choice* 211 SCIENCE 453, 456 (1981).

[16] STEPHEN J. BRAMS, NEGOTIATION GAMES 94 (1990).

difficult unless the other side does make some large concession. Consequently, to permit a return to the table without concession—to save face—negotiators often hedge deadlock and walkout threats with language giving an out if they need to use it.

26. Deadlock and concede[17]

In *deadlock and concede,* the negotiator sets the agenda and organizes her issues so that she raises her least important issue first and her most important issue second. She handles remaining issues similarly, alternating less important and more important issues. As she bargains, she deadlocks on the first issue, but then concedes. Continuing bargaining, she also deadlocks on the most important issue, but then demands that the other side concede on it because she conceded on the first issue and there has not yet been a reciprocal concession. And so on.

27. Friendliness

We are generally well disposed to those who are friendly and more easily persuaded to give or concede to them at least some of what they desire. *Friendliness* can be genuine, reflect a personality or goodwill, or it can be a tactic used to mask an underlying aim to gain advantage. Friendliness elicits friendliness, yet unless a negotiator's aim is to build a relationship, he should not concede simply out of friendliness. This is not to say that one should be hostile, but rather that it is important to distinguish between a friendly demeanor and what is and what is not a good deal. In hard-bargaining, friendly or not, make concessions only for return concessions of equivalent value.

28. Mutt and Jeff, good guy–bad guy, black hat–white hat

Mutt and Jeff, also called *good guy–bad guy* or *black hat–white hat,* is a well-known negotiation tactic combining anger, threats, hostility, and friendliness. In this practice, two negotiators work together to throw the other side psychologically off-balance. One negotiator is hard, aggressive, and angry; the other is soft, friendly, well-disposed, and reasonable. Disconcerted and perhaps threatened by the attacking Mutt, the party being worked on turns to the friendly and reasonable Jeff, whom he or she feels may be an ally of a kind. Softened in this way, the target is more likely to make important concessions, of information or position, to the friendly one.

---

[17] James A. Wall, Negotiation: Theory and Practice 91–92 (1985).

29. Negotiator without authority

Persons negotiating for others may or may not have authority to agree to the resolution of any or all issues concerned in the negotiation. A negotiator without actual authority will have to clear proposed settlements with his or her principal. But the *negotiator without authority* can also use the situation for tactical advantage in a negotiation. This is so particularly where the negotiator misleads the other side into thinking there is apparent authority to settle or the other side is unaware there is no authority. The negotiator who lacks, or pretends he lacks, authority, can explore the other side's positions and even gain concessions without making any real commitments or corresponding concessions of his own. Essentially it is a way to obtain full information while reserving time to make careful, calculated decisions.

Claims of limited authority, or the necessity to seek approval, are also forms of the tactic. A negotiator may invoke limited authority as a tactic to induce settlement within the limits assertedly imposed. The other side may simply not want to take the time or trouble to seek to go beyond the limits.

A negotiator could also assert she had authority to settle—meaning authority to discuss and make tentative agreements without any imposed limits—but later on claim she had to seek approval of any settlement. Although subtly different from the negotiator without authority tactic, it can have the same effect. Note also that the pattern of behavior and inducement is similar to that of low-balling.

30. Representative cloak[18] or phantom player

Sometimes negotiators will assert that while they are personally sympathetic to the other side's position, they nonetheless are acting in a representative capacity and in that capacity must take the stance of their principal. Such statements can be genuine or can be ploys. As a ploy, the assertion of representative status is a subtle combination of negotiator without authority and Mutt and Jeff. It effectively allows a negotiator using it to adopt two postures at the same time—one of sympathy and friendliness, the other of toughness and arm's-length dealing—and play on both. We can also think of this as a *phantom player* phenomenon. Depending on how the competitor plays it, he may proceed as though there were a third party at the table. This is, of course, a party who can make demands, but whom no one can question.

---

[18] Walter A. Maggiolo, Techniques of Mediation 173–174 (1985).

31. Status, authority, association, and credentialing

Although not commonly acknowledged, there are significant wealth, class, and status differences and distinctions in the United States, and most people are aware of them, at least on an unconscious level. Wealth, class, and status distinctions, and their trappings, can sometimes influence negotiations. This occurs when the *status, stature,* or *authority* of the one side impresses the other. The other may defer for that reason or may make unwarranted assumptions about the other side's power, strength, or resolve. One inoculates oneself from such influence by being aware of the phenomenon. If bitten, there are the antidotes of carefully considering the relevance of the displayed array and adopting a ''show me'' attitude; that is, resisting persuasions based on relative social position alone.

Association is a similar negotiation tactic using borrowed authority. There is a certain cachet that attaches to one connected with ''important'' or ''famous'' people. These real or alleged connections impress many, usually the unthinking. Consequently, negotiators sometimes seek to legitimize themselves and their stances by making some claim of important association. (Name-dropping is a form of claiming legitimation or status by association.) The association may be real or feigned. Negotiators sometimes seek to enhance their bargaining position by involving well-known persons or authorities, either by actually bringing them to the table or by in some way obtaining their blessing. Alleged, but false, association is a trickier form of the same tactic. In either case, one should guard against undue persuasions based on authority.

32. Principle

Appeals to *principle* are often highly persuasive. On the other hand, negotiators and others, politicians among them, sometimes use principles in unprincipled ways, cynically, as tools to manipulate. Unless simply horse-trading or haggling, most bargainers invoke principles as justifications for positions they take. Indeed, one good way to prepare for negotiations is to develop arguments of principle for the positions one takes. There is, however, a difference between deriving positions from principles and finding principled arguments to support a position taken for other reasons. The latter may simply be rationalizing, seeking to apply a high moral gloss to what is actually a calculation for private advantage. Arguments of principle sometimes mask other reasons, and one should seek close, reasoned justifications supported by evidence.

33. Time, timing, and endgame

Time is important in negotiations, and parties can use time pressure to their advantage. Usually, the party that is more patient or less pressed for time has an advantage. The need to come to agreement within a specified time may force one to make concessions one would not otherwise make. A negotiator can also pretend that time is important when it is not, forcing the other side to a speedy agreement or to hasty concessions.

Cunning negotiators who know that the other side is under some time deadline or pressure to conclude negotiations can use time to their advantage. As the deadline approaches, they may stall, raise new issues or resurrect old ones, inject new complications, produce documents containing already rejected agreement language, or make other efforts to unravel what appeared settled. The hope is that the need to reach an agreement by a certain time forces the needy party to make significant concessions, even perhaps to concede points already won. Not having a deadline, not announcing one, patience, and a willingness to walk away are ways to deal with such tactics.

34. Deadline

Setting a *deadline* to accept or refuse an offer or position can be a tactic, albeit a dangerous and risky one. It may succeed where the side imposing the deadline commits itself to accepting the consequences of no agreement and the other side has less resolve. Where the consequences of no agreement are severe for the side refusing to agree, the approach of the deadline enhances psychological pressure and wonderfully concentrates the mind on the downsides of refusing to agree. Certainly, if the side refusing to agree is simply bluffing, the deadline calls the bluff and changes the contest to a test of resolve.[19]

35. Draft document or single negotiating text

Sometimes a party to a negotiation will bring a *draft document* to the table as a basic text to set the agenda or to work from in moving toward a final

[19] A most obvious and stunning recent example of deadline was the United Nations-imposed deadline of January 15, 1991, for Iraq's withdrawal from Kuwait. Anyone who followed the events during the last few weeks, days, and minutes prior to the deadline understands how the deadline forced desperate searches for ways out as well as generated immense public pressures and anxieties of all sorts. Notwithstanding, the imposition of the deadline failed to achieve its intended result, and the nations arrayed had to accept the defined consequences of failure to meet the deadline—the prospect of a devastating war. David Hoffman, *US-Iraqi Talks Fail to Break Gulf Stalemate*, WASH. POST, Jan. 10, 1991, at A1; Ann Devroy, *Bush Offers Scant Hope of Averting War*, WASH. POST, Jan. 15, 1991, at A12.

agreement. This is often a useful technique to advance negotiations. It is also a powerful tactic, for a document tends almost irresistibly to set the agenda and focus the parties not only on particular issues, but also on a prescribed resolution of those issues. It's a way to take the initiative in negotiations. The other side's choices are either to work with the document, ignore it, offer a counterdocument, or use enormous self-discipline in dealing with the document for selective advantage.

36. Backtracking or unraveling

Backtracking or *unraveling* can occur when the parties, during a single negotiation, negotiate a number of issues separately and sequentially. After the parties settle a few issues, one party, to get his way on a new issue under discussion, may threaten to undo the earlier agreements. A negotiator can use this ploy as a means to gain leverage over the current issue or as a way to force the reopening of apparently settled issues in order to obtain more gain on them.

37. Irrevocable commitment[20]

One problem a negotiator may have is persuading the other side that the negotiator has reached his bottom line, particularly when he hasn't. One way to do this is to apparently commit oneself to a course of action that shows the other side that the negotiator can't budge. For example, union negotiators could propose a negotiating position to the union and ask the union to vote on it. If the membership adopts it, then the negotiators can claim to management that they cannot agree to any less advantageous settlement position because the union would dismiss the negotiators and strike.

38. Reinforcement and reward[21]

In *reinforcement and reward,* the negotiator in effect uses principles of operant conditioning theory and treats concessions as rewards for desired concession behavior of the other side. The concession follows the other side's concession and is a more than equivalent concession—the excess or "unearned" portion of the reciprocal concession being the reward. The tactic apparently produces more concessions and stimulates concessions to continue even when the negotiator stops making reciprocal concessions.[22]

---

[20] Thomas Schelling, The Strategy of Conflict 24–28 (1963).

[21] Wall, *supra* note 17, at 98–99.

[22] *Id.* at 99.

Chapter 5
DECEPTION IN NEGOTIATION

Many of the competitive negotiation tactics described above involve some kind of manipulative perception management, or more active deception. Whether or not one would ever use such communicative tactics, one must be able to recognize and deal with them. Moreover, some of the tactics and ploys already described certainly seem unethical, immoral, or perhaps counterproductive, and it is necessary to assess the morality and advisability of using them.

Some negotiators manage communications to mislead or deceive in a number of ways, not all of which are always intentional. Most of these ways do not involve any deliberate lying. Their effectiveness depends considerably on the gullibility of the other side, on its lack of acuteness in listening, and on its unwillingness to confront, or draw attention to, what is happening. Although the effect is to mislead, a negotiator who uses the method may later on technically deny that he intentionally misled. He can instead lay the blame on the other side's faulty interpretation of what was said. For example, suppose negotiator A says during the course of a negotiation, "Our company never does that." He then strikes an agreement with the other side, B, that doesn't require his company to do what he said it never does. Later on, in another business deal, A's company does, for B's competitor, what A said it wouldn't do. When B comes raging back to A complaining of unfair treatment, A responds that he was just asserting what his company had refused to do in the past and was not taking a position regarding what it might do in the future. B is in effect forced to confront the possibility that it was his own misinterpretation of the statement which led him astray.

I. DECEPTION

The following are some of the major devices parties use either to cause others to draw inferences the speaker wants them to draw or to control communications and disclosures.

A. Bluffing

Bluffing is a form of pretense. The bluffer may show strength to mask weakness and convince the other side there is no weakness. Alternatively, the bluffer may simulate weakness in order to hide strength and tempt the other side to make some move the bluffer knows he can beat. In a negotiation, for example, the bluffing negotiator may attempt to show strength by confident assertions of claims or by using false threats and promises. Similarly, to avoid giving information and entice the other side to make some disclosing move, the negotiator may feign ignorance or engage in "calculated incompetence."[1]

B. Predictions

Negotiators sometimes make claims that, in the quick and often animated exchanges of a negotiation, seem to be factual assertions, but are actually predictions. "If you do that, I'm afraid we'll have to go ahead and do business with your competitor." Predictions are not true or false, but claims about how the future will be. A prediction about one's own behavior is really either a promise or a threat.

C. Repeated claims or assertions of "fact"

Parties to short negotiations or negotiations with an impending deadline rarely recess to investigate claims or assertions of fact. In these situations, negotiators, particularly inexperienced ones, oftentimes fail to challenge factual claims by asking for proof or support. When a negotiator repeatedly asserts something as a "fact," the negotiation dynamic tends to induce the other parties to treat it as one and not to explore more deeply the nature of the claim. For example, a negotiator representing a company in a negotiation says to the other side, "We can't do X," and repeats this position several times as the negotiation progresses. Unless alert and aware of the repetition phenomenon, the other side is likely to accept the statement as a given.

D. Opinions of value or worth

Persons negotiating often make exaggerated claims of value or worth. Of course, opinions can be informed or uninformed, and can be correct or incorrect.

---

[1] RICHARD E. WALTON & ROBERT B. MCKERSIE, A BEHAVIORAL THEORY OF LABOR NEGOTIATIONS 68 (1965); *See also* Chapter 2, Part I.G., Bargaining Informational Moves, *supra*.

When one makes a claim of value, however, there is generally implicit in the claim some referent or standard of value that supports the claim. For example, when the diamond dealer says, "This diamond is worth $5000," the prospective purchaser tends to assume that the dealer means the diamond would bring $5000 if offered on the open retail diamond market. The dealer could really be saying that *he* places a $5000 value on the diamond or that he thinks that he might induce someone, somewhere—perhaps the purchaser—to buy it for $5000. Consequently, in making claims of value or worth, negotiators sometimes play off the assumptions the hearer makes about the objectivity of the claim. Note also that the repeated assertion of the value claim—unchallenged—tends to make it an operative negotiating fact.

E. Disinformation

Disinformation comprises either untrue statements made to deceive or mislead or technically true statements that give rise to false impressions. In the latter case, the statements are not actually false respecting any material facts, but mislead because the speaker causes the hearer to make a faulty assumption. Some of the tactics and claims described above have that character, but here is another example. Suppose a negotiator says, "In the past, I've made it a practice never to come back to the negotiating table after I've made a final offer and it was refused." The implication is that the speaker will do the same during this negotiation, even though he might not. The hearer concludes that the negotiator will behave in the future as he said he behaved in the past. The speaker, however, doesn't actually say that he will, and he could later credibly claim that he did not say he would. The other party might still feel misled but nonetheless be uncertain whether it was her own lack of shrewdness or attention to detail that resulted in the misunderstanding.

F. Misrepresentations of position

There is no enforceable rule of negotiation that requires bargainers to state their actual, as opposed to their bargaining, position on issues. Indeed, negotiating parties tend to assume that, during the negotiation, each side will move away from its initial, and even some of its subsequent, positions. Consequently, for the most part, statements of position are simply bargaining points. Although not truthful in accurately reporting the party's reservation point or bottom line, within the context of the negotiating "game" and its moves, negotiators view positions taken as "moves," and not as factual statements.

G. Withholding information; general failures to disclose

Even given the general norm that one should not lie, there is an important difference between lying and failing to provide information. Rather than lie, that is, provide false information, negotiators often fail to provide requested information, even when they have it, or sometimes provide only partial information, with misleading effect. Although debatable, there appears to be a customary norm that unless the negotiating parties have some sort of trust or fiduciary relationship, negotiators may treat negotiations as arm's-length transactions in which each party must take care of itself. This usually means that negotiators need not disclose information useful to the other side in the negotiation. (They may choose to do so for practical reasons, but that is another matter.)

Withholding information is advantageous when the other side acts on factual assumptions favorable to the withholder. Suppose, for example, that a manufacturer, under a contract to produce a certain product by a certain date, has had an equipment failure, but has found a supplier of the same product. Unknown to the manufacturer, the supplier has an oversupply of the product and wants eagerly to get rid of it. The supplier could withhold information of its overstock and possibly could even claim that to meet the manufacturer's order on short notice, the manufacturer would have to pay a premium, or rush-order, price. The supplier has no obligation to disclose its actual position, and unless good business reasons—for example, the development of a good, longer-term relationship—suggest otherwise, the supplier could exact a greater gain by simply failing to disclose.

H. Failures to disclose specific requested information

Sometimes negotiators deliberately refuse to provide information they have which the other side specifically requests. There is a difference between a refusal to disclose information voluntarily on one's own initiative and a refusal to disclose following a specific request for information. One may properly ignore general requests for information, for they are open-ended requests to reveal one's hand. Practically speaking, it is more difficult to avoid requests for specific information, for there are few ways, other than diverting the questioner or lying about one's knowledge, to avoid answering. Sometimes a refusal to respond will provide the very information the negotiator seeks to withhold. Denying that one has knowledge, unless very artfully stated, is a lie. If the other side to its detriment relies on the misrepresentation of no-knowledge, the negotiator has, in effect, provided materially false information. To avoid this, negotiators often prefer to evade the question or to provide some plausible excuse for a refusal to give the requested information.

Negotiators avoid both outright lying and answering information-seeking questions in a number of ways. They sometimes combine these techniques to divert the other side and take the initiative in maneuvering the discussion. I should add that time deadlines, or the need to cover a lot of different material in a negotiation, may make the following techniques far more effective. Their efficacy usually depends on the interrogator's failures to require the answering party to stick to the point or to follow up questions and examine responses carefully. Time pressures also induce these failures.

1. Shifting or diverting attention

Rather than answer a direct question, the negotiator ignores it and shifts the subject. One common way to do this is to "answer" the question with a question. Since many persons react rather unconsciously and feel a need to answer questions, this shift returns the initiative to the second questioner.

2. Answering unresponsively

The negotiator answers vaguely or answers a question different from the one asked. He can do the latter either by simply being unresponsive or by restating the question as a different question and then answering the restated question. The psychology of this move is interesting. The response may simply dupe the questioner, who fails to notice that his original question went unanswered or is distracted by the reply. On the other hand, the questioner may notice, but think the hearer misunderstood. Out of politeness, the questioner then chooses not to pursue the matter. For examples of this, watch any question and answer period with a major politician.

3. Answering partially

The party answers incompletely, usually at some length, so that the questioner loses track of the fact that her question wasn't answered.

4. Promising

The negotiator promises to answer at a proper time, but never does so. Instead, the negotiator takes the initiative and begins talking on a point he wants to make. This often results in diverting the questioner's attention to the matter the negotiator is pressing.

5. Tactfully refusing

The negotiator refuses to answer and gives some explanation such as "I'm not at liberty to tell you that" or "I'm not prepared to answer at this time." Such statements are disingenuous and "artful." Note that the lack of freedom to respond or lack of preparation may be matters fully within the speaker's control. If so, what the speaker is really saying is that she doesn't give herself permission to answer now or that she's not ready to answer. The hearer may draw different conclusions, however.

6. Subtle or ambiguous qualifying; creating plausible deniability; artful pleading

In order to avoid giving the requested information, the negotiator adds a qualification to his statement. The qualification, usually unnoticed unless the other side listens carefully and is attuned to subtlety and nuance, makes the statement technically true. For example, if a negotiator says, "I can't offer you more at this time," the phrase "at this time" qualifies the statement. The statement could mean that the negotiator truly can't raise the offer, or it could mean that he has decided that he would be better off in the negotiation if he didn't immediately offer more. The statement is true either way. Indeed, the negotiator in the example may mean the latter but hope that the other side interprets the statement as the former.

A good recent example from the political world concerns President Clinton's claims of pushing through the 1994 crime bill in order to put additional police officers on the streets. In 1996, in a speech in New Orleans, President Clinton said that he had "worked hard to pass the crime bill, to put one hundred thousand police officers on the streets."[2] In fact, at the time of the speech, only 17,000 new officers had been hired and placed on duty. Now, the President didn't *actually say* that he had put 100,000 new officers on the streets—although that interpretation wouldn't be unreasonable and one can be sure he'd be happy to get credit for that—but only that he had "worked hard" to pass a bill to do that. If challenged that he had not actually put the claimed number of officers on the street, President Clinton could, however, also reasonably claim he had never said he had.[3] This is what a lawyer would call "artful pleading."

---

[2] Michael Kelly, *This Year's Model*, THE NEW YORKER, June 17, 1996, at 45, 48.

[3] *Id.*

7. Bargaining; conversational steering

The negotiator treats giving an answer as a concession and requires reciprocal equivalent disclosure, for example, "I will answer your question if you will tell me. . . ." This also may be a ploy to take control of the discussion and steer it in directions toward which the negotiator wishes to move.

8. Listening

The negotiator generally avoids the information disclosure dilemma by asking open-ended and other questions and adopts the tactic of listening much and saying little. Although listening is a good thing that can improve party relations and lead to understanding, people often fail to notice that a questioner can direct a conversation or negotiation. As long as the respondent is compliant, the questioner can control the conversation and its topics. Many people, particularly in dealing with bureaucracies, have had the experience of having extended, but unsatisfactory, conversations with a superior or official. They had much to say or complain of, while the superior or official said little. On walking away they find they feel they were somehow taken advantage of by being dissuaded from doing something. The feeling comes from having been in someone's control without realizing it.

In any case, here are a few ways parties can exert some conversational control through questioning.[4]

a. Loaded or advising questions

Loaded or advising questions are those that a party usually can't answer and that have a message more important than the information they seek. Examples: "Wouldn't it be better if. . . ?"; "Why don't you. . . ?"; "Aren't you being. . . ?"; "Doesn't that make you. . . ?"

b. Semi-innocent or two-level questions

Semi-innocent or two-level questions are those which, while seeking an answer, have some other motivation as well. Examples: "What's so bad about that?" (information seeking and partly advising); "Are you going to give . . . a better deal than me?" (information seeking and a justice or fairness claim); "Haven't

---

[4]The list and the examples are derived from GERALD GOODMAN & GLENN ESTERLY, THE TALK BOOK 119–145 (1988).

you considered our other alternatives?'' (suggesting there may be other alternatives for the questioner without actually saying so).

c. *Closed questions*

Closed questions are those calling for a quick, usually yes/no answer. Trial lawyers and similar interrogators learn how to use closed questions in order to control witnesses closely. Examples: ''Do you understand?''; ''Isn't that right?''; ''Are you ready to proceed?''; ''You read the contract, didn't you?''

d. *Open questions*

Open questions are those questions that, while generally not disclosing the questioner's attitude, invite long, relatively undirected answers. Examples: ''What do you think about that?''; ''How do you feel about that?''; ''What did you do?''; ''What is it that you want?''; ''What do you see are the issues here?''; ''What are your needs?''

e. *Rhetorical questions*

Rhetorical questions are those that expect no answer but that also attempt to create new meaning or to persuade others through offering an interpretation of the situation. Examples: ''How long shall the United States continue to remain impotent while China thumbs its nose at us on human rights and trade matters?''; ''But we can't do that, can we?''

f. *Multiple-choice questions*

Multiple-choice questions are a series of loosely connected closed questions that confront the respondent with a set of choices and may amount to a masked persuasion. Example: ''Do you like the red or the green? Do you want leather or cloth seats? CD or just stereo?''

g. *Disclosing questions*

Disclosing questions are those that disclose information about the questioner. Examples: ''Are you prepared to discuss the antitrust implications of this?'' (suggesting and perhaps disclosing that the questioner understands, or at least, appreciates them); ''Are you aware that I have options other than dealing with you?''

I. Providing false factual information

Providing false factual information material to the negotiation amounts to lying. It's more than a sharp practice, and can amount to fraud. Actual lying in a negotiation happens, but no one would assert it was a proper tactic.

There are those, however, who would argue that the first seven kinds of deception listed above, which amount to different kinds of misleading, are permissible in ordinary competitive negotiations.

> Like the poker player, a negotiator hopes that his opponent will overestimate the value of his hand. Like the poker player, in a variety of ways he must facilitate his opponent's inaccurate assessment. The critical difference between those who are successful negotiators and those who are not lies in this capacity both to mislead and not be misled. Some experienced negotiators will deny the accuracy of this assertion, but they will be wrong. I submit that a careful examination of behavior of even the most forthright, honest, and trustworthy negotiators will show them actively engaged in misleading their opponents about their true positions. . . . To conceal one's true position, to mislead an opponent about one's true settling point, is the essence of negotiation.[5]

The argument in favor of this position is essentially that when each party to a negotiation understands the basic rules of the bargaining game no one playing the game is deceived about its nature. Each side understands that the other may engage in sharp practice, manage expectations, or mislead.[6] This is undoubtedly true in some fields of bargaining where adversarial bargaining practices and norms are common and where the negotiators are generally experienced, for example, in labor-management negotiations or lawsuit negotiations.

Advocacy for a client tolerates, and even requires, taking positions and making interpretations and arguments favoring or promoting the client's cause. That's certainly a basic assumption of the adversary system for lawyers and, in large measure, seems to be an operative norm in competitive business and other contest arenas. In general, this kind of advocacy is acceptable even when the advocate, looking at the matter objectively, believes his positions, interpretations, and agreements are wrong. There is a difference in arguing for a position in which you do not believe and actively lying regarding some material fact. This is so even though the appearance of belief in the argument adds credence to it.

In advocacy arenas, consequently, one should not be surprised by advocacy. In such contexts, negotiators take it as axiomatic that they are advocates for

---

[5] James J. White, *Machiavelli and the Bar: Ethical Limitations on Lying in Negotiation*, 1980 Am. B. Found. Res. 926, 927–928 (1980).

[6] *Id.* at 927.

their side and that the other side is equally capable of advocating its views. They assume that parties can distinguish between bluffing, opinions, and interpretations on the one hand, and factual statements on the other, and understand that one cannot rely on the former. They would also expect that a careful, critical, and perhaps suspicious listener, one concerned to protect his or her own interests, would note that many statements of the other side are not to be taken at face value. Instead, they need discounting, interpretation, and subtle contextual reading.

Under similar reasoning, misrepresentations of position would not be improper. Competitive bargaining assumes that the parties will end at a place different from where they open. One can view such misrepresentations as a form of bluffing or statements of claim, and expect that the other side will so recognize them. Early statements of position, therefore, are viewed as just that—positioning.

Outside structured adversarial negotiation contexts, some proponents of competitive bargaining might assert that the nature of profit-driven competition in business contemplates self-interested, arm's-length behavior. This "norm" assumes that people in business understand—or will soon come to understand—competitive business practices. As long as such practices are not illegal, that is, do not amount to fraud or other deceptive business practice, they are proper. Of course, this view must also contemplate that bargainers can use competitive strategies and tactics defensively, to protect themselves and to deal effectively with a competitive bargainer.

The argument for the legitimacy of competitive or adversarial bargaining turns on the supposition that such bargaining is the norm in certain arenas or contexts, or between certain kinds of parties who can be expected to take care of themselves adversarially.[7] Since the parties are, or should be, aware of the process, and choose to enter it, the process is fair to them and whatever results it delivers are also thereby thought to be fair. While there are many cases where this may be an appropriate assumption, there are other cases where it is clearly false. It is obvious that a sophisticated hard-bargainer can use competitive strategies and tactics to mislead unsuspecting innocents. This raises the issue of the morality of such practices most sharply.

In analyzing the morality of hard-bargaining, it is essential to be precise regarding exactly which hard-bargaining practices are in question. Positional bargaining is one thing, and the active use of misleading or deceptive practices quite another. For example, unless there is some ethical rule of disclosure in arm's-length transactions it's difficult to conclude that basic positional bargaining is morally wrong or unethical. Taking an extreme opening position,

---

[7] *Id.*

making small concessions, and hanging tough on concessions is not being inherently deceptive; it's just being tough. Being tough or firm in this way may mislead, for it may cause the other side to conclude that the negotiator will not settle at any point other than his asserted position. This may, of course, in some sense be untrue, but in a way is also irrelevant. If the parties frame the negotiation as a contest of firmness, the only relevant truth is that the party that is, or gives the appearance of being, the most firm will prevail.[8]

On the other hand, outside of *caveat emptor* arenas, where only those prepared to be wary or be fleeced should enter, competitive negotiation tactics involving active misleading, lying, or deception regarding material facts on which the other party may rely appear simply to be wrong. The principal justification—that context changes the actual meaning of the behavior in ways recognizable by the parties—doesn't apply. It is at least arguable that the nature of adversarial bargaining in certain arenas permits the parties to act on the assumption that all parties are aware of the rules of the game. That being so, *otherwise* misleading practices are not truly misleading, and the parties are treating each other as autonomous moral equals. This is not so, however, where one of the parties goes beyond the rules of the game or when one of the parties, to the knowledge of the other, is plainly unaware of them and has had no notice regarding them.

[8] Of course, that basic positional bargaining may not be morally wrong does not mean it is a wise way to bargain or that it will produce the best agreements, but that is another matter.

CHAPTER 6
COMPROMISE NEGOTIATION

There are two major kinds of cooperative bargaining: compromise bargaining and integrative or problem-solving bargaining. There are similarities between them, and both may use some of the same techniques. Nevertheless they differ in aim and are distinct in purpose and approach. This chapter focuses on compromise bargaining as a form of cooperation. It includes a discussion of the bargaining strategy conflict that occurs when cooperative bargainers attempt to negotiate with competitive bargainers.

I. THE COOPERATIVE BARGAINER

What follows is a composite, or "ideal-type," portrait of a cooperative bargainer. Not everyone who bargains cooperatively will have all the described attitudes and traits, and actual persons will differ in the degree to which they may have them. My cooperative bargainer is, as was my competitive bargainer, a fictional character, identifiably lifelike, and most useful to show how a cooperative bargaining strategy may work.

A. Contrasting competitors and cooperators

Competitive bargainers negotiate opportunistically, competing when possible and cooperating, or conceding, when necessary. They bargain as their perception of the power relationships or dependencies between the parties dictates. The competitor automatically assumes that the other side is also competing, and, except for competitors using unquestionably deceptive tactics, believes that as long as the competition is fair, the result of the negotiation will be fair.

In compromise bargaining, the parties seek to accommodate one another, to a certain degree, in order to distribute possible gain or otherwise settle the issues between them. In contrast to pure competitive bargaining where one or both parties seek to exploit one another to gain as much as possible, the cooperator seeks to settle matters reasonably, fairly, and satisfactorily to all parties.

B. Cooperators as compromisers

One essential strategy cooperators use is compromise. The cooperator gives up part of what he may ideally want in order to get something of what he wants, recognizing and accepting that the other side must do the same thing.

Negotiators compromise for different reasons. Some do so because the situation requires it. Others do so because they perceive it in their interest: the actual and perceived power relationships between the parties may dictate it, as neither party commands an advantage. Other persons are cooperative and compromising by nature. They may approach negotiations with a strong ethic of fairness and equality and compromise bargain as a matter of principle. They are trusting, in that they expect the other side to return their cooperation, and they are trustworthy, in that they do not aim to exploit the other side.[1] Yet others compromise as a matter of personal inclination, out of a desire to harmonize relations, a need to placate, or from an aversion to conflict, competition, or contentiousness.

The cooperative negotiator aims to be reasonable and seeks agreements that appear to be fair and just to the parties. He or she hopes that reasonable behavior will beget reasonable behavior, that the parties can operate on the basis of mutual trust, and that the present dealings may facilitate and enhance future dealings. The cooperative negotiator may thus be concerned with relationships—the present relationship between the parties, as well as the possibility of future relationship between the parties. Even if the cooperator doesn't anticipate future dealings, his own self-image or standard of proper conduct, as well as matters of general reputation, may cause him to bargain cooperatively.

Reasonableness and concerns about relationships and standards of conduct incline the cooperator to use cooperative tactics and not to seek more gain than seems reasonable, fair, and just under the circumstances. Thus the cooperator will generally open a negotiation with actions and words indicating openness and reasonableness. Often, she will make a first proposal that, although perhaps favorable to her side, is not in any way extreme. The cooperative negotiator, in planning her opening proposal, takes into account the claims and concerns of the other side as she understands or anticipates them. She then discounts her potential initial claim in order to make her position appear reasonable to the other side.

---

[1] JEFFREY RUBIN & BERT BROWN, THE SOCIAL PSYCHOLOGY OF BARGAINING 153, 183 (1975).

The cooperative negotiator, at least the cooperator who is not simply a placater, also provides reasoned justifications for her proposals, whether for an initial proposal or for subsequent proposals framed after discussion and concession. Indeed, the cooperator may determine her positions by reasoned justifications, focusing on "objective" criteria, that is, *external* standards such as fairness, market value, the right to a reasonable profit, and the like, on which the parties might generally agree. Invoking these criteria to justify a proposal or a concession makes the action seem reasonable. It shows the other side that the negotiator is not simply seeking to gain all she can, but compromises her interests, in generally acceptable and fair ways, in order to reach an agreement.

Because the cooperator wants to be fair and reasonable, he is willing to listen to the other side. Indeed, as he is open to reasonable persuasions, he wants to know exactly how the other side justifies the positions it takes. The cooperative negotiator thus wants an honest exchange of relevant information. The cooperator therefore generally discloses information in the expectation of a similar disclosure from the other side, even when it is not necessary to do so. This focus on open communication is both an aim and a tactic. It is an aim in that full information is essential to crafting a settlement reasonable and fair, or comfortable, to both sides. It is a tactic insofar as the cooperator seeks to stimulate the other side to disclose by disclosing herself. Similarly, the cooperator makes concessions in order to get concessions, or, in other words, takes cooperative actions in order to get cooperative responses.

When compromise bargainers negotiate with one another, they can often come to quick agreement. There is no particular trick or skill involved in *simple* compromise, except perhaps figuring out how much one is comfortable in conceding. Of course, a discerning cooperator would also know why she was willing to compromise, whether out of principle, as a trade-off for something else such as preservation or advancement of a relationship, or from a psychological need to placate.

As compromisers define success as getting what is reasonable and fair under the circumstances, hardly exact standards in most cases, they are usually satisfied if their bargaining result falls within some range. If they are trusting and open with one another, and thus freely exchange information and engage in mutual concession-making, it usually doesn't take them long to discover where their ranges of satisfaction overlap.

There are, of course, cases where compromise bargaining simply will not work, for example, when the parties bargain about an indivisible item that each wants, but cannot share. This may also be true where negotiations involve fundamental value conflicts. If each party aims at realizing values incompatible with those of the other party, compromise bargaining simply will not work. At such times, there is nothing the parties are willing to compromise.

II. THE ART OF COMPROMISE BARGAINING

Compromise bargaining requires concessions but even cooperative bargainers can find it difficult to concede on particular issues where they find their interests in direct conflict with those of the other side. Sometimes there are results one *must* obtain, otherwise there is no sense in negotiating. In such cases, the parties can yet find a path to productive agreement, a hopscotch kind of path, made of stepping stones each party lays down to reach an agreement, rather than traveling the straightforward two-way road of simple compromise. When there are multiple issues under negotiation, the parties may find a track by creating a mosaic of trade-offs between issues rather than seeking compromise on each issue. In other words, the compromise involves trading across issues rather than within issues.

A. Trade-offs, logrolling, and packaging

Multi-issue negotiations offer possibilities of trade-offs as between issues because the parties may value different issues differently and have different perspectives regarding them. When parties in a multi-issue negotiation negotiate each issue to a separate conclusion, they can't perceive how their different valuations of different issues could lead to trade-offs. Instead, their only way to reach agreement is to give way or compromise on each issue. When the parties explore all issues before striking deals, however, they may be able to see how they can gain what they want on issues of importance to them. By conceding on issues of lesser importance to them but of greater importance to the other, they may make trade-offs as between issues and create a final package more beneficial to each side than compromises on each individual issue.

When parties explore all the issues before seeking to settle any, it is also possible for the parties to logroll, that is, exchange concessions on different issues. Logrolling works when the parties are able to trade off items of lower priority or value for those of higher priority or value. The parties may be able to do this if they have different priorities, and at least one of them is aware of their respective priorities and can therefore perceive the trade-offs.

Negotiations open up the possibility of logrolling when the parties systematically explore the various issues between them, seeking to discover how strongly each side feels about the respective issues. This usually occurs either through express information exchanges or their substitutes, exchanges of proposals and counterproposals. In effect, in a trial-and-error process, the parties explore each other's limits or preferred outcomes over the full range of issues. Knowing their own priorities and preferences on the various issues, they are then in a position to propose packages.[2] That is, the parties contingently propose different combinations of concessions over the various issues, some more favorable to one side than the other, until each side concludes it's done as well as it can.[3]

To get a sense of how this works, take the example of two parties, Gina and Mike, negotiating over three issues. To simplify matters, let's assume that there are three possible outcomes on each issue and that Gina and Mike have prioritized or valued the possible outcomes by assigning a point-value to them, as displayed in Figure 6–1.[4]

Figure 6–1

	Gina			Mike		
	outcomes			*outcomes*		
issues	A	B	C	A	B	C
Γ	40	20	10	10	15	30
Σ	10	20	30	20	30	10
Δ	20	30	10	40	20	10

Now, as Gina and Mike bargain, they discover that on issue Γ outcome A is very important to Gina, but not as important to Mike, who values outcome C more highly than A. On issue Σ, however, Mike values outcome B over other possible outcomes, while Gina values C over other outcomes. As they continue

[2] Logrolling presumes some way for each side to determine the other side's priorities. This is not difficult when the parties trust one another and are equally revealing. It can be problematic when the parties may behave opportunistically, however, for disclosure of priorities can open one up to exploitation. If a party reveals that certain items are important to it, the other side could use the information, in effect, to hold those items hostage. Consequently, parties consciously attempting to logroll need first to ascertain whether it is safe to do so.

[3] Obviously, even if the parties enter negotiations knowing their priorities, information they receive in the negotiation may cause them to reassess and alter them. Indeed, there is a clear risk in too rigid prenegotiation prioritization, for if the parties prioritize the same way, they will end in competitive conflict. In such a situation, a break in negotiation to allow each side to process the information and reassess its priorities may work wonders.

[4] Plainly, most people don't quantify their valuations of outcomes. Indeed, although it is a useful exercise to try to do it, many outcomes we might value in a particular negotiation don't lend themselves to quantification. Then, too, quantification may introduce a false precision in valuation which really doesn't exist in life. Nonetheless, quantifying valuation is useful, helps parties become much clearer about their values, and facilitates comparisons and judgments otherwise difficult to make.

to work through the issues, they will progressively discover how each values the possible outcomes on the different issues—most likely through the intensity with which they respectively bargain for various outcomes.

To begin to work toward agreement, they will likely each propose trading off outcomes on some issues for outcomes on others. When the parties incorporate all issues in the bargaining and proposals, they will in effect be proposing different possible packages. For example, Mike might propose package Γ–C, Σ–B, Δ–A. Gina would propose package Γ–A, Σ–C, Δ–B. Mike's package gives Gina 50 value points on her scale and himself 100 on his scale. Gina's package gives her 100 value points and Mike 40 value points. Neither would likely accept those packages because each would perceive the possibility of greater gain from some other package.

As a second packaging effort, Mike might then propose Γ–B, Σ–B and Δ–A. This package would give him 85 points and Gina 60 points. Gina could respond with package Γ–B, Σ–B, and Δ–B. This package would give her 70 points and Mike 65. The parties would continue to experiment with packages in this way until it became clear to each of them that some particular package was the best that they could get.

B. Bargaining efficiency

Suppose that Gina and Mike negotiate the three issues between them one at a time. Assuming that each is trying to maximize gain for each issue, the likely result is a compromise on each issue. For example, they might agree on outcome B for each issue. If we tally their total points for such an agreement, Gina ends up with 70 points and Mike with 65.

Assume now, however, that the parties consider all issues and outcomes together. They discuss them serially, but hold off making offers and counteroffers until they have discussed all issues, and then they make offers and counteroffers as packages of preferred outcomes over all the issues. They experiment with different packages and finally settle on the following: Γ–A, Σ–B, Δ–A. If we again tally their points, we see that Gina ends up with 80 points and that Mike also ends up with 80. In other words, through the trade-offs they made across all the issues, *they are each better off* than they would have been in the first scenario. In the first scenario, each party "left gains on the table," that is, the parties did not bargain efficiently. Had they shared information about the way they valued the issues, through proposing trades and possible packages of outcomes across all issues, they would have discovered, and could each have claimed, additional value.

This phenomenon of inefficient bargaining or gains left on the table is a well-known and studied feature of negotiation.[5] In all multi-issue negotiations where outcomes are quantifiable, it is possible, with full information from all sides, to construct and graph the set of all possible solutions to the negotiation problem. Here, in Figure 6–2, is an example of such a graph in a hypothetical negotiation.

Figure 6–2

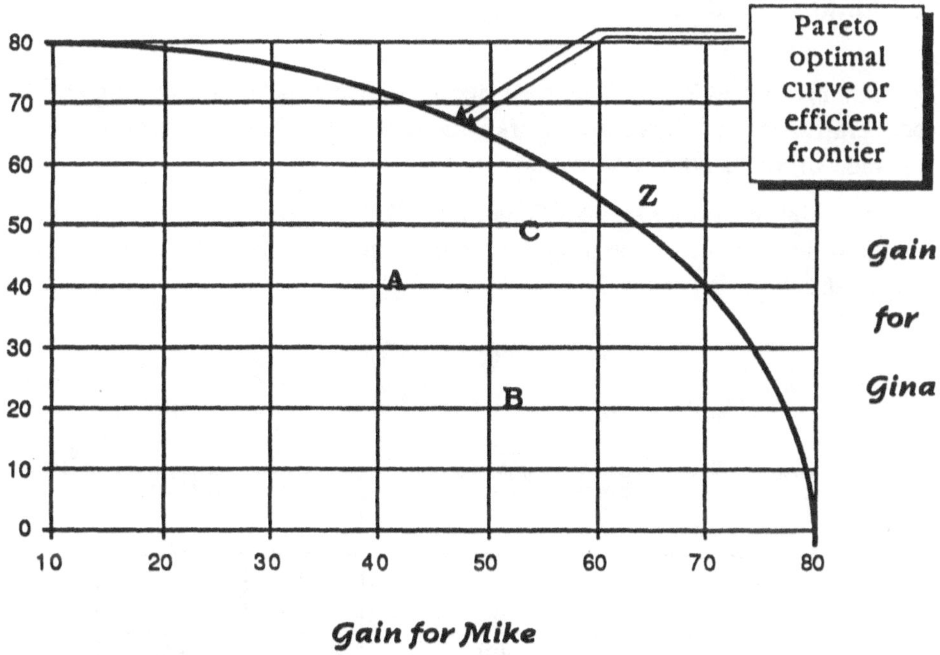

The curve, which defines all the possible maximal solutions to the negotiation problem, is called the *pareto optimal curve* [6] or the *efficient frontier*. In the negotiation, no one can do better than to reach some point on this curve.

Looking at negotiation solutions that fall within the quadrant defined by the curve, for example, solution A, we see that the parties left some gains on the table. They could have reached the curve, but did not. Now compare solution C to solution A. Each party did better. Such a solution is said to be *pareto superior*. That is, in terms of bargaining efficiency, any move that leaves at least one party better off without leaving the other party worse off is a move toward greater efficiency.

In negotiation, it is clearly desirable for the parties to attempt to bargain efficiently in this manner; indeed, the ideal is to reach solutions like Z, which

[5] Howard Raiffa, The Art of Negotiation 138–142, 148–165 (1982).

[6] After Vilfredo Pareto, the Italian economist and sociologist.

are on the frontier. Parties stand only to gain, not lose, if they can find and trade all potential gains on the table between them. They are most likely to do this if they share information or if the negotiation process permits them contingently to compare possible outcomes across all issues. Those parties who assume that there is more value to be gained, which they can find if they systematically exhaust the permutations and combinations of issues and outcomes, are most likely to find it.

C. Linking Issues

Linking, or adding, issues to a negotiation can be either a competitive or cooperative tactic.[7] This move works cooperatively when it creates possibilities of trade-offs that otherwise would not exist.

As a linking example, take Gina and Mike's negotiation and let us suppose that initially they are negotiating only issue Γ, and that their payoffs for outcomes are as shown in Figure 6–3.

Figure 6–3

Gina

	outcomes		
issues	A	B	C
Γ	40	20	10

Mike

outcomes		
A	B	C
10	15	30

Gina will argue most strongly for outcome A, Mike for C. They might compromise on B, where they each, in effect, lose half of their maximum possible gain. If they add issue Σ (as displayed in Figure 6–4), however, and agree on package, Γ–A, Σ–B, then Gina obtains 60 of a possible 70 points of value. This is six-sevenths of what she wants, while Mike gets 40 of a possible 60 points, or two-thirds of what he wants.

---

[7] Linking can be competitive when parties add or link issues to a negotiation not because they are implicit in or logically related to the central issues in the negotiation, but because they seek leverage in it. Successful linking will require the other side to address the linked issue, which might not occur but for the need to negotiate the other issues in the negotiation. Linkage may also enhance the linker's bargaining position and power regarding the issues central to the negotiation, and is a likely tactic for negotiation parties with less power.

Figure 6–4

	Gina			Mike		
	outcomes			*outcomes*		
issues	A	B	C	A	B	C
Γ	*40*	*20*	*10*	*10*	*15*	*30*
Σ	*10*	*20*	*30*	*20*	*30*	*10*

D. Unlinking issues

Negotiations can stymie over particular linked issues that the parties cannot reconcile. In such cases, the parties must re-examine their priorities to determine, with the benefit of information gathered in the negotiation, what is most important to them. Sometimes, by dropping or unlinking an issue holding up agreement, the parties can successfully negotiate remaining issues.

As an unlinking example, let's now suppose that Gina and Mike are negotiating all the issues Γ, Σ, and Δ, except that the array of outcomes has the following payoff schedule for them, displayed in Figure 6–5.

Figure 6–5

	Gina			Mike		
	outcomes			*outcomes*		
issues	A	B	C	A	B	C
Γ	*40*	*20*	*10*	*10*	*15*	*30*
Σ	*10*	*20*	*30*	*20*	*30*	*10*
Δ	*10*	*5*	*50*	*50*	*10*	*5*

Obviously, issue Δ has a lot of value to each of them, but they value outcomes in opposite ways. Their negotiation of this issue is likely to be highly competitive and contentious. There's just too much value riding on it for them not to fight over it. In fact, there's so much value that issue Δ bargaining is likely to distort or seriously complicate bargaining on issues Γ and Σ. Either Gina or Mike would have to accept their worst outcomes on the other issues to prevail on Δ. If Δ thus is a major impediment to agreement on other issues, they can agree not to discuss it and more productively work on issues Γ and Σ.

Realistic examples of linking and unlinking to facilitate compromise and agreement are not difficult to create. To take a prosaic instance of linking, suppose a company executive wants a particular employee to take on a new and difficult task. The employee, however, already feels overworked and would resist the assignment. This particular employee, however, has also complained that she lacks the proper resources to do her job well. In particular, she claims that she needs a state-of-the-art computer workstation. It's easy to see how linking these two issues may produce movement on each, some sort of compromise satisfactory to both parties, whereas keeping them separate may result in a stalemate on both issues.

More dramatically, the abortion controversy illustrates the possible value of unlinking. Those who favor and those who oppose abortion often confront one another on issues that each feels implicates their fundamental values regarding basic choices and human life. On these matters, the parties take irreconcilably opposed views. Suppose representatives of these two opposed groups meet to discuss a possible parental notification law concerning underage girls seeking abortions. If these groups can agree not to discuss the abortion issue itself, they may be able to make some progress toward agreement on a parental notification statute. Otherwise, continued fighting awaits them.[8]

E. Trade-off bargaining and contingent agreement

There is good advice in the old negotiation saying, "Nothing is final until everything is settled." When there are many issues to consider, the parties can take up issues sequentially, but make resolution of each issue dependent on the resolution of others. This procedure opens the possibility of trade-off bargaining. The parties can do this expressly, by agreeing in advance that their discussion is exploratory and tentative and that they will decide at the end of the negotiation whether to settle. As they move through the issues, they can indicate the possible agreements. Alternatively, the parties can simply signal they will consider making a concession on a given issue and then move on to explore a new issue; for

---

[8] Linkage is also likely to occur in negotiations on behalf of a group composed of parties having differing, but perhaps related, interests. The need to maintain group cohesion means that the negotiator may not be able to unlink issues important to part of the group. When there is such group pressure to keep an issue linked, the only way to unlink it may be to otherwise address or satisfy the needs of that element of the group responsible for the linkage.

example, "I think we'll be able to resolve that one without too much difficulty. Now let's talk about the next issue."

Keeping agreements tentative permits their amendment in the light of new information. This suggests that it is well for negotiators to attempt to work through issues sequentially from least to most contentious. Handling easier issues first facilitates cooperation, and success in resolving issues may improve cooperation on more contentious matters.

F. Agreement costs as linkable and tradable

A party can experience a direct cost from an agreement, and resist agreeing for that reason. Sometimes it is possible for the party benefiting from the agreement to pay those costs and thereby induce the other to agree. Airline practices on overbooking flights provide a simple example. Anticipating no-shows, airlines sometimes overbook flights, but then must deal with angry and frustrated passengers when they all show up, as the airline cannot accommodate them all. Typically, the airline will ask for volunteers to take a later flight. It may also provide a sweetener, in the form of a cash payment or voucher for free travel, to pay for the delay costs the volunteer experiences. Dealing directly with the costs a proposed agreement may entail thus links that issue and permits the parties to create a trade-off agreement incorporating it.

This example actually demonstrates two different ways of trading off or making compensation in order to secure an agreement, *specific* and *nonspecific* compensation. In making specific compensation, a party pays or alleviates exactly those costs the other side experiences. In making nonspecific compensation, a party pays the other in different kind or different "coin." In the example, providing a later flight pays the other in the travel originally desired. The money or voucher pays for—or buys out—the intangible cost of delay.

In any given negotiation, the specific compensation required is apparent, at least to the side experiencing the cost, for it comprises exactly that loss it has sustained.[9] Nonspecific compensation, however, is another matter. Only the other side can determine whether it values something else, which the party can provide, sufficiently to constitute a satisfactory replacement for those costs the agreement imposes. In the airline example, if someone is trying to get home in an emergency, money may not compensate for the delay.

---

[9] Obviously, in some cases the costs of a proposed agreement may not be clear, even to the party which will experience them, for those costs may turn on contingencies. In such a case, the parties may find a compensation formula which incorporates the contingencies as variables. There will also be cases where the parties dispute what the costs of agreement may be, which would make either the existence or amount of the costs themselves an issue in the negotiation.

In other words, nonspecific compensation pays the side experiencing the costs in some ''coin'' *that* party values, coin that the issues under negotiation do not implicate. Plainly, it is a kind of trade-off introduced into the negotiation in order to secure agreement. To do this, however, the party willing to pay nonspecific compensation must discover what else, other than those interests specifically involved in the negotiation, the other party values.

A recent, and important, example of nonspecific compensation involves the alliance the United States drew together to face Iraq in the Persian Gulf. Apparently, in order to secure Egypt's agreement to send troops to Saudi Arabia, the United States agreed to forgive the $6.7 billion military debt Egypt owed the United States.[10] While Egypt's direct costs in joining the Gulf forces are not clear, Egypt undoubtedly contemplated domestic problems arising from allying itself with the West against a Muslim state. In addition, Egypt had many thousands of its citizens working in Iraq, sending considerable income home and greatly assisting the Egyptian economy. Forgiving Egypt's foreign debt alleviated some of these costs and plainly was important enough to Egypt, together with perhaps other factors, to persuade it to accept the direct costs of joining the allies.

G. Future costs and precedent

There are other ''costs of agreement'' concerns parties may have which cause them to resist agreement. Two related concerns are that other parties may misinterpret the agreement and that the agreement may establish a precedent for other negotiations. A party who fears either of these things worries less about the present agreement than its future consequences.

When future consequences are an issue, there are a number of possible trade-offs. Most evident are agreements keeping agreement terms confidential or stating that the parties will not treat the settlement as precedent. Similarly, if the concern is that the agreement may create an undesirable precedent, some image problem, or loss of face,[11] the parties may be able to devise some formula that avoids these problems. They might do this, for example, through the shaping of the agreement itself or through an agreement about how to describe and publicize the agreement. Similarly, the parties can deny that the settlement constitutes a precedent and emphasize the special circumstances that gave rise to it.

---

[10] *Bush Forgives Egyptian Debt*, WASH. POST, Dec. 29, 1990, at A16.

[11] Apparently, Saddam Hussein's refusal to withdraw his forces from Kuwait involved, in part, some issue of potential loss of face and credibility as a leader in the Arab world. Obviously, if loss of face is a cost a party may experience, it's important for the parties to find some formula that permits the affected party to protect or maintain its image or save face.

III. DEFENSIVE COOPERATIVENESS

A. The innocent or naive cooperator and the cooperative negotiator's dilemma

Competitive and cooperative bargaining strategies conflict, and a simple cooperative strategy leaves the cooperator vulnerable to exploitation by a competitor. There is also good evidence that competitive negotiators who use the high demand, firmness, small concession strategy get better negotiation results than cooperators, at least where "better" means getting the most immediate gain.[12]

Cooperative bargainers vary greatly in their sophistication. Innocent cooperators who, consciously or unconsciously, uncritically adopt the premise that cooperation begets cooperation, may unwittingly engage in risky behavior—risky in the sense that it exposes them to possible exploitation. Potentially detrimental information disclosures, unilateral concessions, or excessive concession-making are all examples of risky behavior. Some cooperators may even exhibit invariant, nonadaptive, or "pathological" cooperation. That is, they consistently and detrimentally misinterpret the other side's exploitive moves, or otherwise always respond to persistent hard-bargaining with increasing deference or reasonableness and with more, and possibly greater, concessions.

If the hard-bargainer overreaches too much, the cooperator may feel pushed beyond his own boundaries of reasonableness and cooperation and break off the negotiations out of frustration and anger at the other side's unreasonableness. A canny hard-bargainer, however, skilled in reading the other side and sensitive to the possibility of pushing too far, can always take advantage of a naive and inexperienced cooperative negotiator. Innocent or naive cooperators tend to assume that the other side is bargaining nonexploitively. They want others to trust them and tend in general to trust others. In their desire to be reasonable and friendly, they assume that the other side will act the same way, even in the face of contrary evidence.

Cooperators may worry more about having a good relationship and keeping things calm, reasonable, and agreeable than they do about getting exactly what they want. Indeed, going into the negotiation, they may not specifically know what they would deem a good disposition. Instead, rather than enter the negotiation with certain specific ends in mind as desirable results, they may enter with vague, more malleable and manipulable notions. For example, they may think

---

[12] RUBIN & BROWN, *supra* note 1, at 267.

that they only want "what's fair" or "what's reasonable" under the circumstances. The lack of a clear reference point makes them less able to discern their own interest and therefore more subject to competitive bargaining.

The cooperator's desire to be a certain kind of person—to be noncompetitive, nonaggressive, fair, decent, and honorable—may also cause her to turn the other cheek to the other side's hard-bargaining tactics. Naive cooperators may undercut getting what they want by assuming that they must make unilateral concessions, or compromise without a return, just in order to get an agreement. They sometimes fail to distinguish between their behavior toward others and their behavior toward the problem they are trying to resolve. In other words, they are "soft on the people" and "soft on the problem."

The cooperator faces a dilemma:[13] the reasonable, compromising conduct in which she wishes to engage in order to obtain a fair and just agreement puts her at risk. If the other side is in fact also cooperative, all is well and good. The other side, however, may not be cooperative, but instead may be overtly competitive or cooperative in demeanor and competitive in substance. If, for example, management reasonably volunteers important information—say, that it is planning a plant expansion—the union may simply use it to its advantage without volunteering information in return or reciprocating in any other way. Similarly, if Susan, being cooperative, makes a concession hoping to trigger a concession from Jerry, Jerry may simply take the concession and either give nothing in return or give a noncommensurate concession. Indeed, the cooperator's concession may encourage the other side to seek more or greater concessions. In this situation, the truly naive cooperator may respond by conceding more in the hope of inducing a concession and movement toward an agreeable settlement. She would be better off if she noted the lack of reciprocity and adjusted her own behavior to protect herself.

The cooperator faces the dilemma that the way she wants to negotiate may put her at risk of being taken advantage of or exploited. Obviously, cooperative negotiators should not naively *assume* that the other side will also act cooperatively. Indeed, they must recognize that they cannot successfully bargain cooperatively unless the other side cooperates. They also need to devise ways to protect themselves from the other side's possible competitive moves—which a reasonable, cooperative demeanor may mask.

Cooperators, aware of the potential risks involved in their cooperative behavior, could adopt a hard-bargaining strategy. But this would certainly not be necessary in all cases, and many cooperators might object to hard-bargaining in principle. How does a wise and careful cooperative negotiator protect herself from competitive bargainers?

---

[13] David A. Lax & James K. Sebenius, The Manager as Negotiator 30–33, 41–42 (1986).

B. Defensive cooperativeness

During the initial stages of a negotiation, the parties feel each other out. They do so not only to gain information respecting positions, wants, and desires, but also to get a sense of whether, and how far, they can trust one another. As trust, or providing security that one can trust, is a key issue, cooperators should try to anticipate negotiation. They should work on developing information about the other side, and even on building relationships with it, prior to negotiation.

Cooperative behavior, because it promotes trust, tends to induce reciprocal cooperative behavior.[14] Once in a negotiation, the careful cooperator adopts a cooperative, if wary, demeanor, and indicates a general posture of flexibility on issues, perhaps signaling or hinting at a willingness to make concessions on certain issues. Nevertheless the defensive or cautious cooperator does not make significant concessions before determining whether the other side is trustworthy.

C. Building trust

Parties who trust one another may have difficult negotiations—for example, the issues may be truly difficult or conflictual—but not because they are suspicious of one another. Lack of trust or mistrust creates its own set of negotiation difficulties. Trust, particularly among nonacquaintances, is fragile, and many negotiations, let's call them unstable negotiations, may "tip," that is, move toward cooperation or competition, depending on the words and actions of the parties.

Researchers have usefully distinguished between three different kinds of trust: calculus-based trust, knowledge-based trust, and identification-based trust.[15] Calculus-based trust essentially is trust based on a calculation of possible benefits and losses.[16] Knowledge-based trust is based on predictability of behavior, which, of course, derives from knowledge of a party.[17] Identification-based trust derives from mutual understanding and mutual endorsement of individual aims.[18]

Unstable negotiations appear predominantly to involve situations of calculus-based trust or knowledge-based trust where one negotiator knows another will

---

[14] MORTON DEUTSCH, THE RESOLUTION OF CONFLICT 365 (1973); RUBIN & BROWN, *supra* note 1, at 263.

[15] Roy J. Lewicki & Barbara Benedict Bunker, *Trust in Relationships: A Model of Development and Decline*, in CONFLICT, COOPERATION, AND JUSTICE 133–169 (BARBARA BENEDICT BUNKER, JEFFREY Z. RUBIN, AND ASSOCIATES, EDS., 1995).

[16] *Id.* at 145.

[17] *Id.* at 149.

[18] *Id.* at 151.

bargain competitively. Tipping such negotiations away from competition and toward cooperation calls for a deterrent strategy. That strategy, in effect, informs the other side inclined to compete that nontrusting actions will result in retribution that outweighs any short-term gain.[19] Contingent cooperation, reformed sinner, and tit-for-tat strategies, all discussed below, do just that.

In the interactive and communicative processes of negotiation, negotiators constantly make ongoing evaluations and assessments of one another, and make responsive moves or choices based on these assessments. These evaluations and assessments are interpretations of the "evidence" at any given moment. The "evidence" is often ambiguous or unclear, and interpreting it to draw inferences and conclusions involves filling the gaps. Trust fills these gaps by generating favorable inferences; mistrust by drawing adverse inferences.

Because trust between the parties often makes negotiations easier and more productive, a negotiator should certainly aim at building trust. It will certainly aid in negotiations that could tip either towards cooperation or competition. Roughly, that's the set of negotiations in which no side enters trustingly. It includes negotiations between parties new to one another, or new to dealing with one another. It also includes arm's-length transactions between parties who may have reasons to compete, and negotiations between parties who have reason, because of prior interaction or information, to be mistrustful.

We tend to trust those who are similar to us, who appear to like us, who initiate cooperative behavior, and who confer benefits on us (make concessions to us).[20] This suggests that a negotiator who wants to bargain cooperatively should act cooperatively, focus on commonalities, and make some early, even uninvited, concessions. Such behavior may be sufficient to tip a possibly unstable negotiation situation toward cooperation. On the other hand, while cooperation may work with parties who are merely initially uncertain whether or not to cooperate, it will not likely work with committed competitors. With them, acting cooperatively might put the negotiator at risk. Unfortunately, however, transparently wary behavior may create suspicion in one not otherwise inclined to be suspicious. In this regard, it's important to remember that it is hard to create trust once there is suspicion. What's to be done therefore?

Here, it seems that a strategy of cautious cooperativeness would work: one behaves cooperatively, but doesn't take substantial risks—i.e., makes no significant concessions—before determining that the other side is trustworthy. Then, as the other side cooperates, the negotiator can increase his own cooperativeness.[21]

---

[19] *Id.* at 146.

[20] DEUTSCH, *supra* note 14, at 147–159; RUBIN & BROWN, *supra* note 1, at 272.

[21] "[A] sequential change in the other's behavior from low to high cooperativeness induces greater cooperation than either a shift from high to low or a pattern of high unchanging cooperation." RUBIN & BROWN, *supra* note 1, at 272.

D. Contingent cooperativeness and the reformed sinner strategy

There is good evidence that even those who wish to bargain cooperatively can succeed with competitive negotiators by adopting a shifting "competitive to cooperative," or "reformed sinner" strategy.[22] This strategy involves making a high initial demand, initially remaining firm, and then moving to a "contingently cooperative" strategy. Contingent cooperativeness involves behaving cooperatively if the other side reciprocates cooperative behavior, and increasing cooperative behavior as the other side does so. Interestingly, the cooperator's initial firmness may signal to the other side that competitive behavior will not work. By making high demands,

> a bargainer avoids the pitfall of adopting a stance that may prove to be too "generous"; he is thus less likely to accept a smaller division of the resources than the other is willing to offer. Second, by making extreme initial demands, the bargainer often gives himself more time to assemble information about the other's preferences and intentions. Third, he communicates his expectations of how he should be treated by the other—namely that he should not be exploited. Finally, his extreme initial offers provide the other with valuable information about his subjective utilities.[23]

The contingently competitive strategy appears to work by giving the other side evidence that its own cooperative behavior, but not its competitive behavior, has a desirable effect.[24] In carrying out this general strategy, the cooperator may expressly negotiate over the negotiation ground rules, seeking the other side's commitment to negotiate cooperatively as well, but in any case asserting a norm and expectation of cooperative behavior. The cooperator may then attempt to structure the negotiation agenda to handle small issues first, where the risk of loss is not great. When ready to take risks, the cooperator makes contingent proposals. He may expressly offer a concession or adopt a position closer to the other side's demands, but makes such moves contingent on some specific concession or change of position from the other side.

E. Strategy imitation or response-in-kind; tit for tat

Response-in-kind, or tit for tat, is a kind of contingent cooperation a negotiator can use to handle a competitor. If the cooperator observes competitive tactics, she can call attention to them and state that she knows how to bargain that way too, and will respond in kind, unless the other side bargains cooperatively.

---

[22] *Id.* at 273.

[23] *Id.* at 268.

[24] *Id.* at 277; DEAN G. PRUITT, NEGOTIATION BEHAVIOR 115–116 (1981).

Alternatively, the cooperator can just respond in kind, using tit for tat to discipline the other side.

Using a tit-for-tat or a matching strategy of conditional niceness appears to be an effective way to induce cooperation.[25] The strategy makes it clear to the other side that it risks retaliation and increasing conflict if it bargains competitively.

F. Role reversal[26]

Role reversal, either open and explicit or indirect, also sometimes works to generate cooperative behavior. In role reversal, the negotiator pretends he is the other side, and from that perspective, states the other side's positions, claims, and reasons. If successful, role reversal reveals that the negotiator truly understands the other side, and this will likely induce cooperative behavior.

G. Firm and fair

When negotiators disclose they have fairness concerns, but are not firm in what they themselves want, they expose themselves to possible exploitation. When they appear firm, but are unconcerned with fairness, they seem unfair and invite resistance. By contrast, when negotiators appear to be both firm and fair, others are likely to make the most concessions.[27]

H. Cost-cutting strategy

In human decision making, losses always loom larger than gains.[28] This means that people will resist suffering losses more than they will relish obtaining gains. It also means that they will take risks to avoid losses, but will not take equal risks to secure gains.[29] In this sense, people evaluate possible losses and gains asymmetrically. This suggests that "the most effective concessions you can make are those that reduce your opponent's losses,"[30] and that the least effective are those that merely confer additional gains.[31]

---

[25] ROBERT AXELROD, THE EVOLUTION OF COOPERATION 118–120 (1984); PRUITT, *supra* note 24, at 116–117.

[26] HERB COHEN, YOU CAN NEGOTIATE ANYTHING 50 (1980).

[27] PRUITT, *supra* note 24, at 38.

[28] Daniel Kahneman & Amos Tversky, *Prospect Theory: An Analysis of Decision Under Risk*, 47 ECONOMETRICA 263, 287 (1979).

[29] *See infra* Chapter 9, Cognitive Problems in Negotiation, note 13.

[30] Daniel Kahneman & Amos Tversky, *Conflict Resolution: A Cognitive Perspective*, in BARRIERS TO CONFLICT RESOLUTION 57 (KENNETH J. ARROW, ROBERT H. MNOOKIN, ET AL., EDS., 1995).

[31] *Id.*

In competition-cooperation terms, a party is most likely to be competitive when faced with a risk of loss. To avoid this competitive turn, a negotiator, aware that the other side may view a requested concession as a loss, should follow a cost-cutting strategy. He should find ways of reducing the costs the other side experiences for requested concessions.

I. Fractionating concessions

The careful cooperator can also help fashion a self-protective concession strategy by fractionating concessions.[32] One fractionates concessions by dividing an issue into smaller issues and therefore into smaller concessions. The cooperator can thus make a small concession and wait to see how the other side responds. If the other side makes an equivalent concession, the cooperator can move on.

J. Ambiguous or disownable signals

A negotiator makes a "disownable" concession move[33] when he makes an ambiguous statement that suggests a willingness to make a concession, but which can also be plausibly interpreted as not expressing such willingness. If the other side takes the statement as offering a concession and reciprocates, then the cooperator confirms the other side's interpretation in some way. If the other side seeks to grab the assumed concession without offering a return, then the cooperator denies making it. Suppose, for example, that one party to a negotiation has repeatedly argued that the other side had to meet two conditions before he would consider changing his position. After a time, however, he begins to mention only one condition. This may signal a willingness to drop the unmentioned condition.

This sort of signaling amounts to a testing of the other side, but a testing that does not run the actual risk of making a concession or exposing weakness. At most, it is an unclear expression of a willingness to concede contingently. As another example, consider two parties negotiating over contract terms. The buyer wants the seller to give her the same discount on equipment that the seller gives some of its other, much larger, customers. The seller says, "We can write something like a 'favored nations' clause into the contract." The buyer then says, "I'll take that, and I appreciate getting the same discount as your larger customers," but makes no concession in return. The seller then responds. "Well, you can have the clause, but it doesn't apply to discounts." Alternatively, had the buyer shown a willingness to concede, the seller could let the buyer's first interpretation of the statement stand.

---

[32] Roger Fisher, ed., International Conflict and Behavioral Science: The Craigville Papers 104 (1964); Pruitt, *supra* note 24, at 99.

[33] Pruitt, *supra* note 24, at 94.

If there is little trust, this process of signaling can be quite subtle, for the target of the signal may be uncertain whether to interpret a statement as expressing a willingness to concede. If he is uncertain, he may fear responding in a way that clearly shows his willingness to reciprocate, for that may put him at risk. Consequently, the parties sometimes engage in trading ambiguous statements until one side feels secure enough to make a clear proposal or until both sides simultaneously make a clear move.[34]

K. Directional information[35]

A negotiator may sometimes encourage cooperative bargaining by simply indicating on which issues the other side should improve its proposals. This tactic provides the other side with some information about the negotiator's priorities, but without clearly committing to anything.

L. Demanding reasoned justifications

The cooperator should make a practice of asking the other side to justify the positions it takes in terms of some objective criteria. If the other side is simply behaving competitively and attempting to extract whatever gains it can, it may have difficulty in stating satisfactory justifications for its positions. It thus reveals itself as a simple, grasping, competitive negotiator.

M. Time-outs

Negotiating parties deadlock when no side is willing to make a further concession to bring the parties closer together. When the parties are nearing a deadline and are in deadlock, they may realize that the negotiation will fail completely unless they cooperate. Declaring a time-out gives the parties time to assess the situation without continued conflict, reconsider their reading of the negotiation thus far, and more coolly determine whether to risk trusting the other side. Often enough, when the parties return to formal negotiation, each side signals a willingness to move or makes concessions leading to agreement.[36]

---

[34] *Id.* at 96.

[35] *Id.* at 173–174.

[36] To this point, I have principally considered ways that a cooperative bargainer might negotiate to protect herself from a competitive bargainer, gain security, increase her confidence that the other side can be trusted, and discipline the other side to cooperate. But the other side may bargain competitively because it itself is so insecure or untrusting that it fears the other side will exploit it. While the tactics discussed above should also apply in this situation, it may sometimes be necessary for the cooperator to take greater risks, such as making a unilateral concession, in order to gain the trust of the other side. There is no rule or guideline which will help the cooperator determine when to do this. It is simply a judgment call dependent on the negotiator's skill and sensitivity in reading the other side and assessing its real needs and interests.

IV. COMPARING COMPETITION AND COOPERATION

People bargain competitively for various reasons, and negotiators and mediators need to understand competition in negotiation in order to respond to it appropriately. Some people bargain competitively without giving much conscious attention to the matter. Others compete in response to the other side's competitive behavior. In this, they follow the common pattern that a particular kind of behavior elicits a similar behavior in response. In other words, one party frames the negotiation as a contest, and the other party picks up the competitive cues and behaves accordingly. Further, people naturally incline to competitive bargaining when they are untrusting. In such situations, in order to avoid putting themselves at risk, they act guardedly and adopt elements of the competitive strategy, for example, withholding information or misrepresenting positions. Finally, one can readily imagine ambiguous bargaining situations, as many in fact are—in which at least one party is untrusting—as quickly devolving into a competitive negotiation between both parties. The untrusting party acts defensively; the other side senses this as competitive behavior, and therefore acts in a similar fashion.

Negotiators, however, can also consciously adopt a competitive strategy. Negotiators are most likely to compete purposely when:

- the parties have an adversarial relationship;
- a negotiator has a bargaining power advantage and can dominate the situation;
- a negotiator perceives an opportunity for gain at the expense of the other party;
- the other side appears susceptible to competitive tactics;
- the negotiator is defending against competitive moves; and
- there is no concern for the future relationship between the parties.

This list suggests that competitive bargaining is most likely in labor and lawsuit negotiations, insurance and similar claims-type settlements, and in one-time transactions between a relatively experienced party and a relatively inexperienced party. One would, for example, expect to see it in sales transactions where the parties are unlikely to see one another again.

Representative bargaining, or bargaining for a constituency, may also prompt competitive bargaining, even when there will be future negotiations between equally sophisticated parties. The negotiator's accountability—her need to show success, and the client's or constituency's desire for it—may override relationship concerns and reasons for cooperation.[37] The concerned audience—a client,

---

[37] PRUITT, *supra* note 24, at 41–43.

constituency, or coalition partner, or other phantom party at the table—is, in effect, looking over the negotiator's shoulder. The negotiator therefore takes positions and makes moves she believes her client either expects or would approve.[38] International negotiations between countries, union-management and lawsuit negotiations, and negotiations between different parties in a coalition of interest-groups thus sometimes evince this pattern.

Aside from circumstantial or situational pressures, there are some persons who bargain competitively because they believe that's the way to do business. There are also persons who are simply constitutionally disposed to bargain competitively, and will incline to do so opportunistically in any bargaining situation, if they can.[39]

Finally, it's important to note that one can bargain competitively on some issues in a negotiation and not on others. In other words, a negotiator can selectively use competitive strategy or tactics on particular issues, while using a cooperative or problem-solving strategy on other issues. In such a case, extracting gain competitively may not greatly endanger future relationships—or, at least, there's a judgment call about that—and the negotiator attempts to calculate the net effect of the overall results, skewing the benefits, insofar as possible, to his side. In this kind of calculation, its clear there's some kind of assessment, or balancing, of short-term versus long-term gain. Again, there's no formula for this, and in any given case, the parties probably follow rules of thumb prevalent in the industry, developed from prior experience, or based on hopes or individualized assessments.

Similarly, it's possible for negotiators to use an integrative or problem-solving bargaining strategy in order to attempt to increase the amount of gain possible to the parties. At some point, however, notwithstanding cooperation to produce greater gain, the parties will have to distribute or divide the gain, and they may therefore also engage in competitive bargaining.[40]

Obviously, competitive bargaining covers a continuum of behaviors from the simplest, unreflective adversarial actions to highly conscious and virtually scripted contests. As such, competitive bargaining moves are natural responses in some negotiation situations and advantageous or profitable actions in others. This being so, what are the downsides to competitive negotiation?

---

[38] RUBIN & BROWN, *supra* note 1, at 50–54.

[39] The fabulously wealthy and sometime oil entrepreneur Calouste Gulbenkian appears to have been such a person. "He could not respect himself unless he 'drove as good a bargain as possible.' In other words, he wanted as much as he could get." DANIEL YERGIN, THE PRIZE 418 (1991). His son reported that his practice was "to make his demands step by step, so that having obtained satisfaction on one point he would raise another and yet another, thus achieving all he wanted or, at least, much more of what he wanted than he would have obtained if he had started by putting forward all his demands at once." *Id.* at 417.

[40] LAX & SEBENIUS, *supra* note 13, at 115–116.

Competitive negotiation, at least in its full-blown form, is risky bargaining. The competitor takes risks in order to secure gains. Among the risks a competitor takes is the risk that there will be no gains at all. The competitive strategy of staking out a position and holding firm, particularly when joined with various devious tactics, runs the risk of alienating, frustrating, or angering the other side and thus precluding a possible agreement.

Even if there is an agreement, it may not be a sustainable one. On reflection, the other side may conclude it doesn't really like the deal or come to feel that it was "taken" in some way. Furthermore, even if there is a deal and it survives, the bargaining that took place may adversely affect future relations between the parties. This is certain to happen if one side discovers that the other actively misled or manipulated it. It may also happen just because of residual hard feelings or mistrust arising from the tactics used.

Beyond these concerns, competitive bargaining is neither efficient nor productive bargaining. It is inefficient and nonproductive in that parties who withhold and manipulate information miss possibilities of cooperating to find or create additional value to divide between them. In this way, they can be said "to leave gains on the table."

Along this line, two real gains competitive negotiators are unlikely ever to realize, and bring to bear in immediate or prospective negotiations between themselves and others, are genuine cooperation and positive relationship. To put it another way, although a competitive negotiator may realize a gain in a particular negotiation, he may forgo far greater possible gains in doing so. The greater foregone gains are those that may arise from enlisting the willing cooperation of others to assist him in maximizing the satisfaction of his interests, while at the same time advancing their own. That's an entirely different way of looking at the negotiation situation—one that competitors usually don't attempt.

CHAPTER 7

PROBLEM-SOLVING OR INTEREST-BASED NEGOTIATION

The problem-solving or interest-based negotiation[1] model approaches negotiations quite differently than do the competitive and simple compromise negotiation models. In essence, the problem-solving strategy treats the coordination and conflict of interests as a joint problem of the parties, a problem that may create opportunities for them to benefit mutually. If parties approach negotiations with this attitude, their negotiation tasks are clear. They must work together to identify their common problems, undertake a search for alternative possible solutions to their problems, and mutually choose courses of action. I explore this model in greater detail below.

I. PROBLEM-SOLVING AND COMPETITIVE NEGOTIATION COMPARED

In distributional bargaining, parties compete or fight over presumed fixed sums or positions to get the most for themselves out of a deal. In problem-solving bargaining, however, the negotiators seek instead to find ways of satisfying the interests of all parties. The aim is not to beat the other side in a contest for gain, but to work together with it for the benefit of both. One way the parties might do so would be to cooperate to increase the sum, or amount of gain, available to them. Where the parties' join efforts to increase the sum total of possible gains, it may result in more to divide between them. Each party may thus do better in a final share allocation than it would by competing over an assumed fixed amount. For example, two companies were competing over warehouse dock loading space; the space was so small only one company could use it at

[1] This form of bargaining is also referred to as integrative bargaining, as the parties are said to integrate their interests. The meaning of "integrative," however, is less self-evident than "problem-solving," and I believe that the latter better captures the processes involved in this kind of negotiation.

a time. Rather than continue to compete, the companies agreed to extend the loading platform so that both could use it simultaneously.[2] Through their cooperation, they increased the resources they had to share, and both were better off after their agreement than they were before.

A. Common or complementary goals or interests

Problem-solving negotiation assumes that parties often have common or complementary interests that they can agree to coordinate for mutual benefit. Parties have a common interest when they share a goal and would benefit in the same way, although not necessarily to the same degree, if they could realize the goal. For example, two persons starting a business partnership have a common goal of developing business.

Parties' interests are complementary when they have different aims or goals, but the goals are compatible, and each party, in pursuing its own goal, can assist the other in reaching its goal. For example, air express delivery companies need persons to act as couriers to speed documents through customs following international flights. These companies do not wish to bear the expense of full-time courier employees. There are, however, many travelers who would like to fly internationally at a reduced rate. Courier companies often employ such people to accompany documents, *charging* them what amounts to a highly discounted airfare. In effect, the company buys a regular airfare ticket for the courier, but reduces its cost by having the courier pay some portion of the airfare. The courier gets her flight, but at a considerably reduced cost; the air express company gets its documents through, also at a reduced cost. The express company and the courier's travel goals are complementary, and they are able to work together for their mutual benefit.

Rather than requiring that one or both parties give way, as is the situation in competitive bargaining, the discovery that the parties have common or complementary interests creates possibilities of mutually beneficial joint action. By contrast, competitive negotiation assumes that the parties' interests or goals are antagonistic. The two strategies thus differ in their initial definition or perception of negotiating situations. Problem-solving negotiators conceive bargaining situations as open and amenable to cooperative development. Competitive negotiators look upon bargaining situations as closed, viewing the amount of available gain as fixed and as subject merely to division.

---

[2] MARY PARKER FOLLETT, DYNAMIC ADMINISTRATION: THE COLLECTED PAPERS OF MARY PARKER FOLLETT 3–4 (1982).

B. Conflicting goals or interests

Problem solving, however, does not ignore the possibility that bargaining parties may sometimes be in conflict. Parties' goals conflict if they cannot realize them at the same time. Suppose you and I are sitting in a library working, and you want to open a window to get fresh air. I want to keep it closed because I'm cold and want to avoid a draft; we can't both have our way.[3] Even in such circumstances where aims or desires apparently conflict, it may be possible, with effort and ingenuity, for the parties to reconcile their conflicting aims. In the library example, we might do this by opening a window in another room in the library, assuming the air circulation is such as to bring fresh air to you without chilling me.

Problem-solving negotiation thus recognizes that parties may have different needs and interests, but finds that such differences or conflicts do not necessarily require the parties to compete. Instead, such conflicts are often useful in crafting an agreement. Even where the parties have conflicting interests, they may nonetheless creatively devise ways to serve their respective interests, as in the loading dock and library examples. If they succeed, they may obtain results benefiting both parties more than would strategies of competing to win or simple compromising.

C. Compromise in problem-solving negotiation

Unlike simple compromise bargaining, problem-solving bargaining does not focus on compromising for the sake of agreement. Instead, it recommends that parties work toward agreement by means other than compromise. It calls upon the parties to search for agreements that serve their respective interests as well as possible. This operative premise against easy compromise facilitates ''constructive conflict.'' Where the parties resist easy solutions—and simple compromise is an easy solution—they must be inventive or creative, and undertake a wide-ranging search for ways to benefit both parties. The premise is that creativity can lead to greater gains for each party than can simple compromise, which, at best, merely mitigates losses. Surprisingly often, when negotiating parties search beyond simple compromise, they discover there are ways to integrate their interests so that both gain. If they work at it, they can often find creative solutions that will leave them better off than would a simple compromise.

Even with the best of will and cooperative effort, however, the parties will sometimes find that their interests apparently conflict and that they cannot find a clear way to satisfy all their interests completely. Their interests may so conflict that the *only* solution to the conflict is compromise.

---

[3] *Id.* at 3.

There are, however, different ways to compromise. In particular, trade-off compromising[4] results in making greater possible gains available to the parties than does simple division compromising. Redefining a bargaining situation to include a greater number of interests and issues creates trade-off possibilities, making greater overall gains available to the parties. Thus, in those cases where parties cannot create *new* gains, in the sense of creating new resources, they can nonetheless work together to expand their bargaining. In doing so, they may find other possible gains already available, but not initially perceived, and distribute them as well as possible. In other words, compromise *is* a solution to conflict, but some kinds of compromise are better than others. More specifically, trade-off compromising may leave each party better off than would simple division compromising.

The problem-solving model of negotiation, therefore, does recognize compromise as a useful and creative tool to reach agreement. Resorting to an easy compromise, however, may inhibit other more creative and more gain-producing solutions to conflict. The problem-solving model, therefore, looks to compromise as a *last*, rather than a *first*, resort in attempting to fashion agreements.

II. BASIC PROBLEM-SOLVING NEGOTIATION

Problem-solving negotiation follows the same process involved in any sort of problem solving. There is first a definition of the problem, a search for solutions to the problem, and then an evaluation of alternative solutions against some set of criteria. The process is a dynamic one, however, and all its stages are subject to refinement based on developing information and reassessments. Thus, as a person reflects on possible solutions to a problem, he may also begin to redefine the problem, and any redefinition, of course, will lead to new possible problem solutions. Similarly, as he evaluates solutions and focuses on the most promising ones, he may discover that his criteria for evaluation are inappropriate, and this would cause him to develop new criteria. New evaluative criteria might also lead to new ways of looking at the problem, and therefore a new problem definition, or to a renewed search for possible solutions to the problem.

Individual problem solving is a dynamic learning process, and can be complex. Problem-solving negotiation, while following the same process, adds potential complexity by adding parties who must work together to solve problems they share. The parties may differ in their initial definitions of the problem, in proposed possible solutions, and in criteria they use to evaluate possible solutions. They will likely have differing respective best alternatives to a negotiated settlement. Not only is each party proposing its own views,

---

[4] HOWARD RAIFFA, THE ART AND SCIENCE OF NEGOTIATION 156–160 (1982).

interests, preferences, and values, it is also learning about the other's. Indeed, in complex problem-solving negotiation, negotiators constantly reassess their interests and preferences as they gain information and their perceptions of problems, possible solutions, and agreements, and even their sense of alternatives to agreement change. In short, they revalue their situations. This means that problem-solving negotiation is a process open to novel and mutually beneficial solutions to joint problems. The process is diagrammed in Figure 7–1.[5]

The model as presented seems rather idealistic, for it operates on the premises that the negotiating parties cooperate fully and do not seek to take advantage of one another. Thus, for example, the model calls on the parties to share information fully, to define problems mutually, and to work as allies to find solutions to their problems. One might agree that this would be a good process to resolve differences, but doubt that parties could or would act in such a trusting, possibly altruistic, manner. Thus the model seems naive.

The problem-solving model does recognize that parties, in their self-interest, may attempt to skew, or manipulate these supposed open and mutual processes in their favor. For example, even where parties cooperate or collaborate to increase gains, they must still divide any value they jointly create. This means that even when the parties work together to create or increase available gain, opportunities remain for competitive self-seeking. Note here that the problem-solving model takes such possibilities into account and offers ways of dealing with them.

For the present, however, the first task is to develop an understanding of how problem-solving bargaining basically works. We shall return to this more general issue of competition within problem-solving negotiation after exploring the basic features of the model, sketched by elements and process stages.

A. Information gathering in problem solving

Problem-solving negotiation involves an attempt to understand both one's own needs, values, and objectives and those of the other side. Problem solvers *share* information to discover what their real conflicts are and what they each think is important, and to facilitate problem-solving efforts. By contrast, competitors *withhold* and *manipulate* information to maximize their own individual gains. Problem-solving negotiation is thus a full information perspective of bargaining that calls upon the parties to create and maintain a free, open, and rather complete flow of information.

---

[5] The graphic is adapted from RICHARD E. WALTON & ROBERT B. MCKERSIE, A BEHAVIORAL THEORY OF LABOR NEGOTIATIONS 138 (1965).

Figure 7–1

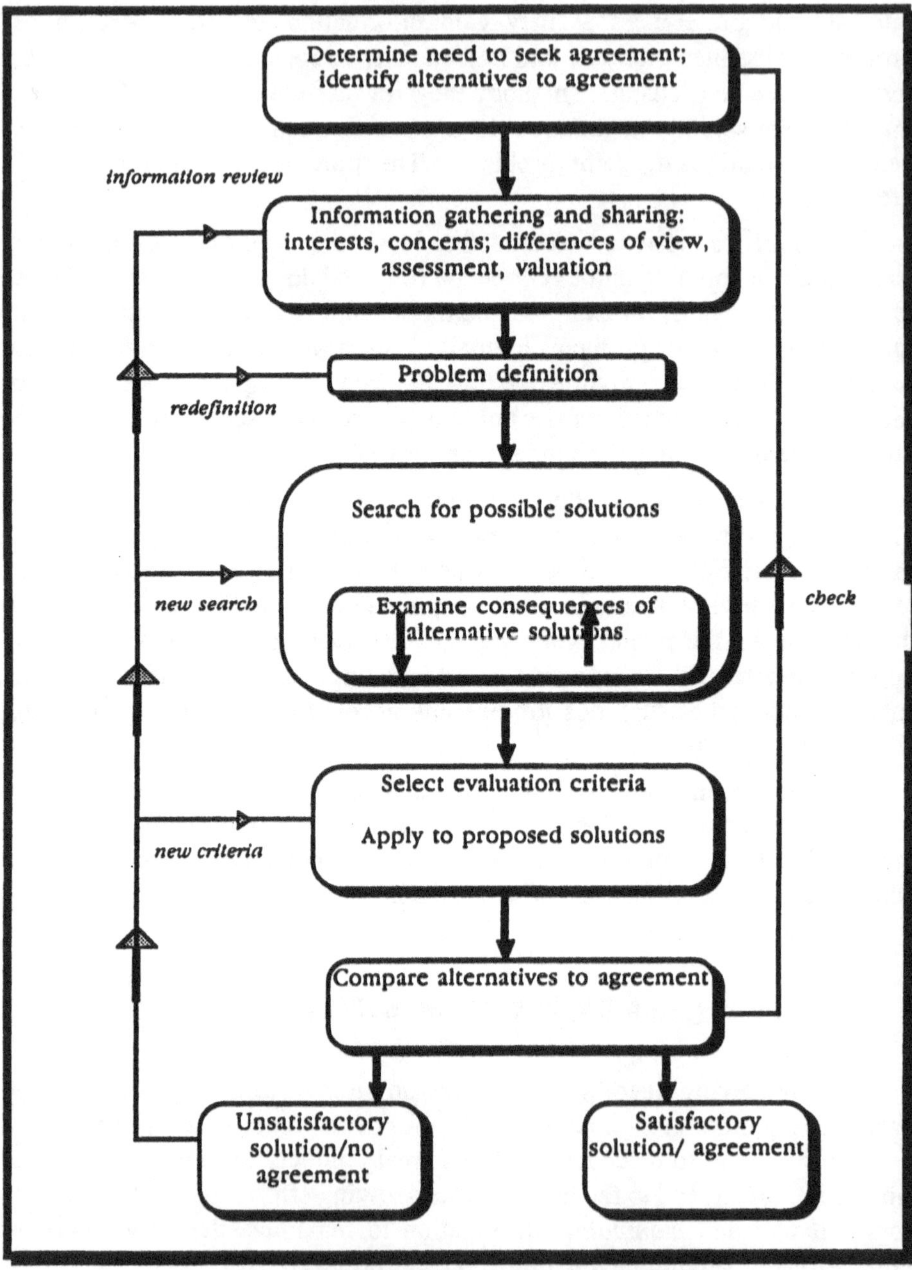

Problem-solving process in negotiation, mediation, and consensus-building

If the parties each have full information, they will know what their actual conflicts are. They will know which interests they share and which they do not. They will also know how each of them perceives the situation and what each hopes to accomplish through negotiation. If the parties have this information and accurately perceive each other's point of view, they can turn to a collaborative search for solutions that meet the goals and objectives of both sides. When each knows what the other wants, they may see how together they can help each other get what they want.

B. Interests and positions

Problem-solving negotiation is *interest-based* bargaining. Competitive negotiation and simple compromise negotiation, on the other hand, involve *position-based* bargaining. *Interests*, as used here, comprise the more abstract and perhaps intangible goals parties have in a given negotiation. That is, what the parties really care about for themselves, what they aim to achieve through the negotiation, what general needs—economic, psychic, moral, relationship, short-term, long-term—the parties hope to realize or serve. Such interests should be contrasted with particular *positions* the parties may take in a negotiation. Positions are the specific demands parties make in order to realize their interests, and the relationship between positions and interests is essentially a means-end relationship.

To take a simple example, suppose Noah decides to ask his boss for a raise. Noah has a good job and already has a good income, but he feels he wants a raise. He doesn't really need the extra money, but, of course, would like to have more disposable income. In his negotiation with his boss, Noah asks for an additional $2000 a year, which would give him the same salary as the highest paid employee in his department. Were Noah to examine his motives more deeply, however, he would realize that he feels undervalued. What he really desires is recognition and a status equal to that of the highest paid employee in his department. Although he is not clear about it, when Noah asks for $2000 more a year—takes the *position* that he needs a raise of $2000—he is primarily trying to serve his status interest, not his financial interest. Were Noah and his boss clear about this, rather than make his salary the issue in the negotiation, they could focus on ways to give him the status within the company that he desires.

This example shows that parties take *positions* in negotiation because they believe that achieving them is a way to serve their deeper purposes or *interests*. They may not have thought this through clearly or carefully enough. Espousing a wrong position, even promoting a particular position at all, may cause a negotiation to focus on the wrong issues. If Noah's boss has a strong need to save money, Noah's position that salary is the issue will make the negotiation a difficult one. If, however, both parties focus on why Noah wants a higher salary, they may discover that the real issue is status, and that issue may be easier to resolve. In other words, discovering the parties' real interests allows negotiators to avoid defining the issues in terms of positions that may not implicate those interests. In short, focusing on interests rather than positions helps the parties to define the real issues in the negotiation.

Interest-based negotiation opens up settlement possibilities not only because it helps parties focus on the right issues, but also because there may be many ways to satisfy the parties' actual interests. Paying Noah an extra $2000 a year is one way to give him enhanced status. Giving him a special title, a new position, or some other form of recognition are other ways—all ways that may serve his employer's interests better than the requested raise.

When bargaining positionally, the parties are in effect attempting to impose their own *unilateral* solutions to the issues between them, for a position is really a preconceived proposal for resolving a difference or dispute. Position-based bargaining inclines parties to bargain competitively, for staking out positions frames a negotiation as an "either-or" contest: "Either we do what you want or we do what I want." This leads to efforts to dominate to have one's way. If these do not succeed, the parties each give way a bit—compromise between their positions—in order to reach agreement. Position-based bargaining thus locks the parties into predetermined solutions, possible contests of wills over positions, or simple compromises between positions.

Interest-based bargaining by its nature also expands the set of possible outcomes with which the parties can work. Working at the deeper level of interests gives parties a broader perspective on what the negotiation may involve. This means that the parties increase the set of possible trade-offs or considerations they can take into account and use to shape packages. As a simple example, if the parties focus on winning positions, they will likely ignore the implications their contest has on their future relationship. Focusing on short-term gains may entail future losses because the parties may not wish to deal with one another again. By focusing on interests, however, they can see the value in continuing and developing a relationship and consider what that may be worth, comparatively speaking. Interest-based bargaining thus permits parties to examine their complete set of interests, rather than a single one, and consider ways in which potential agreements can serve multiple ends. As a final, practical matter, interest-based bargaining opens up the possibility of persuading parties to agree to proposals on the basis of what they themselves value.

C. Motivating Interests

It is natural for parties to incline toward positional bargaining. Positions are specific demands, clear and direct responses to a question, "What do you want?" Consequently, even the most experienced negotiators may not initially frame a negotiating problem in terms of the aims they're trying to accomplish, and the motivating interests they're trying to serve. The business deal that created the joint oil company giant, Royal Dutch/Shell exemplifies this.

Royal Dutch was principally an oil producer and refiner, with secure sources of oil. Shell was an oil trader, transporter, and distributor. Although it had also begun to produce and refine oil as well, its supply was not secure and it was in difficulty. The two companies competed for markets, and they also competed with other strong oil companies such as Standard Oil. Royal Dutch and Shell decided to amalgamate, for their respective strengths were complementary and the combined company would be better able to compete with the other major oil companies. Under the terms of the proposed agreement, the Royal Dutch management was also to manage Shell. However, Shell's principal owner, Marcus Samuel, objected, taking the position that Shell should continue to manage itself. His reason for taking that position was his fear that Royal Dutch would not manage Shell in Shell's best interests, but rather its own. To overcome this problem, Royal Dutch offered to buy one quarter of Shell's shares, creating an important stake in Shell's best interests.[6] Samuel conceded his position, but gained his apparent real objective or deeper interest. Moving away from his original position to the interest he was trying to serve made the final agreement possible.

What parties seek to realize in a given negotiation depends very much on the parties and the circumstances, and it is impossible to list all motivating interests. The parties themselves may not be clear about their underlying interests, but may be more focused on positions. This may be true, in part, because motivating interests are background factors, often seem intangible, and may be difficult to value concretely. Nonetheless, it is useful here to list some general interests and values that may motivate most people. Doing so gives a clearer sense of the bedrock level of interests it's necessary to reach to undertake useful problem-solving bargaining.[7]

- Economic interests: profit, reducing future costs, reducing inefficiencies, developing new business opportunities.
- Moral and psychological interests: integrity, principled behavior, fairness, self-respect and esteem, freedom from anxiety and stress, adventure, excitement, peace of mind.
- Ego or psychic interests: personal satisfaction, security, career, good performance, respect.
- Influence interests: reputation, authority, credibility, status, good will.

---

[6] This story is related in Daniel Yergin, The Prize 126 (1991).

[7] The nonexhaustive, roughly categorized list of interests is meant merely to be suggestive. Clearly, many of the interests listed fit into more than one category or cut across categories.

- Ideological interests: religious, political, or social beliefs.
- Relationship interests: maintaining good relationships, developing or enhancing possibilities of future relationships, terminating detrimental relationships.
- Freedom of action interests: avoiding undesirable precedents or restrictive commitments.
- Efficiency or security interests: establishing a good precedent, developing a settled and reliable procedure or process for resolving problems or issues.

D. Initiating problem-solving negotiation

The problem-solving strategy contemplates that each side in a negotiation will seek to satisfy its own interests and that each side should collaborate with the other parties to define and solve the problems between them. For the problem-solving strategy to work, it's important that the negotiators establish problem-solving ground rules, either implicitly or explicitly. This ensures that each party is engaged in and, hopefully, equally committed to, the same activity.

1. Negotiating the negotiating procedure

If the parties do not agree that they will bargain in a problem-solving manner, at least one of them has to propose, or initiate the strategy. Thus, in dealing with relatively unknown parties or parties who are inclined to negotiate competitively, one who wishes to solve problems may need to begin the negotiation by negotiating the negotiation procedure. A negotiator can do this expressly by openly making the negotiating process itself an initial subject of negotiation. Alternatively, a negotiator could simply use the strategy, for example, by probing for full information, working to discover the other side's interests, revealing one's own, and so on.

2. Using problem-solving tactics

Depending on how competitive the other side appears to be, the problem-solving negotiator may need to be very insistent on the way she wants to bargain. She can do this by seeking the other side's commitment to problem-solving bargaining. She can also use tactics that move the other side into a reciprocal problem-solving stance. During negotiation, the problem-solving negotiator simply refuses to accept positions as a basis for bargaining. Instead, she asks hard questions about what interests justify the positions the other side takes. She works to create a free flow of information and insists on clear and accurate communication, where the parties state their needs concretely. If it is safe to do so, she is explicit about her side's needs, values, and objectives. She seeks to discover the other party's as well, making a genuine attempt to understand the other side and how it perceives its interests and the situation.

3. Exploration of interests and differences

There are two general ways to increase the possible gain available to the parties or to "create value": to find common and complementary interests and to exploit differences. Where parties share interests, they may be able to devise some agreement which satisfies their shared interest or find some way in which their different interests can mesh. Sometimes parties' interests are different and conflict, but the parties also have different goals, values, stakes, outlooks, predictions, risk-aversions, and time-preferences. In that situation, it may be possible to exploit those differences in ways that satisfy all the parties' perceptions of the situation.

Joint gains come from exploiting differences, and it is the parties' differential perception and assessment of situations that leads to trade-offs.[8] For example, suppose we are negotiating a contract under which I will supply you, for a relatively long term, a unique article I manufacture. I depend on a foreign supplier for materials to make the product. My concerns are about my supply, and I fear my supply costs will increase. Therefore, I want to charge you the highest price I can. You, on the other hand, think foreign supplies are, and will continue to be, stable, and that therefore the price should be lower. Rather than compromise on a specific price, we can set it by using a formula that takes into account the cost of the foreign supply. In other words, our predictions about the available foreign supply differ. If we are each willing to act on our own predictions, we can use this difference to craft an agreement satisfactory to each of us.

These kinds of differences between parties, if somehow reflected in a final agreement, allow each party to get what it wants, or thinks it needs. It's therefore essential for the parties to discover and thoroughly explore the differences between them. The parties need to examine quite carefully their respective interests, values, goals, and perceptions of the situation. In particular, negotiators should attempt to discover differences in beliefs or forecasts, in risk-aversion, and in time-preferences.[9] This will open up possibilities of exploiting differences by matching what one party finds valuable or desirable to obtain with what another party finds relatively costless to relinquish. For this process to work, of course, the parties must also depersonalize conflict by accepting differences in viewpoints, rather than seeking to impose their respective viewpoints on one another.

---

[8] RAIFFA, *supra* note 4, at 155.

[9] DAVID A. LAX & JAMES K. SEBENIUS, THE MANAGER AS NEGOTIATOR 94, 99–102 (1986).

4. Problem definition

Once there is full information exchange and exploration of viewpoints, the particular negotiating problems the parties have should be fairly apparent. In general, they will take the form: "How do we work together to satisfy those interests we've articulated in our discussion?" It's worth noting, however, that the parties may not agree in their views of what the common problem is, and this may take some negotiating. This is important because it means that the parties have not communicated well, that they really haven't understood one another's points of view. Consequently, problem definition is an opportunity for the parties to determine whether they really understand one another, and they should take it seriously.

5. Problem solving and value creation

Once the parties agree on what their problems are, the negotiation can turn to problem solving, the actual search for solutions. As the parties wish to solve their common problems in the best possible way, their initial aim is not to jump to some solution. Rather they hope to create a process for discovering as many alternative solutions as possible in order to compare them.

The parties may use any process they wish to help devise alternative solutions or options. For example, they each could simply offer their own ideas or they could more actively brainstorm. Brainstorming is particularly useful because the rules of brainstorming[10] reduce inhibitions in idea-generation and preclude discussion of ideas as they surface.[11]

---

[10] Brainstorming is a simple and effective technique used to generate possible solutions to problems. Here are the rules for brainstorming:

- Get an agreement from each participant to use brainstorming as a means to generate a list of possible solutions to a problem.
- Get an agreement on the definition of the problem to be addressed, and write out the problem definition for all to see.
- The object of brainstorming is to develop a list of ideas which the participants can thereafter refine. To this end, every participant is encouraged and permitted to offer any ideas he or she has as possible solutions to the problem. This is, in effect, an anticensorship rule: all ideas, whether apparently relevant or irrelevant, serious or facetious, are acceptable for inclusion on the list.
- Participants may state any ideas they have, but may not comment on them during the brainstorming session. Similarly, other participants are also barred from commenting on ideas as they arise. These anti-justification and anti-judgment rules operate to stimulate creativity and avoid ego and proprietary investments in particular ideas.
- Repetition of ideas is all right.
- Silence is all right.
- At the conclusion of the brainstorming time period, the participants should have a list of ideas on which they can begin to work. They should proceed systematically through the ideas, discussing each, and its ramifications, as a possible solution to the problem presented. It may be useful to have the participants rank-order the ideas and then discuss them in order of perceived significance.

[11] Those who propose an idea often take a proprietary interest in it, and their desire to see it accepted diverts the process from idea-generation, the essential task at this point.

6. Ways of working toward integrative agreements

There are four general ways to work toward integrative agreements, and negotiators can consciously focus on these to help them generate a list of options. The first of these ways is to increase resources so that the parties no longer compete for them. The parties can also look for *bridging solutions*. Bridging involves finding some way of advancing both parties' interests simultaneously. The air courier example discussed earlier is an instance of a bridging solution.[12] If an agreement option imposes costs that might cause a party to resist it, it may be possible to cut, minimize, or compensate the other side for the costs it incurs in agreeing.[13] Finally, the parties can pose and explore options that involve trade-offs, logrolling, and packaging, as discussed in the last chapter.[14]

7. Separating solution generation from evaluation

As the parties seek the *best* solution to their problem, they should undertake a thorough and systematic search for optional ways to do so. In this, it is most useful for the parties to separate the processes of developing options from that of deciding which option is the best solution to their problem. Evaluating ideas as they arise tends to stifle idea development, precludes cross-fertilization between ideas, and cuts off packaging opportunities. There is a risk, when parties evaluate ideas as they arise, that they will argue about them rather than treat them as tentative and exploratory proposals. In addition, there is always the possibility that a party will advance only those ideas most likely to benefit it the most. Separating the evaluation process from that of idea-generation somewhat weakens the force of this kind of calculated behavior.

8. Evaluation: narrowing options and value claiming

Once the parties have a list of alternative ideas or options for solving the problem, they must evaluate them and decide the terms of their agreement. A party should evaluate options by considering how well any particular option serves its interests, rejecting options not advancing its interests or requiring undesirable compromise. In considering options, a party should compare the

---

[12] Another simple example of bridging, sometimes used as a simulated negotiation problem, involves two parties negotiating over a small shipment of rare oranges. One party wants the oranges for the pulp; the other for the skin, which is to be used to extract a rare, naturally occurring, medicinally useful chemical. If each party enters the negotiation positional and simply demands that it have the oranges, it's obvious they will be in serious conflict. If they reveal to each other why they want the oranges, and exactly what their interest in them is, however, they will discover they have no conflict at all, but that their interests are complementary.

[13] *See supra* pp. 80–81 for a discussion of cost-cutting strategy.

[14] *See* Chapter 6, Compromise Negotiation.

outcomes any option confers with its best alternatives to a negotiated settlement. Obviously, if the proposed negotiated outcomes are not better than the other alternatives, the party should not agree to them.

9. An example of a problem-solving negotiation

Assume there is a large manufacturing company that is experiencing high production costs at several of its older plants. It has examined its costs carefully and has concluded that these plants are technologically inefficient. The company also believes it would be better off to close these plants and build new ones, taking advantage of robotic manufacturing processes. If the company does this, however, many employees will lose their jobs when the company closes plants. The union, therefore, makes plant closures an issue in the next round of bargaining with the company.[15]

In these circumstances, each party could hard-bargain, the company going forward despite union objections, and the union striking if it does so. The parties' alternatives to a negotiated settlement are not good. The company could close plants and suffer a strike. The union could accept plant closures with attendant job losses or it could strike. The strike script, however, would convert the situation into a contest of strength and economics that would undoubtedly be very costly to both sides.

Reducing the situation to just a few interests, the company has important interests in profitability, efficiency, and a stable, experienced, and cooperative workforce. The union has the important interest of protecting worker's jobs, but that interest must take into account the continued competitiveness and vitality of the company. If the union accepted the company's inefficiency and noncompetitiveness claims, the parties could define their joint problem as a question of how to increase productivity in the inefficient plants without unduly threatening worker job-security. As alternative solutions, they might propose more rigorous production standards, restrictions on new hires following retirements, selective layoffs, and possibly even wage reductions.

When the company evaluates these proposals, however, it decides they will not solve the productivity problem, which it deems due to plant design, location, and equipment. Assume that the company's studies convince the union that the company's conclusion is correct. The parties might then define the problem as how to close the plants with the least harm to the workers. As possible solutions to this problem, they might pose training and job relocation programs, a special worker-assistance fund, and synchronizing old plant closures with new plant openings so that workers can transfer. Both the company and union would find

---

[15] The example is based on a case discussed in WALTON & MCKERSIE, *supra* note 5, at 160.

these possible solutions, or some combination of them, better than their no-agreement alternatives and would likely agree to them.

E. Evaluation problems: value claiming in problem-solving negotiation

In problem-solving negotiation, there are two different kinds of bargaining activities. These are value creation, that is, devising "increasing sum" solutions to the parties' common problems, and value claiming,[16] that is, dividing any gain the parties create. In other words, the parties collaborate to increase the possible available gain and they find some way to distribute it between them. How they distribute this gain may be a significant problem, for while there may be more to share, the parties may opportunistically seek to appropriate for themselves as much of it as possible.

This is easy to illustrate. Suppose Delta and Sigma have just been involved in an integrative bargaining session. They have come up with five different ways to create value, but each of these ways of adding value also differently allocates the value gain as between the parties. The situation is graphed in Figure 7–2.

Figure 7–2

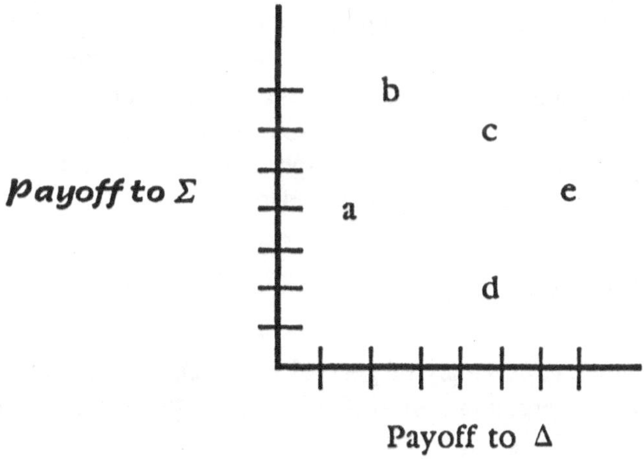

In this payoff schedule, solution b confers the most gain on Σ and solution e the most gain on Δ. Solution c, roughly and in terms of relative share, is equally good for both parties. It is not, however, the maximum gain either party could get. The parties will likely perceive this. There is therefore a good chance that each party will promote or argue for the particular solution that favors it most. In the example, Σ will argue for b and Δ for e.

[16] LAX & SEBENIUS, *supra* note 9, at 30–33.

This example clarifies the distributive problem in integrative bargaining. Although the parties may create value, they must still divide it. Often, they will divide it by agreeing to accept some particular solution as a way of satisfying their interests, but some solutions may be better for one side than for the other. In dividing the gain, or deciding which particular solution to accept, the parties can use any of the basic bargaining strategies: they could bargain competitively, compromise, or problem solve.[17] Of these, competitive bargaining is of most concern, for it may not be readily apparent that it is occurring. An innocent negotiator may fail to realize that the other side is appropriating the greatest part, or at least a disproportionate share, of the joint gain.[18]

In the simplest case the parties would bargain integratively to increase the amount of available gain, and then bargain openly and distributively to allocate the gain between them. But negotiations do not usually divide into such neat and distinct phases, and it is difficult, during the course of a negotiation, for negotiators to shift from integrative to distributive bargaining. This is simply because the two strategies are generally inconsistent with one another.[19] For example, genuine integrative bargaining requires full information disclosure and a joint search for solutions to a common problem. Distributive bargaining, on the other hand, requires, at best, selective information disclosure and information manipulation to insure intended effects, and seeks to control proposed solutions to insure maximal gain. Thus, in cases where the parties initially bargained integratively to increase gain, they will have disclosed the very information they should have concealed in order to maximize their gain from the negotiation. For example, suppose I want to sell you an item that my company has overproduced, given the market for the product. If I disclose the overproduction to you, I cannot later, in order to get from you as high a price as possible, pretend I will have no difficulty in selling it to someone else.

F. Mixed bargaining

Because of this inconsistency of general approach, phase shifts from integrative to distributive bargaining are difficult to manage. What is more likely is

---

[17] The idealistic, and rather simplistic, problem-solving model promoted by some in effect proposes that the parties seek to divide gain fairly by agreeing to use some mutually selected, objective principle, e.g., fair market value. In essence, this appears to be an effort to extend the problem-solving model one step further—not only to create gain but to search for some mutually acceptable and fair way to divide the gain created.

[18] As basic bargaining strategies, problem solving and hard-bargaining are inconsistent with one another. For example, where the problem-solving strategy calls for full information disclosure, hard-bargaining contemplates withholding information. It's nonetheless possible for a bargainer both to attempt to increase available gain and to appropriate most of that gain. In doing so, however, the bargainer would, to a certain degree, have to cooperate in problem solving and also nontransparently use some hard-bargaining techniques and tactics.

[19] *See generally* WALTON & MCKERSIE, *supra* note 5, at 161–183.

that parties may attempt a simultaneous complex blending of integrative and distributive moves. For example, in order to take advantage of the other side's willingness to engage in integrative bargaining, the hard-bargainer, while pretending to give full information, could selectively withhold information. Similarly, a hard-bargainer might not engage in a genuine search for creative alternatives to solve the joint problem. Instead, he might offer and advance only those solutions that would, if accepted, confer the most gain on his side. The hard-bargainer could also dissemble about his preferences or priorities or distort the actual amount of gains or losses certain alternatives might confer or impose on him. Alternatively, a negotiator could selectively bargain integratively in good faith on some issues while merely pretending to do so on other issues. This might allow him to make clever and advantageous trade-offs later.

In such cases, the negotiator follows a complex "mixed bargaining" strategy[20] involving apparent integrative bargaining moves which screen actual distributive aims. The result is what is called "variable-sum" bargaining, as distinguished from "zero-sum" and "positive-sum" bargaining. In variable-sum bargaining, the gains realized in the negotiation depend on the actual amount of genuine integrative bargaining taking place. If a party manipulates integrative bargaining in order to secure a greater share allocation of any gains, there may be less overall gain than there would had both parties genuinely engaged in integrative bargaining.

The concern, however, is not so much the bargaining efficiency, that is, whether the parties have failed to realize all potential gains, but rather exploitation of one party by the other. Negotiators engaged in problem-solving negotiation should be alert to this possibility. Unless justifiably trusting of the other side, they should adopt an overall strategy of working to increase gain and acting defensively to prevent the other side from getting a disproportionate share of it.[21]

1. Agreement on evaluation principles

One possible way to limit competitive claiming is to insist on principled evaluation of the options the parties are considering incorporating into their agreement. For example, suppose the negotiation involves a factual dispute, or a dispute about the value of some item. Obviously, depending on findings of fact or value, one party may stand to gain more than the other. Consequently, in such a case, a party may seek to persuade the other that its own version of the facts or its own valuation formula is the one they should use. To avoid this problem, which could entail a competitive conflict, the parties could agree to

---

[20] WALTON & MCKERSIE, *supra* note 5, at 161–168, contains a good discussion of mixed bargaining.

[21] *Id.* at 82.

some "objective" determination of the facts or valuation, e.g., using a neutral fact finder or taking the average of three appraisals. In other words, rather than selecting an option just because one party prefers it, the negotiators can attempt to agree on objective criteria for choosing among the options. The negotiation may thus, for a time, shift from a discussion about various proposals to a different discussion, or negotiation. That is a discussion over what principles the parties' can mutually agree to accept to help them choose between options.

Note, however, that while the parties can attempt to solve the gain distribution problem in a principled way, they can also attempt to deploy those principles most advantageous to them. Suppose, for example, that you and I each need a good computer and agree to share the $3000 cost of buying one. Neither of us has enough spare money to buy the computer on our own, and neither of us needs to use it full time. Now, of the $3000 cost, I put in $2000 and you put in $1000. How do we allocate use of the equipment?

Two of the obvious principles we could use to allocate our use-share are equity and equality. I am likely to assert that we should share the computer in proportion to our contributions to its purchase. You could respond that we should share equally, for although I contributed more, I would have no computer but for you. If I agree with you, and we adopt the equality principle, you obtain a share beyond your contribution. This example illustrates the share-division problem and demonstrates that, even when parties attempt to come to principled agreements, particular principles will often favor one side more than the other in share-distribution. It also suggests that parties are likely to advance those division principles which are most advantageous to them. Negotiators must therefore closely attend the division of gains and scrutinize preferred division principles with great care.

When parties perceive particular and obvious principles as clearly favoring one side or the other, they may find it better not to invoke them or argue about principles at all. Advancing such a principle will likely appear to be a competitive move. In such a situation, it's necessary either to move to other principles that the other side deems fairer, if possible, or to resolve the issue without regard to principles at all.

2. Fair division

Various "principles" that negotiating parties could use to divide gains actually divide them unequally or have results that at least one party can object to as being unfair. Parties will generally perceive that various "principles" divide gains as between them in different ways and deliver different results. Even if all parties might agree that, in the abstract, a particular principle—say, equal division, for example—is fair, when actually applied to a particular case, some will view it as unfair. This is the case in the shared computer purchase example given above. Whenever applying a "principle" results in conferring more gains on a party than he appears to deserve, the "losers," who get proportionately less, may feel injustice in the distribution or envy the unwarranted gains.

Theorists have devised a number of techniques and decision procedures, or algorithms, such as "one party divides, the other chooses,"[22] to deal with this problem. One technique is a *post-settlement settlement.*[23] With this technique, the parties first work out a settlement acceptable to them. Afterward, perhaps with the help of a third party, they seek to improve on the original settlement. Although primarily concerned with enhancing negotiation efficiency, the technique does have fair-division implications. "Efficiency" here means that in bargaining the parties do not "leave gains on the table," that is, that they find all the gains they have to divide between themselves and that they divide them. The basic rule of the post-settlement settlement is that the parties can change their original agreement as long as any new agreement improves on the old. It will do so if it makes at least one of the parties better off (receive more gains) while not worsening the position (reducing gains) of any other party. To the degree that a post-settlement settlement actually does improve the position of the least well-off parties, it enhances or improves the fairness of the original deal.

Two algorithms, the "adjusted winner" procedure (AW) and the "proportional allocation" procedure (PA), by contrast provide means to produce efficient, envy-free, and equitable divisions.[24] The AW procedure works as follows. When parties seek to divide goods between themselves, allocate 100 points to each party, and let each party value the separate goods by allocating and distributing the 100 points among the goods. Then, give any particular good to whichever party has allocated the most points to it. Where there are ties, give the good to one or the other party. Tally the points each party "realizes" from the award of goods, and then make goods transfers to equalize the parties' point totals.[25]

For example, Bob and Carol must divide three goods between them.[26] Their initial point allocation is set up in Figure 7–3.

Because he has allocated the most points to Goods 1 and 2, Bob gets them, while Carol gets Good 3. Bob has realized the value of 73 points while Carol has realized a value of 61 points. If Bob transfers Good 1 to Carol, she will realize 66 points. This is a close approximation of equality. (To achieve perfect

---

[22] RAIFFA, *supra* note 4, at 297–299.

[23] LAX & SEBENIUS, *supra* note 9, at 180–181.

[24] STEVEN J. BRAMS & ALAN D. TAYLOR, FAIR DIVISION 65–85 (1996).

[25] *Id.* at 68–69.

[26] *Id.* at 68–70.

Figure 7–3

	Good$_1$	Good$_2$	Good$_3$	Total
Bob	6	67	27	100
Carol	5	34	61	100

equality, Bob would also have to transfer a small portion of Good 2 to Carol as well.)

AW works properly only when the parties are truthful about their valuations. PA, by contrast, works by inducing parties to be truthful. Under PA, as with AW, parties allocate 100 points among goods. The parties then add their allocations for particular goods, and each party receives its proportionate share of each good. This is illustrated in Figure 7–4.[27]

Figure 7–4

	Good$_1$	Good$_2$	Good$_3$	Total
Bob	6	67	27	100
Carol	5	34	61	100
Total by good	11	101	88	

Bob receives $6/11$ of Good 1, $67/101$ of Good 2, and $27/58$ of Good 3. Carol receives the remainder. On examination, it turns out that both parties receive value worth the equivalent of 55.9 points to each of them.

Both AW and PA would appear to work well in negotiations where parties must divide something between them "equally." That is, when the parties seek to achieve equal satisfaction although each party values things differently. Cases involving nonmonetary inheritances that the legatees must divide equally and divorce property settlements provide examples. They would also work in any negotiation in which the parties agreed in advance to divide "equally" any gains they created through negotiation where the gains were not fungible goods.

[27] *Id.* at 75–78.

A final useful method of securing fair division is through a two-stage auction process.[28] In stage 1, all parties submit sealed bids. These are then opened and made public. In stage 2, each party can choose one of the first stage bids—his own or another's—as a second stage bid. If her second stage bid is the high bid, she wins the auction. If more than one party makes the high bid, the party who made the highest stage 1 bid wins the auction.

Not many negotiating parties will have the sophistication needed to invoke the post-settlement settlement technique, and the AW, PA, and two-stage auction procedures on their own. These methods are neither intuitive nor well known. They are, however, useful devices that a third-party intervenor in a negotiation, e.g., a mediator, might wish to propose in order to resolve particular share allocation problems in particular disputes.

G. Possible limits on interest-based bargaining

Interest-based bargaining opens possibilities foreclosed in position-based bargaining, and can result in more creative and satisfactory agreements than is possible in position-based bargaining. It is not, however, a bargaining strategy that succeeds in all bargaining situations.[29] Parties' fundamental interests sometimes conflict so strongly that focusing on them might cause a breakdown in negotiations. In such circumstances, it is better for the parties to focus on concrete and pragmatic issues, involving lower-level interests, which they may be able to resolve. Beyond this, in bargaining situations where there is a considerable power imbalance between the parties, the party with the greater power may see no benefit from interest bargaining and resist it for that reason.

1. Fundamental value conflicts

The most obvious example of a case where interest-based bargaining will not work involves parties who frame issues in terms of fundamental values or ideologies which conflict. A few years ago, it would have been impossible for the United States and the former Soviet Union to negotiate over fundamental changes in their political systems and basic ideologies. The countries, however,

---

[28] *Id.* at 179–181.

[29] Some of the popular literature promoting interest-based bargaining is a bit Pollyanna-ish, following a rhetorical strategy of trying to convince readers that interest-based bargaining is a "magical" tool for producing problem-solving results. The truth, however, is that some problems do not have ingenious solutions, but are resolved simply by a decision. The solution, if you want to call it that, is a decision that people can live with. In such circumstances, negotiating is not so much a question of finding a "right" answer that will meet everyone's interests, but really is a matter of "working through." That is, facing the ambiguities of the situation, the conflicting feelings and values, accepting what each has to give up, becoming comfortable with the less than optimal result.

reached many lower-level agreements ranging from cultural exchanges to arms control. Similarly, the United States and Ayatollah Khomeini's Iran could not negotiate about the respective values of Western capitalist civilization and Islamic fundamentalism. They were nonetheless able to negotiate over the American hostages and Iran's frozen assets in the United States.[30]

In both of these cases, the parties did engage in some kind of interest bargaining, but did not even attempt to negotiate over their fundamental belief systems. The lesson is that where parties have strongly opposed basic interests, a likely case when they attempt to realize conflicting ideologies, they will do better if they focus on intermediate, pragmatic interests instead.

2. Bargaining power imbalances

Nothing requires parties to bargain in problem solving rather than competitive ways. Because problem-solving bargaining can lead to gains or better results for both sides than can competitive bargaining, and enhance relationships as well, it generally appears to be a better way to negotiate than competing. Why then, apart from inveterate competitors, would a party ever choose to bargain competitively rather than integratively?

Most starkly put, when a party has the power to get what it wants from another, and is unconcerned with any potential negative consequences of doing so, it has no reason to engage in interest bargaining. In other words, parties roughly equal in bargaining power, parties actually dependent on one another, are most likely to use interest bargaining because neither can dominate the negotiation. Where a party can dominate without cost to itself, however, it has no reason to refrain. Thus there will be occasions when a party will choose not to engage in interest bargaining because it perceives that positional bargaining on a particular issue serves it better. This might occur when a particular issue and its surrounding circumstances give a party enhanced power or leverage in a negotiation.[31] For example, an employee, concerned *only* with negotiating a possible salary increase, should probably reveal she has a higher salary offer from another employer. Similarly, if a real estate development company fails to prepare an adequate environmental impact report on a project, groups seeking to reduce the project's adverse environmental consequences could use that issue to exact gains.[32]

---

[30] James B. Stewart & Peter Tyrell, *US Firms Win Some, Lose Some at Tribunal Arbitrating $5 Billion in Claims Against Iran*, Wall St. J., Nov. 15, 1984, at A36; Bernard Gwertzman, *Iran and US Seek to Clarify Terms for Freeing Hostages*, N.Y. Times, Jan. 18, 1981, at A1; *Negotiations History: An Array of Deadlines Posed and Passed*, Wash. Post, Jan. 19, 1981, at A16.

[31] Lax & Sebenius, *supra* note 9, at 70.

[32] Both examples assume that the dominant party has considered the full range of its possible interests yet has found no reason not to attempt to appropriate most of the gain for itself.

Even so, efforts to interest bargain may, in many cases, moderate domination moves. By moving the negotiation to the level of interests, the parties expand the scope of their considerations. They may learn they are dependent on one another in ways they hadn't realized. The development company may have other planned projects of interest to the groups now opposing it. It might therefore be willing to trade off significant mitigating changes in its other projects to avoid the delay that litigation over the environmental impact report would create. Even when parties do not uncover such dependencies, the dominant party may nonetheless discover that potential benefits from working together outweigh the gains from noncooperation.

III. SUMMARY

The following are the general steps in integrative or problem-solving bargaining.[33]

- Determine what your interests or the interests of your principal really are.
- Establish your best alternative to a negotiated agreement.
- Negotiate a cooperative, problem-solving bargaining process—that is, attempt to make the negotiation a mutual search for ways to satisfy both parties' interests.
- Identify issues and problems between the parties by revealing interests and discovering those of the other side. Explore interests and differences of views and perceptions of the situation. In this process, do not compromise interests, or "give" on them in an effort to be reasonable. Instead, stay committed to attempting to satisfy your interests completely.
- Focus the discussion on the parties' interests, not on their positions.
- Clearly state the parties' interests, needs, and values, and define any conflicts or problems they create as between the parties. Avoid emotion-laden conflict by accepting the other's viewpoints and by focusing discussion on interests and problems.
- Separate the process of inventing solutions from deciding what solutions to adopt.
    - Create value or alternative possibilities for agreement by jointly devising solutions to the problems the parties perceive they are trying to solve.

---

[33] The text here generally follows the models found in ROGER FISHER & WILLIAM URY, GETTING TO YES (1983); LAX & SEBENIUS, *supra* note 9.

    - Attempt to surface solutions satisfactory to both sides by exploiting shared interests and differences of valuation, forecasts, risk-aversion, and time-preferences.

- Although the parties may collaborate to increase possible gains or to devise various possible solutions to their jointly defined problems, they must yet devise some way to decide which alternatives to select. As that decision will distribute value as between the parties, they must take care to analyze how it will do so.

- To avoid a competitive struggle, the parties may attempt to find "objective criteria" to help them select among proposed alternative solutions.
    - They can do this by framing this final problem-solving issue as a mutual search for objective criteria during which the parties ask for and seek *principled* justifications for accepting, or deciding between, proposed solutions. This is more difficult than it may seem, for few principles distribute neutrally, and it is important to examine proposed principled distributions carefully.

- Measure possible settlements by reference to concrete no-agreement alternatives.

CHAPTER 8
FACILITATING EFFICIENT TRADE-OFFS

In order to negotiate well, it's essential to know what issues are likely to arise in a negotiation. In simple negotiations, or standardized negotiations such as employment contracts, the issues are usually quite predictable. For example, in employment contracts, the obvious issues are salary, length of contract, position, duties, and vacation time. In a typical negotiation concerning a lease of office space, price-per-square-foot, building-maintenance fees, common-area fees, space redesign and remodeling, parking spaces, and length of lease are issues certain to arise.

In other negotiations, some issues may be clear or anticipated, while others are uncertain or even unsuspected. Suppose that, seeking to take advantage of lowered interest rates, Jane seeks to refinance her house. Her current home loan is at 9 percent interest, and she wants to refinance it at a lower rate of 7.5 percent. There seem to be no issues there, other than her ability to qualify. When she talks to the bank about refinancing, however, she discovers she will have to pay 2 "points," or 2 percent of the total loan amount, to the bank as its fee for making the loan. The bank also says it will reduce its fee to 1.5 points if Jane keeps a checking account at the bank and authorizes an automatic deduction for her monthly payment. The bank further tells her it will refinance her house at an even lower rate of 7.25 percent if she agrees to open a credit line of at least $10,000, also secured by her house. While Jane may find these offers attractive, she did not anticipate them, and they raise issues she will need to decide.

I. INTERESTS AND ISSUES

Negotiation issues arise from the interaction of the negotiating parties' interests. If Jane is a good credit risk, the bank's interest in making a profit on money it lends, and assuring payment, explains its offer to Jane. The automatic checking account deduction gives it payment priority and security, and the line of credit offer, if accepted, makes for a larger loan, also secured by the house. For her part, Jane's interest in a lower loan fee and a lower interest rate make the bank's offer attractive. Nonetheless, she may have other interests that make it problematic to accept. For example, she may keep her money in another bank, with which she has good relations that she wants to keep. She may also think it unwise to have access to a $10,000 credit account, as she wishes to keep her overall debt load as low as possible and doesn't want an open temptation to spend. Jane will have to weigh her several interests carefully in order to make a decision regarding these issues the bank's offer raises for her.

Plainly, figuring out one's interests is important because they will, together with the other party's interests, define the issues in the negotiation. Furthermore, one's interests vary from situation to situation, and have varying weights in different contexts. Negotiations often affect multiple interests that a party has. The possible ways the negotiation can resolve the issues will affect those interests in different ways and to different degrees. Multi-issue negotiations open possibilities of different "packages" or combinations of ways the parties can use to resolve issues. In such circumstances, a negotiator often finds decisions whether to accept negotiation proposals difficult to make because he confronts choices not considered before and does not know how to compare and value the possible trade-offs. In addition, the speed and pace of such negotiations, and the involvement of multiple parties can compound the difficulty of figuring out how a particular proposal affects one's interests.

For example, the Law of the Sea Treaty negotiation involved more than 150 countries, with very different interests and ideologies.[1] There were hundreds of complicated, often interlocking, issues. These concerned territorial seas, the rights of landlocked countries, fishing zones, navigational freedom, ownership of the seabed, seabed mining, commercial-mining rights, the role and authority of the United Nations, and the like.

While few negotiations are this large, momentous, and complicated, many negotiations do present choices that are difficult for the negotiator to value and assess. When parties are not clear about exactly what it is they seek from a negotiation, or when other parties raise issues that surprise them, they may not be able to protect or further their interests. Consequently, it's important for a party to think through impending negotiations, how they implicate her interests, how she values or weighs them, and what are her preferences and priorities. This knowledge will help her to compare different possible agreements and determine which is best for her. In these cases, the negotiator should have some

---

[1] James K. Sebenius, Negotiating the Law of the Sea 7–12 (1984).

method or process for carrying out a comparative assessment of relative preferences.[2]

A. Figuring out fundamental interests

Deciding what you value, how much you value it, and what you are willing to give in return, require you to analyze your fundamental interests and how the pending negotiation might affect them or contribute toward realizing them. Usually, as you begin to think about an upcoming negotiation, you have some sense of what you want to get out of it and of what the likely issues are. To discover your fundamental interests, simply begin by making a list of what you think will be involved in the negotiation, and the issues you think are important to you. Then go over the list, and for each item on it, ask yourself why that item is important. Analyze the reasons you offer for holding these items important, and ask again why those are important to you. Eventually, you will reach a bedrock level where you cannot go further, where you cannot find any reason for an item's importance other than a recognition that it is important. When you have reached that level, you have identified an interest that's fundamental to you.[3]

Assume a company is negotiating to buy a 100-acre tract of land from a farmer who owns 1000 acres. The company intends to build family housing and a commercial center on the property. One item it wishes to discuss in purchase negotiations is the question whether there are any toxic chemicals on the site. Why is that item important? Well, if there are any on the site, it may not be developable. Cleanup may cost the company more than it can pay and still make a profit. The company may face toxic chemical liability suits at some time in the future after it has developed the site. Why are these important to the company? Obviously, all these reasons relate to the financial viability of the project. But the last reason also implicates the company's reputation, future business prospects, and a desire to avoid debilitating litigation. Why are these important? They too relate to financial viability or profitability, but also to company survival, integrity, and stature. Why are these important? It's hard to push them back further. They just *are* important; they are fundamental.

Having identified one's own fundamental interests in this way, the negotiator should try to identify the other side's fundamental interests as well. This allows

---

[2] This is true whether one negotiates for oneself or a client. When working for a client, the negotiator must have a way to get the client to address, and decide, what is most important and what configuration of packages or outcomes will best satisfy his or her interests. The text discusses quantification procedures, but for an outline, *see* p. 117.

[3] RALPH KEENEY, VALUE-FOCUSED THINKING 65–69 (1992); Ralph Keeney & Howard Raiffa, *Securing and Analyzing Values*, in NEGOTIATION ANALYSIS 148–149 (H. PEYTON YOUNG, ED., 1992).

the negotiator to determine which issues are likely to be important to the other side. There may be issues that are of mutual importance to each side. Other issues may be of immediate concern only to one side or the other. Nonetheless, whatever is an issue for one side will be an issue in the negotiation, and the other side will have to deal with it in some way. Anticipating the other side's issues enables a negotiator to figure out possible trade-offs.

In the land purchase example above, suppose the development company discovers that the farmer is in financial difficulty and has a large farm-mortgage balloon-payment due within three months. The farmer has a clear financial interest in making the sale, and his financial need is likely to make the transaction closing date quite important to him. The closing date may or may not be as important to the development company, but it is most useful to the company to know it may be important to the farmer.

B. Figuring out possible outcomes

Issues grow out of interests, and identifying each side's fundamental interests is essential to figuring out the possible issues in a negotiation. Once you have listed the issues the negotiation will likely involve, it is important to try to specify the possible resolutions, or range of outcomes, for each issue. For example, in the land sale hypothetical, we have thus far posed two issues. For each issue, we can pose possible outcomes. (See Figure 8-1.)

After the negotiator specifies the range of outcomes for each issue in this fashion, she can then rank or weight issues and outcome preferences. If the issues and outcomes lend themselves to it, the planner can quantify them, as with the additive-scoring model described below.[4] If not, the planner can make a qualitative assessment of issues and outcomes, trying to determine the relative importance or weight she accords each issue and her outcome-preferences within and across issues.

C. Valuing outcomes

Merely identifying issues and possible outcomes, however, is not quite enough. In order to trade, a negotiator must have a sense of the value of the items traded. In other words, the negotiator needs to look at the array of possible or probable interests and outcomes implicated in the negotiation, and assign values to them, for himself and the other participants. Assigning

---

[4] *See infra* notes 5–6 and accompanying text.

Figure 8–1

Issue	*Outcomes*
Toxic Chemicals	• None on site • Minor presence, readily remediable • Significant presence, but reduced purchase price • significant presence, no reduction in price, but hold harmless clause • significant presence, no reduction in price, take land as it is • chemicals are an insuperable problem
Transaction Closing Date	• 6 months • 3 months • 1 month

value may be a matter of identifying preferences, outcome priorities, or even attempting to quantify particular outcomes by giving them a relative numerical weight.

Valuing possible outcomes in this way greatly facilitates intelligent and efficient bargaining. Having assigned relative values to different outcomes prior to negotiation, the negotiator can readily assess different packages of proposals during the negotiation. He can then make package adjustments or counterproposals having more value to him.

Valuing potential outcomes is not easy work. We often do not know, without considerable thought and without obtaining more information, whether we value outcome A more than outcome B. Do you prefer a contract for one year at 8 percent or a contract for three years at 4 percent? The answer depends on how well a particular outcome serves your interests.

There may even be a tension or some conflict between your interests of which you are unaware until forced to confront it. As a simple example, suppose you have to choose between two job offers, one, well-paying, in a large, congested city, and the other, not as remunerative, in a small, attractive city in the mountains. Each possibility attracts you. You like the culture, excitement, and opportunities of the large city. You also love the mountains and outdoor sports while urban squalor and congestion repel you. This may be a hard choice. Choice of a job implicates many more interests than those stated. For example, it bears on career opportunities, relationships to partners and relatives, other opportunities, lifestyle, and many other consequences as well. Resolving which job to take is not necessarily an easy question. To do so may require much weighing and sorting. It takes time to find out what you really value.

So too regarding choice and decision making in complex negotiation. Unless well-organized and given sufficient time, the negotiators may have extraordinary difficulty in sorting out how possible choices bear on their own best interests. Sorting this all out in advance, insofar as possible, is the ideal way to do this.

D. Quantification

One useful way to value interests for purposes of assessing possible trade-offs and the attractiveness of various packages is to attempt to quantify them. Many people are uncomfortable with the thought of quantifying decisions, particularly where issues to be decided are qualitative and appear unquantifiable. But the aim of quantifying decision making is not to impose a false mathematical precision where none can exist, but simply to give rational guidance in situations involving confusing trade-offs. Quantification is a means of preparation. It forces a party to think through what it really values, and how much it values it, as compared to other things implicated in the decision.

The quantification procedure itself is not difficult. It is simply a matter of deciding the relative importance of issues, and then, within issues, deciding the relative importance of the possible outcomes. A negotiator can do this by assigning points or various weights to issues and outcomes. Here is an outline of the quantification procedure.[5]

a) Identify the interests the negotiation may involve. Consider both concrete interests such as, for example, job security, and more abstract interests, such as the client's desire to vindicate a principle or the precedential value of any particular settlement.
b) Assess the situation, role-playing if necessary, from the other side's point of view and identify its interests.
c) Array the respective interests, note common and complementary interests, and consider carefully where the parties' interests may conflict. Determine the probable issues in the negotiation and the range of possible outcomes over all issues.
d) Figure out the least and most attractive set of outcomes. Use these to compare other possible outcomes.
e) Work out other possible outcomes and compare them. Try to determine which outcomes are preferable to others. To help decide whether one outcome is preferable to another, quantify outcomes as outlined below. Quantification may seem a bit artificial, but the procedure is not rigid and is designed to reflect subjective valuations and weightings.

1) Allocate 100 points over the range of issues. Assign weights, as among issues, by allocating points, or values, to each issue according to subjective feelings about their relative value.

2) After dividing up the 100 points among issues, allocate the points assigned to a particular issue by assigning weights to each possible outcome on that issue.

3) This procedure will produce a schedule or matrix of issues and outcomes with point values assigned to each outcome on each issue. Comparing different packages then simply involves adding up the points the different packages produce. The package with the most points should be the most preferred outcome.

f) Once a party works through this exercise, it should attempt to do the same thing for the other side, role-playing if necessary, to get an understanding of its interests, preferences, and priorities.

Let's assume you represent a cable television company, and you want to buy customer-billing services from a data-service company. The data-service company provides television-usage monitoring devices, computers, and software that will allow your company to do its billing automatically, no matter what level of service your individual customers have. To simplify the example, further assume there are only five issues to negotiate: price, features, delivery date, training, and service.

---

[5] This procedure is adapted from DAVID A. LAX & JAMES K. SEBENIUS, THE MANAGER AS NEGOTIATOR 74–84 (1986); *see also* KEENEY, *supra* note 3, at 129.

After thorough discussion within your company, the CEO decides that, given the range of possible outcomes for each issue, the company should weight the issues as apportioned in Figure 8–2.

Figure 8–2

Issue	*Points*
Price	30
Features	20
Delivery Date	10
Training	20
Service	20

Having determined the relative weight of the issues on a 100-point scale, the CEO proceeds to analyze possible outcomes on each issue. After she identifies them, she also weights them—by allocating point values based on the total number of points assigned to that issue. (See Figure 8–3.)

Quantifying in this fashion allows the cable company to compare the value to it of alternative packages that the vendor may propose.

The hypothetical presupposed that the issues in the negotiation were independent of one another. When issues are independent, a negotiator can value them separately, as in the example, and simply add points for each issue. In other words, simple, additive-scoring systems work where issues are independent of one another.

Where issues are interdependent, however—that is, where the value of one issue depends on how the negotiators resolve another issue—it may be more difficult to quantify. Suppose in the cable company example that the vendor ties the monthly contract price to the number of features each billing service package provides. In that case, the parties can't consider those two issues separately. Nonetheless, they could think of them as comprising a unit, that is, as a single issue, weight it appropriately, and then add it to the other, independent issues.[6]

[6] Keeney & Raiffa, *supra* note 3, at 138–139. Simple additivity also does not work, without adjustment, where a party must impose a reservation level or bottom line on one or more issues. In that case, it isn't possible simply to add points to compare different deals, for it is necessary to insure that a minimum score is achieved on the designated issues. *Id.* at 139.

Figure 8–3

Issue	*Outcomes*	*Points*
Price	$1,000/month	20
	$900/month	25
	$800/month	30
Features	10 Features	20
	7 Features	15
	5 Features	10
Delivery Date	1 Month	10
	2 months	8
	3 months	5
Training	In house	20
	Mixed: in-house and at vendor's	15
	At vendor's	10
Service	24 Hour call/7 days a week	20
	Within 1 day	15
	Within 2 days	10

E. Prioritizing or preference ordering interests

Prioritizing or preference ordering interests is another way to value them. It is useful when negotiators have difficulty quantifying interests. Essentially, prioritizing is a matter of thinking hard about interests in order to become clear about their relative importance or value. Indeed, this is the only way to figure out what trade-offs to make. In other words, in order to do this, one needs to know what an interest is worth compared to other interests one has. However, valuing interests, particularly intangible interests, can be quite difficult. While one can't expect exactness in weighting intangible interests, almost any method of relative weighting brings greater clarity to trade-off decisions.

F. Comparative valuation

Another way to comparatively value an intangible interest is to ask how much one would be willing to pay for it if one could buy it on the open market. For example, how much would a trial-averse plaintiff in an automobile accident case be willing to pay to avoid the anxiety of trial?

> [Someone] asks her to imagine that a pharmacist offered to sell her a magic potion that would completely eliminate the feeling of anxiety from court proceedings. What would be the most she would pay for the potion before going to trial? Would she pay $10? "That's silly. Of course." Would she pay $100? "Sure." $100,000? "Certainly not, that's one-third of my minimum settlement!" What about $50,000? "Probably not." $1000? "I think so." $10,000? "Well, that's a tough one. But, if push came to shove, the trial would be an awful experience so, probably yes." $25,000? "Maybe not, but I'm not sure. . . ." And so on.[7]

G. Scoring alternatives to negotiation

When quantifying, weighing, or preference ordering possible issues and outcomes to help in negotiation decision making, it is important to attempt to do the same for one's alternatives to agreement. When the possible alternatives to agreement involve the same issues the negotiation does, this is not difficult, for there is direct comparability. In that case, the alternatives to agreement essentially set the reservation prices for the issues under negotiation.

For example, suppose you are a manufacturer seeking new contracts for the purchase of raw materials. You have existing suppliers, and you can continue

---

[7] LAX & SEBENIUS, *supra* note 5, at 75.

using them if you cannot obtain better materials and terms with new suppliers. As your basic alternative to agreement is to renew the old contracts, you can use those contract terms as your basis for comparing possible new contracts. Some of the existing contract terms such as price and quantity will already be quantified, and you can readily quantify others, like quality, on some appropriate scale. Once you have done this, you can easily compare old supplier contract terms with those offered in negotiations with potential new suppliers.

Scoring your best alternatives to agreement will be more difficult when they involve some issues other than, or in addition to, those which the negotiation concerns. Suppose, in the manufacturing example, that one of the manufacturer's old suppliers has proposed entering a joint venture with the manufacturer. The manufacturer has some interest in this proposal. Whatever issues and possibilities the joint-venture prospect raises, they would not be a direct part of the manufacturer's negotiations with potential new suppliers. In this case, the manufacturer's best alternative to a new agreement seems noncomparable with the price, quantity, and quality issues involved in negotiations with new suppliers. This is because its best alternative to a new agreement involves an altogether different and large issue of a possible joint venture.

Even in this situation, however, it is possible to assign values to the issues in the alternative and those in the negotiation and obtain at least rough comparability. There should be no difficulty in scoring those issues that are common to the negotiation and the existing alternative, that is, price, quantity, and quality.[8] The manufacturer could also estimate the joint venture's value and add that to the scores for the common issues. It could then use this figure to compare new supplier proposals.[9] To be acceptable, any new proposal must deliver a value greater than that which the manufacturer calculated as deriving from remaining with the old supplier and entering a joint venture with it.

II. SUMMARY

Generally, problem-solving negotiation is the most productive way to negotiate and to resolve disputes. While the problem-solving model is a simple one, it is not necessarily simple to execute effectively. Many negotiations and disputes may involve conflicting interests that the parties can reconcile only through trade-offs. Lacking an understanding of how compromise and trade-offs work in problem-solving negotiation, parties may bargain ineffectively, not maximizing their interests as well as possible under the circumstances. Even if they know how these matters work, they may continue to bargain inefficiently if they

---

[8] Keeney & Raiffa, *supra* note 3, at 145.

[9] *Id.*

failed to clarify in advance what they seek from the negotiation and what they are willing to trade. The negotiator needs to identify all possible issues and outcomes, not only from her own perspective, but, insofar as possible, from that of other negotiating parties as well.

The negotiator should identify his own fundamental interests and those of other parties. Examining the array of interests allows a negotiator to anticipate the issues, and, in particular, the issues having relevance for other participants. Having identified possible issues, it is also possible to identify a range of outcomes on each issue and to value them. Not all the issues and possible outcomes a party identifies will have any immediate value to them, but some may have value as tradable items. In other words, the negotiator may identify outcomes that are of little or no concern to himself, but have value to other parties. During the negotiation, the negotiator can trade these items for items he values.

CHAPTER 9

COGNITIVE PROBLEMS IN NEGOTIATION

Notwithstanding the fullest understanding and the most careful planning and preparation, efforts to undertake problem-solving bargaining can go awry. This is because the parties do not take into account some of the ways in which humans tend to make decisions in uncertain situations. Researchers studying human problem solving and decision making observe that human beings possess "bounded" rationality.[1] Humans make choices based on a simplified mental model of a real situation. We unconsciously use judgmental strategies to make decisions when asked to take risks or when interpreting ambiguous or otherwise unclear information. In certain circumstances, these cognitive strategies, sometimes called judgmental heuristics[2] or cognitive illusions,[3] can even cause us to make objectively inconsistent or irrational choices. While useful and efficient, shortcuts enable us to draw conclusions about situations without consciously analyzing them. These strategies can lead to misjudgment and erroneous decisions.

Negotiations usually require negotiators to make decisions under conditions of uncertainty where choices depend on interpreting information and taking or avoiding risks. This is particularly true where parties, because they are somewhat untrusting, have not agreed to share information fully. Even in problem-solving bargaining, parties often have to infer the information they need to make decisions. Where parties must make trade-offs, they do so through package proposals. These the parties must both propose and evaluate. Negotiators must assess the information they obtain in negotiation, and integrate it with other information

---

[1] JAMES G. MARCH & HERBERT A. SIMON, ORGANIZATIONS 136–142, 151, 203 (1958).

[2] *See generally*, DANIEL KAHNEMAN, PAUL SLOVIC, & AMOS TVERSKY, EDS., JUDGMENT UNDER UNCERTAINTY: HEURISTICS AND BIASES (1982).

[3] *See generally*, DETLOF VON WINTERFELDT & WARD EDWARDS, DECISION ANALYSIS AND BEHAVIORAL RESEARCH (1986).

they have. They must assess other negotiators, examine and compare various possible outcomes, and decide whether to agree and on what.

I. REFERENCE POINTS

There appear to be two phases in common decision making. The first is a simplification or "editing" phase, where the decision maker engages in a preliminary analysis of the decision situation in order to simplify it. The second is an evaluation phase, where the decision maker decides which of the "edited" choices is the best.[4]

Editing involves coding possible choices and assessing gains or losses with respect to a defined reference point. For example, if I am considering taking a new job, I will most likely take the characteristics of my present job as a reference point. These will help me compare the new job and make a decision about whether to accept a new position. I will take my current salary, benefits, duties, and so on, as givens and attempt to figure out how the new job may better or worsen those items.[5]

Obviously, if we make judgments by reference to a defined point, what that point is and how we define it are quite important. In a negotiation, a party's overall decision reference point is its reservation price, that is, whatever it feels it must minimally obtain in order to agree at all. In interest-based bargaining, a party establishes that point for itself by figuring out its best alternatives to a negotiated agreement.

A. Framing

People tend to adopt their status quo, whatever that may be in what is at issue, as a reference point for their decision making. What people value, positively or negatively, are changes in their wealth or welfare from their defined reference point.[6]

However a party establishes its reference point for assessing negotiation offers, what is important to understand is that it may be possible to induce a party to change its judgmental reference point. If a party changes its reference point, it will, out of necessity, perceive its decision situation differently. This

---

[4] Daniel Kahneman & Amos Tversky, *Prospect Theory: An Analysis of Decision under Risk*, 47 ECONOMETRICA 263, 274 (1979).

[5] Indeed, focusing on differences between one situation and another appears to be a fundamental feature of human perception. We notice sound or color intensity only in relation to current levels that we are experiencing.

[6] Kahneman & Tversky, *supra* note 4, at 273, 277.

is what occurs when an interest-based negotiator negotiates with a positional bargainer and persuades the latter to look at the situation from the point of view of his interests rather than his positions. Consequently, it is possible to shape the decisions people are likely to make by inducing them to consider their decision from a different reference point.

In simpler terms, the way parties state a problem affects the way they approach and resolve it. The way negotiators define and view issues affects the way they bargain and the concession and settlement decisions they make. Issue-framing therefore can affect negotiation results, and there are a variety of factors that negotiators should take into account in framing their negotiations.

1. Risks of loss or gain

For most people, losses loom larger than gains. We are generally more willing to gamble to prevent or minimize losses than to secure or maximize gains. Put otherwise, people are loss-averse; that is, inclined to protect their current position and willing to take risks to prevent losses. They will not, however, take similar risks to secure gains. People are risk-positive or even risk-seeking in taking action to prevent a loss, but risk-averse in taking action to secure a gain.[7]

We can even expand these propositions somewhat. Persons presented with a choice between a certain small gain and a possible larger gain also tend to act conservatively, taking the small gain and not gambling for the larger. On the other hand, where people see the situation as a choice between a small sure loss and a larger possible loss, they will gamble to avoid the smaller loss. Consider the following example.[8]

Choose between:

a. a sure gain of $3000;

b. an 80 percent chance of winning $4000 and a 20 percent chance of winning nothing.

In this situation, most people choose alternative *a*. Consider, however, the following example.

Choose between:

a. a sure loss of $3000;

---

[7] Amos Tversky & Daniel Kahneman, *The Framing of Decisions and the Psychology of Choice*, 211 SCIENCE 453, 456 (1981); Margaret Neale & Max Bazerman, *The Effects of Framing and Negotiator Overconfidence on Bargaining Behaviors and Outcomes*, 28 ACAD. MGMT. J. 34, 37–38 (1985).

[8] Kevin McKean, *Decisions*, DISCOVER, June, 1985, at 28.

b. an 80 percent chance of losing $4000 and a 20 percent chance of losing nothing.

Most people choose alternative *b*. In other words, people will take risks to try to prevent a loss, but will not take equal risks to try to secure a gain.

It is often possible to frame a situation positively or negatively, as a case of maximizing gains or minimizing losses. Consider a bettor at a race track, having lost $140 on prior races and thinking about making a $10 bet, in the final race, on a horse running at 15:1 odds.[9] The bettor can look at the final bet as offering a $140 gain versus a $10 loss. He may also think of himself as having lost $140, with the prospect of losing another $10, for a total of $150. It is easier to forego a gain than to suffer a loss, and parties facing possible losses are more likely to take a chance than parties faced with the prospect of a possible gain. Furthermore, a loss is less painful if thought of as part of a larger loss rather than considered alone.[10] Consequently, the bettor is more likely to risk the bet if he frames his situation in terms of losses than in terms of possible gain. He is more likely to make the bet if he thinks of himself as trying to break even (no overall losses) than if he focuses on winning $140.

The way one frames an issue, therefore, affects the decision made. In a negotiation, framing the issue, especially as it bears on risk, can affect both the character of the bargaining and negotiation results. Negotiating parties risk nonagreement by the positions they take and maintain. If the parties are some distance apart, there will be no agreement unless one or both concede to close the gap. In this situation, refusing to concede or conceding too little constitute risky behavior. Making concessions, by contrast, moves toward securing an agreement and is therefore an attempt to avoid the risk of no agreement. Consequently, a party that views a negotiation as an effort to minimize losses is more likely to engage in hard-bargaining (risky behavior) than a party focused on potential negotiation gains.

If all parties to a negotiation look upon it as an opportunity to maximize gains, they will all make concessions and come to agreement more easily and productively. Indeed, this is part of the theory of problem-solving bargaining. If a negotiator frames the negotiation as an opportunity to secure a gain or prevent a loss, she presents choices in a way most likely to encourage the other side to make concessions.[11]

---

[9] This example is taken from Tversky & Kahneman, *supra* note 7, at 456.

[10] McKean, *supra* note 8, at 31.

[11] Doing so obviously requires the negotiator to listen carefully and try to discern just how the other side is framing the negotiation or particular issues in it. Suppose, for example, that a real estate broker is trying to negotiate the sale of some property. The prospective buyer is hesitant and unenthusiastic, but the broker discovers that the buyer is worried about the cash outlay. In other words, the buyer views himself as losing his financial liquidity. In this situation, the broker might do well to frame the purchase as one which will protect the buyer's wealth from inflation (no loss) and which may lead to a profit on resale in the future (possible gain).

On the other hand, if a negotiator attempts to hard-bargain, she may do so by framing her own position in the negotiation as an effort to prevent losses. With a risk-positive frame, she will be less likely to make concessions and perhaps more likely to get them. Similarly a negotiator seeking to get as much gain as possible from a negotiation may frame her own situation negatively, as an effort to minimize losses. At the same time she might attempt to persuade the other side to view its situation positively, as an opportunity to secure gains.[12] This analysis counsels the problem-solving negotiator that she must determine the other party's negotiation frame, and, if necessary, seek to change it from a risk-positive to a risk-averse frame. It becomes apparent that understanding how parties frame a negotiation choice, and understanding how to reframe it are essential to effective problem-solving negotiation.[13]

2. Anchoring and adjustment

When people are uncertain, it is possible to center their attention on a particular point merely by mentioning it. Then, when asked to make a decision, the person, once focused, unconsciously uses that point as a reference point for their decision. In other words, decision makers adjust their decision up or down from the noticed reference point. Focusing a person's attention on a certain point tethers or anchors his judgment to the vicinity of the point.

This psychological phenomenon, appropriately called anchoring, is easiest to demonstrate through estimation exercises. For example, experimenters asked subjects to estimate what percentage of countries in the United Nations were

---

[12] Max Bazerman & Margaret Neale, *Negotiator Rationality and Negotiator Cognition: The Interactive Roles of Prescriptive and Descriptive Research*, in NEGOTIATION ANALYSIS 121 (H. PEYTON YOUNG, ED., 1992).

[13] People also analyze a decision-situation by dividing it into riskless and risky components, and focusing their attention on the risk. In comparing choices, they focus on the differences between choices and disregard what is the same in the choices.

Suppose you want to start a business and invite a few people to invest in it. You acknowledge that it is a risky venture and that anyone who invests in it could lose their capital. Suppose you frame the offer in the following ways:

> (1) the investor will have a share in the business and its profits equal to the percentage of her investment as a share of total investment, and a complete loss of capital if the business fails;
>
> (2) the same, except that, on business success, the investor will receive a fixed return plus a percentage.

Simplified, the first formulation presents the investor with a risk while the second presents her with a risk followed by a certainty. While both formulations involve the same amount of risk, the second appears more attractive, and the investor is mostly likely to focus on the difference.

> One may invest money in a venture with some probability of losing one's capital if the venture fails, and with a choice between a fixed agreed return and a percentage of earnings if it succeeds. The isolation effect implies that the contingent certainty of the fixed return enhances the attractiveness of this option, relative to a risky venture with the same probabilities and outcomes.
>
> Kahneman & Tversky, *supra* note 4, at 272.

African.[14] Before making the estimate, however, experimenters asked the subjects to state whether the percentage was greater or less than a number chosen by spinning a wheel having the numbers 1 through 100 on it. Unknown to the subjects, who supposed the number selection was by chance, the experimenters rigged the wheel to stop at 10 or 65. The subjects who saw the 10 made an average estimate that the percentage of African countries was 25 percent. Those who saw 65 made an average estimate of 45 percent. Obviously, seeing the 10 and the 65 influenced the later estimates of the subjects, even though they believed that chance determined the numbers they saw.[15]

This experiment, and others like it, make it clear that it is possible to affect people's judgments through using an anchor. Once focused on a point or alternative, people confine their search for solutions within an area centered on the focus. People use the focus as a reference point for judgment, and adjust from there.

The anchoring phenomenon is important in negotiation. A negotiator can consciously attempt to anchor another party, and a negotiator needs to be wary of being anchored. Interest-based bargaining focuses on satisfying interests rather than on particular means of satisfying interests. This may make interest bargainers less susceptible to anchoring than positional bargainers, for a particular means may act as an anchor. However, interest-based bargaining divides into phases of problem-definition—option generation and selection of solutions—and involves both value-creation and value-claiming.[16] Roughly speaking, the option-generation phase is the value-creation stage, while the solution-selection phase is the value-claiming stage. It is at the value-claiming stage that interest-based bargaining may turn competitive and where anchoring may occur and shape decisions. Anchoring is likely to occur during the solution-selection phase, and many parties attempting interest-based bargaining focus inordinately on just one or two solutions rather than consider all thoroughly and systematically.

3. Attribution error

In the United States, most people, when observing someone making a choice, attribute the choice to the actor's character or disposition. In other words, most people operate from the unconscious premise that people behave as they do because of their dispositions. The actor, however, usually explains his choice by reference to the immediate situation, that is, the factors he thought he faced causing him to choose one way rather than another.

---

[14] ROBYN M. DAWES, RATIONAL CHOICE IN AN UNCERTAIN WORLD 121 (1988).

[15] *Id.*

[16] *See supra* Chapter 7, Sections II (D)(5–8) and (E).

I once observed a classroom during a lecture-discussion. During the lecture, several women students raised their hands, but the professor did not call on them. At last, he did call on a male student who had raised his hand. A female student then challenged him, asserting that he was obviously sexist as he had not earlier called on women students. The professor, while taken aback, responded, "Well, perhaps. You will have to judge, but I really wasn't ready to take questions or comments earlier. I wanted first to cover some more material." Clearly, the female critic attributed the professor's behavior to his character or disposition, while he attributed it to the situation.[17]

Attributing a person's action to his disposition could be a correct assessment, but could also be wrong. It will almost certainly be wrong from the actor's viewpoint, and the actor is not likely to be responsive to assessments, offers, or suggestions not salient to his own perception of the situation.

It is easy to imagine how different observer and actor perceptions of this kind could affect negotiators' judgments about one another. If each negotiator, observing the other, attributes the other's choices to disposition rather than to the situation, each may draw conclusions, and make predictions, which may be incorrect. One might think, for example, that because the other side was very resistant to one's proposals, it was basically competitive. To counter, one might bargain competitively as well. This could be mistaken, however, for it could be that the other negotiator was simply responding to the way the proposals were framed as he perceived them to bear on his interests.

"[Persons] tend to simplify their decision task by ignoring the *contingent decision processes* of competitive others. They assume the other side will act in a certain way, rather than realizing that the opponent's behavior is contingent on a variety of factors."[18] Attributing behavior to disposition simplifies judgment, but leads to misunderstandings that impede or distort judgment. To avoid such errors of understanding, the negotiator must attempt to enter the other side's "problem space,"[19] that is, to see the negotiation issues and situation as the other side sees them. The negotiator, rather than offering his own positions and rationales, needs to elicit talk. He needs to get a good sense of the other

---

[17] We may even hold strongly to character beliefs in spite of contradictory evidence. When evidence appears to disconfirm our beliefs, we carefully scrutinize the disconfirming evidence rather than examine our beliefs. Usually, with intense scrutiny, we can find problems with the disconfirming evidence and therefore reasons to discredit it. Often, people confronted with evidence which conflicts with their beliefs come away holding their beliefs more strongly than before. They either find the evidence to be too flawed to be credited or less damaging than it originally appeared to be. THOMAS GILOVICH, HOW WE KNOW WHAT ISN'T SO 64–67 (1991).

[18] Bazerman & Neale, *supra* note 12, at 112.

[19] Max H. Bazerman, Elizabeth A. Mannix, & Leigh L. Thompson, *Groups as Mixed-Motive Negotiations*, in ADVANCES IN GROUP PROCESSES: THEORY AND RESEARCH, vol. 5 (EDWARD J. LAWLER & BARRY MARKOVSKY, EDS., 1988).

side's values, preferences, concerns and interests, the pressures it feels, the aspirations it has, and so on.

4. Schema and scripts

People generally interpret new situations in terms of schematic conceptualizations, or schema, about what people are like, the ways events play out, and how people act.[20] A stereotype is a good example of a schema as applied to persons. We know that when people use stereotypes in characterizing others, they base their judgments about what others will do on generalizations inherent in the stereotype rather than on an individualized assessment. A "script" is a schema applied to events or situations. It is easiest to think of a script as a stereotyped sense of how events, or cause and effect sequences, progress.

When we communicate with one another, we of necessity interpret or decode what the other says and does. But communication and behavior are often ambiguous, and subject to differing interpretations. The incident of the college professor described above is an example. We also use schemas of various sorts to help us interpret others and their behavior.

5. Setups

While there are countless cognitive schemas, it is possible to predispose people to use one particular interpretative schema rather than another by setting up their expectations. Psychological studies have shown that people given positive introductions to a speaker or lecturer consistently rate her more positively than people given negative introductions to the same speaker. Indeed, "[t]hose expecting a 'warm' instructor perceived him to be relatively sociable, informal, even-tempered, friendly, and so on, and they responded accordingly. . . . In contrast, subjects expecting a cold instructor rated *the same person* as relatively self-centered, unsociable, and formal, and they showed a corresponding reluctance to participate in the class."[21] In other words, by manipulating a person's prior expectations, one can dispose him to interpret another person's behavior or a situation favorably or unfavorably, in line with the setup.

It is even possible to predispose people to act in certain ways. In an experiment involving persons playing the prisoner's-dilemma game,[22] the experimenters exposed players to human interest stories prior to undertaking play. In one

---

[20] RICHARD NISBETT & LEE ROSS, HUMAN INFERENCE: STRATEGIES AND SHORTCOMINGS OF SOCIAL JUDGMENT 28 (1980).

[21] *Id.* at 68 (emphasis added).

[22] In brief, in the prisoner's-dilemma game two parties are presented with a matrix of potential options. For example:

case, the story was a "heart-warming account of someone who offered a kidney to someone whom he did not know who was in need of a transplant. In another instance, subjects heard a ghastly account of an urban atrocity."[23] Those players who heard the heartwarming account played the game much more cooperatively than did those who listened to the atrocity story.

The best explanation for what happened in these experiments is that the manipulations caused the subjects to access certain interpretive schemas that they then used to "read" ambiguous information or to cue their own behavior. The application of these ideas in a negotiation context is fairly obvious. A negotiator can "setup" or predispose the other side to bargain in certain ways by manipulating its prior expectations. For example, when preparing to negotiate against someone anticipated to be a soft-bargainer, the negotiator could insure that the other side receives the message that his own side has little to give. If there is to be a bargain, the other side will have to be willing to concede. Similarly, if one wants to promote cooperative or problem-solving bargaining, it would be useful, prior to bargaining, to regale the other side with stories likely to elicit a positive, cooperative, or problem-solving frame of mind.

6. Commitment and escalation[24]

Commitment to a goal and high aspiration secures persistence, tenacity, and often success. There is good evidence that commitment and high aspiration also

---

	A	B
A	2,2	-4,4
B	4,-4	-4,-4

In each round of the game one party must choose a row, and the other must chose a column. The square in which the chosen column and row overlap contains the values awarded to the parties (the first number going to the party choosing the row, and the second going to the party choosing the column). In this example, if Frank chooses row B and Jim chooses column A, then Frank and Jim would receive 4 and -4, respectively. If they chose column B and row B, each would receive -4, and so on.

If one party chose both the column and the row, he would choose a result leading to either BA or AB, whichever yielded his side the greatest gains and the other side the greatest losses. However, because the parties are dependent on each other, A becomes the obvious choice because the possibility of getting AA in successive rounds is much better than the possibility of ending up with BB. What makes this game interesting, though, is that there is no communication allowed between the parties, and there is the opportunity for greater individual rewards if the individual chooses to take advantage of the cooperator. At that point, however, the former cooperator may seek retribution by becoming competitive and causing joint losses.

For a more detailed discussion of the prisoner's-dilemma game, *see* DEAN G. PRUITT, NEGOTIATION BEHAVIOR 102–110 (1981).

[23] NISBITT & ROSS, *supra* note 20, at 37.

[24] *See generally*, DEAN G. PRUITT & JEFFREY Z. RUBIN, SOCIAL CONFLICT (1986).

contribute to negotiation success. The reasons are obvious. They both lead to firmness, and, as long as the other party is less firm, to concessions from the other side. In problem-solving bargaining, commitment to maximizing one's interest leads to an intense search for ways to do just that.

But commitment can lead to failure, or worse, to escalating and expensive conflict as parties raise stakes and invest more in winning until winning becomes a single-minded prize apparently worth almost any cost.

Decision making in negotiation requires interpreting the moves and actions of other parties. Commitment to an end, however, tends to bias a negotiator's interpretation of information and his judgment. When one stakes oneself on, and makes investments in, a commitment, there is a tendency to justify oneself. Rather than look at the situation objectively, one interprets it in ways that favor one's preconceived view of the situation. The poker player, having invested all of his chips in a hand, borrows more to stay in, believing the other player, who continues to raise, is just bluffing. When the defendant refuses to settle for a high figure, the trial lawyer remains confident that she can destroy the defendant's case before the jury. A country, having lost many lives in a war, believes the enemy is about to collapse, and that more troops, equipment, and just a bit more fighting will bring victory. "It's not possible to stop now, in sight of victory, when we have already sacrificed so much. Hang on just a little more."

Continued investments in the face of large losses is just another example of risk-taking to avoid a loss. What is important for present purposes, however, is not so much this phenomenon, but the rationalization process that accompanies it. Parties who invest heavily in commitments are likely to entrap themselves in escalating conflict, even irrationally so, yet remain unaware of their lack of objectivity. This is most likely where parties have not set limits on their commitment; when they do not, or cannot, take time-outs to reassess their investment. It is also likely when they are not clearly aware of the costs they are incurring; and where they must "save face," that is, justify their actions to themselves or some audience.[25]

Mere statement of these factors contributing to escalation points to obvious precautions that will help prevent spiraling conflict. Setting investment limits beforehand clearly helps. Periodic "objective" assessments of the investment in the conflict or negotiation are also useful. In such assessments, it is important to focus on the current and prospective set of costs and benefits rather than past expenditures. When parties focus on additional losses they may incur, they are more likely to adopt courses of action designed to prevent future loss. One evident course is simply to accept those losses already suffered and not to invest more.

---

[25] *Id.* at 124–125.

7. "Sunk" costs

Suppose you have purchased an expensive ticket to a musical production, let's say at a cost of $100. On the evening you had planned to go and see it, you feel tired and think, "Golly, I wish I hadn't bought that ticket. I'd much rather stay home tonight than go to the theater." Should you go to the theater or stay home? Would you stay home if you could get your $100 back? Should you treat your ticket purchase as an investment you do not want to waste, or should you conclude that the money you paid for the ticket is gone, *whatever you do*?

Money you have already paid out, or investments of any kind that you have made, which you will lose no matter what you do are called "sunk" costs.[26] If you actually prefer to stay home rather than go to the theater, but you go to the theater anyway, you are doing something that you don't want to do in order to avoid a loss that you will have in any case. You invest more, or impose additional costs on yourself, in order to feel that your prior expenditure has not been in vain, has not been wasted. But, while it is rational to base a decision on future consequences, it is irrational to base it on past events you cannot change. It is irrational to act merely to honor sunk costs, that is, to let a past investment govern a future choice simply in order to feel that you have gotten something for your investment. In other words, sunk costs, by themselves, do not provide a rational justification for incurring additional costs or maintaining a course of action.

If there are reasons *other than* sunk costs for continuing a course of action, then perhaps it is rational to do so. For example, if you have made a commitment to someone else that you would go to the theater, in not going you break your commitment. Then you might become known as someone who breaks commitments. In such a case, however, it is the future consequence of reputational loss that might persuade you to go to the theater, and your choice would be rational.

The irrational inclination to honor sunk costs may arise in negotiations in a variety of ways. One might, for example, try to conclude a deal, rather than look elsewhere, because of the time, effort, and resources expended in the negotiation so far. But such costs are not necessarily an appropriate focus of negotiation decision making. Instead one should focus on the future consequences of the deal and the other alternatives one has, including all associated costs.

In a similar way, a concern with sunk costs might incline a negotiator to hard-bargain rather than problem solve. If a party focuses on losses as a reference point, he will take risks, including risks of nonagreement, to avoid suffering the loss. If it were possible to persuade the party to think of the loss as sunk costs,

[26] Dawes, *supra* note 14, at 22.

however, it would be easier to focus on how a possible agreement would affect its interests in the future. A company sues an architect for an allegedly flawed building design that the company has spent $500,000 to correct. The suit, which is not by any means a sure winner, will cost the company $250,000 to pursue through trial, including all attorney fees, discovery and expert witness costs, and lost staff time. In negotiations with the architect and her insurer, should the company hold out for $500,000 because that is how much it is out of pocket? Clearly, the company should base its decision making solely on the probabilities of winning its suit. If they are good, it should perhaps press for maximum recovery; if not, it should settle for what it can get, notwithstanding the losses it will be unable to recoup.

In summary, rational decisions are based on an assessment of future possibilities and probabilities. The past is relevant only insofar as it provides information about possible and probable futures. Rational decision making demands the abandonment of sunk costs, unless such abandonment creates problems outweighing the benefits of abandonment.[27]

8. Saving face and "giving" face

How one addresses the question of saving face is not so obvious. Saving face involves finding some interpretation of the situation, including losses, that permits a party to feel, or credibly claim, that it acted or decided justifiably. In other words that what it did was not senseless, but instead had meaning.

To give an example, I once represented a group of migrant farmworkers who organized to protest and fight substandard living conditions at a farm labor camp. After getting little positive response from the authorities running the camp, the farmworkers escalated their tactics progressively, moving from demonstrations to refusals to pay rent. Eventually, they took over the camp and refused to leave, even after the harvest season had ended. The struggle had cost them much, and authorities were threatening to enter the camp and evict the farmworkers. In private meetings, the workers said they would chain themselves, their spouses, and children to beds and radiators to prevent eviction. It was clear, however, that the authorities would take over the camp, using police forces to arrest the workers, and that they would prosecute them. The farmworkers knew they would lose this battle. They were willing to go to jail to affirm the justice of their cause and to justify to themselves, and others, the actions they had taken up to this final confrontation.

After a long meeting, we resolved the issue by persuading the farmworkers to declare a victory. They had been successful in bringing their plight to public

[27] *Id.* at 31.

and official attention (even the governor had sought to intervene). To demonstrate this, they could hold a farewell fiesta at the camp as a way of celebrating and thanking supporters. This is what the farmworkers did.

In retrospect, the negotiation or conflict resolution strategy behind this solution is clear. The farmworkers were in an escalating conflict leading to a showdown they would lose. Even a loss would give meaning to their protest, but declaring victory and holding a fiesta also gave meaning to their prior actions as well as providing a rationale for ending them. By allowing the farmworkers to save face, it spared them further costly confrontations quite unlikely to create any gain.

When caught in a spiraling conflict, a party wishing to cut its losses and get out often needs to find a satisfactory interpretation of its withdrawal. It needs an interpretation that justifies its whole course of conduct to that point rather than making it appear senseless, foolish, cowardly, or weak. This is particularly true where the party must explain itself to a constituency or some public. There is simply a need to avoid or blunt belittling criticism.

Saving face is important in successfully concluding some conflicts and negotiations. Indeed, it is so important that negotiators need not only be sensitive to it, but also willing to "give face." By giving face, I mean helping the other party to make face-saving claims about the course of the negotiations and the results achieved. One can do this by constructing some agreed upon, dignifying, justifying, public description of the parties' activities, and agreements or non-agreements. Alternatively, a negotiator can give the other side something it can publicly use to assert that it did not come away from the negotiation defeated, empty-handed, nor in any way taken or humiliated.

II. COGNITIVE OVERLOAD

As the number of parties, issues, and possible outcomes in a negotiation increase, so too does its complexity. Every party may take a different position on each issue, and each issue may have many possible outcomes. If the parties make trade-offs between issues and different possible outcomes on each issue, the complexity may seem unmanageable. Take, for example, a six-party negotiation over six issues with six possible outcomes on each issue. The parties will have thirty-six possible outcomes to bargain over, and as each may value the outcomes differently, as many as 216 trades to make. Actually, there may be more, as parties experiment with different possible packages.

To the potential complexity of trades, we must add different personalities, communication styles, bargaining expectations, and strategies. If the negotiators at the table represent organizations or constituencies, there will be additional bargaining problems. These may occur as negotiators either attempt to carry out bargaining instructions or provide information to their principals so the latter can reassess their positions. Finally, depending on the nature of the issues involved, parties at the table may seek to form coalitions in order to secure an agreement. Forming such coalitions comprises a subnegotiation within the larger negotiation and will affect it. Coalition members may strike subdeals among themselves. Countercoalitions may form.

Every such change—and the situation may be quite fluid and dynamic—affects the bargaining space and the configuration of bargaining positions within it. As each new item appears in the bargaining—a new piece of information, a concession, a proposal, a change of position, an apparent coalition—parties may responsively reassess their positions and further change the bargaining configuration. Multiparty, multi-issue bargaining operates much like a kaleidoscope, a small change, a slight twist of the viewing cylinder, precipitates a complete reconfiguration of scene.

In such complex bargaining, the negotiating parties may have to process and deal with more information than they can handle, a situation of cognitive overload. It is in just such situations that people attempt to simplify decision making by resorting to various rules or guidelines. For example, rather than deal with the complexity, a party may decide to follow its predetermined course of action, in effect ignoring information acquired in the bargaining. Another response might be quick compromise; rather than work through the complexity, the negotiator, feeling overwhelmed, capitulates. In a sufficiently complex bargain, the negotiators might conclude they are just going around and around, without getting anywhere, and give up altogether. A party, not seeing any favorable or acceptable way through the complexity might fear the other parties might strike a deal that freezes it out or is otherwise disadvantageous to it. The threatened party might then attempt to form a blocking coalition killing any such deal.

Aside from patient, painstaking, hard work, there are three general ways to handle cognitive overload in negotiation. The first is simply awareness of the phenomenon, which can serve to inoculate a negotiator from the frustrations of complexity and check the tendency to seek easy solutions.

More important, negotiators involved in complex bargaining must have a concern for the processes they are using to attempt to reach agreement. Since they will be involved in a shifting dynamic of trade-offs, they need some process that will help them sort out their relative preferences and priorities in a fair way. The parties need to establish a clearinghouse for information, a neutral market for making trades, and a group problem-solving process to help them create additional value.

If the parties are trusting of one another, they can do this on their own. If not, they will have difficulty, for they will not be sufficiently disclosing to make efficient trades. In such a situation, straw-voting on proposed packages sometimes works. In a straw vote, without any party disclosing its bottom line, all parties can get information about where others stand, at least enough to allow reassessment of positions and repackaging. If the parties follow this procedure repeatedly, they can often construct final packages acceptable to all.

Sometimes one party takes on a leadership or facilitative role, framing and preparing packages and eliciting responsive information that it then uses to reformulate proposals. Finally, parties involved in complex bargaining should consider using a neutral facilitator or mediator. A trusted neutral party sometimes creates the information clearinghouse and trading-market, and invents problem-solving processes the unaided parties cannot.

A final way to improve decision making in complex negotiations, and to get better results, is intense preparation of the kind discussed in the prior two chapters. Indeed, carrying out those analyses and steps, with due attention to potential cognitive difficulties in negotiation, will greatly improve negotiation decision making and results.

CHAPTER 10

COALITIONS AND REPRESENTATIVE BARGAINING

Coalitions aggregate, catalyze, mediate, and forward interests. Like neurons in a neural net, coalitions are both junctures of communications and information processors, and through their interactions, connections, and field effects become nodes of influence and decision.

In bodies politic, coalitions play key roles in public policy negotiations and in organizational and corporate decision making. Alliances, leagues, associations, unions, groups, and federations of all sorts engage in political and quasi-political negotiations in legislative politics at all levels, from city councils to Congress. This activity may be informal or official, spontaneous or planned, or temporary or enduring. Coalitions clash, contend, skirmish, and compete in fields overseen and refereed by regulatory boards and administrative agencies. Internationally, coalitions of nations, and coalitions of groups within and across nations, shape and determine the terms of major multinational treaties, such as the Law of the Sea Treaty[1] or GATT.[2] Coalitions also mold and influence decisions in other domains of international action. These range from grand joint-exertions such as the recent efforts to end the Serbian-Bosnian-Croatian crisis,[3] to the pursuits of private international corporations seeking business, or government contracts or favors, abroad, to the humanitarian labors of nonprofit international relief agencies, and to the struggles of nongovernmental organizations to influence the handiwork of nations. Within more private realms, coalitions sway and often control the decisions, internal and external, of myriad corporate bodies,

[1]Official Text of the United Nations Convention on the Law of the Sea with Annexes and Index, The Law of the Sea 1–157 (1983); *See generally*, JAMES K. SEBENIUS, NEGOTIATING THE LAW OF THE SEA (1984).

[2]General Agreement on Tariffs and Trade, Protocol of Provision Application, 61 Stat. (5), (6), T.I.A.S. No. 1700, 55 U.N.T.S. 639.

[3]William E. Schmidt, *Croats and Muslims Reach Truce to End the Other Bosnia Conflict*, N.Y. TIMES, Feb. 24, 1994, at A1.

from business corporations, boards of directors and faculties, to committees, task forces, working groups and gangs.

Coalitions penetrate and infiltrate all collective decision making, and anyone whose work engages the decision making of groups needs to understand how coalitions may affect group processes and decisions. In particular, negotiators, mediators, and consensus-seeking facilitators involved in multiparty negotiations where coalition activity is likely—I will call them focal negotiators for ease of reference—need to understand coalition formation and the nature and dynamics of coalition bargaining. Alliances and alliance activity affect both *what* and *how* decisions are made. Alliances may both enable and disable effective and efficient bargaining, and may facilitate making good agreements or precluding them. Alliances and coalitions, however, are neither fixed, permanent, nor relentless entities. One can both work with coalitions—often there is no other way of proceeding—and shape and reform them to effect desired decisions and agreements.

Understanding coalitions and coalition-bargaining dynamics endows the focal negotiator with the cognitive schemata to form, track, and reconfigure coalition paths and plays. Knowledgeable ways respecting coalitions, however, are not quite enough. Beyond coalition dynamics, in many arenas and negotiations in which coalitions are active, the allies who form coalitions are themselves aggregates, sometimes even collectivities of collectives. They comprise large groups that are but represented in coalitions. Those seated at the coalition table speak for others—groups, organizations, constituencies, and groups of organizations and constituencies. Acting as an agent for others entails role-directed and constrained behaviors creating dynamics different from those occasioned by acting on one's own behalf. When some or all parties at the table represent groups or constituencies, and table-coalitions and countercoalitions form, the negotiating game can become quite complex. The complexity increases when there is coalition play *within* the represented parties. Coalitions away from the table affect coalitions and coalition action at the table, not least by affecting the agents at the table. In their cognitive blueprint, therefore, focal negotiators should trace not only the circuitry of coalitions, but also the connected circuits of agency bargaining.

I. COALITIONS

Increasing the number of parties involved or interested in a negotiation can seriously complicate it. Adding parties can add issues, increase interaction, communication, and coordination problems, multiplies possibilities of conflict, and may create new constraints on settlement. Bringing in parties may also alter the power relationships in a negotiation and change its bargaining dynamics.

All of these effects may occur where negotiating parties create alliances or coalitions, either to achieve negotiation goals or block those of some other party.

A. Coalition formation and dynamics[4]

A coalition is an alliance of two or more parties agreeing to engage in joint or coordinated action against other parties or coalitions.[5] Coalitions form when parties perceive that allied action is the best way for them to gain or maximize desired outcomes. Allying forces to enhance the power of coalition members constitutes a problem-solving response to competitive situations in which coalition members, acting alone, cannot gain desired results from others. In other words, in negotiations, as in other circumstances, coalitions form to remedy or offset power imbalances among the negotiating parties.[6]

1. Coalition formation

Negotiation coalitions arise when unallied parties lack the bargaining power to get what they want from a negotiation. Coalitions then form to gather enough power for the allied parties to achieve their common and individual goals. They ally to improve their alternatives for getting what they want. They can do this either by finding an alternative to dealing with the more powerful party, or by favorably and more directly altering the dependency relationships between the negotiating parties.

Coalition formation is one major way parties change their relative dependency on those with whom they wish to, or must, deal. Allying with others may create new alternatives, change the alternatives available to other negotiating parties, or bring additional resources. An employer may be able to withstand a strike by a single one of its unions, but when all its unions ally, it may have to

[4]Game theorists, social psychologists, and political scientists have produced a significant literature on the theory of coalitions and coalition formation. Because it is theoretically oriented, much of the literature is concerned primarily with the question of what a rational actor would do in acting to form, and divide the gains of a winning coalition, in highly constrained, competitive circumstances. This literature provides useful insights about what constitutes rational behavior under limited assumptions or in experimental game conditions. Without attempting to provide a review of this complex literature, I have selectively used some of its insights to suggest some of the dynamic and complexity that goes into coalition formation.

Aside from game theory, the works I found most indispensable in helping me understand coalitions are SAMUEL B. BACHARACH & EDWARD J. LAWLER, POWER AND POLITICS IN ORGANIZATIONS (1980); HOWARD RAIFFA, THE ART AND SCIENCE OF NEGOTIATION (1982); and David A. Lax & James K. Sebenius, *Thinking Coalitionally: Party Arithmetic, Process Opportunism, and Strategic Sequencing*, in NEGOTIATION ANALYSIS 153–193 (H. PEYTON YOUNG, ED., 1991).

[5]BACHARACH & LAWLER, *supra* note 4, at 8, 45, 106.

[6]*Id.*

bargain. When asked by a single homeowner to install a speed bump on her street, the city council may ignore the request. When all the homeowners in the residential district make the same request, it will more likely take action. Three nations create a free-trade bloc, eliminating tariffs between them in order to stimulate trade, reduce its costs, and lessen trade with other countries whose tariffs add to the costs of goods produced in those countries—in other words, to reduce damaging trade dependencies.[7]

In all situations where parties are dependent on a decision maker, and the decision depends either on voting or an assessment of the "politics" of the situation, coalitions can form to change the alternatives available to the decision maker. A coalition does this by increasing the risk of adverse consequences flowing to the decision maker from decisions unfavorable to the coalition or its members.

Typically, coalitions form in voting bodies, such as legislatures or councils, where every member has an equal vote. They form as well in any situation where a party faces a more powerful party and alone lacks the resources to achieve its ends or protect itself. An investor wants to buy a company but does not have sufficient funds, so he brings in other investors. One of several unions wants higher wages for its members, but the company can maintain production even if these union members strike. The union therefore seeks alliances with other company unions and with the union members who transport the company's goods. A developer wants to develop acreage within a city and needs a zoning change, but powerful no-growth advocates oppose it. The developer then seeks allies among local contractors, building trade unions and suppliers, local banks, and merchants.

Coalitions also form when some external circumstance forces parties to agree, in some way, in order to receive a benefit or avert a problem or catastrophe. Under clean air and transportation legislation, the federal government designates certain geographic regions as ozone "nonattainment zones."[8] In order to receive federal highway and transportation funds, cities and counties within the zone must agree on a transportation plan that reduces auto pollution below a certain level. As another example, the owner of a major league baseball team proposes to sell the team to investors in another state. City officials, fans, merchants, and local investors rally to cobble together a local investment group to make a competing bid.[9]

2. Intracoalition and intercoalition negotiation

There are two rather different negotiation processes of interest as coalitions form and attempt to maintain themselves during a negotiation with other parties.

---

[7] The example is based on the recently concluded North American Free Trade Agreement.

[8] 23 U.S.C.A. §104 (1993).

[9] Marc Sandalow, *S.F. Group Says Giants Lack Votes to Move*, S.F. CHRONICLE, Nov. 3, 1992, at A1.

The first is the intracoalition negotiation, that is, the negotiation involved in forming the coalition. Intracoalition negotiation concerns the particular issues of how the prospective coalition members identify potential alliances and how they decide to divide or distribute between themselves the gains the coalition realizes. The second is intercoalition negotiation, that is, the negotiation between a formed coalition and other parties to, or coalitions involved in, the overall negotiation. These two different negotiations are interrelated and affect one another. This is so in part because coalition formation may stimulate countercoalition formation and defensive efforts. Equally important, however, the deals struck to form and maintain a coalition will shape the coalition's bargaining with external parties.

3. Simple coalition dynamics[10]

Coalition formation occurs when parties negotiate an alliance agreement, formally or informally, expressly or tacitly.[11] In order to form a coalition, prospective coalition members must perceive that an alliance between them will confer advantages unavailable acting alone. From the point of view of rationally calculated advantage or gain, prospective coalition members decide whether to enter a coalition by comparing their respective potential gains from either acting alone or from entering whatever various alliances are possible. A simple example illustrates this.

Consider a negotiation among three parties: Anna, Emma, and Paul.[12] Assume, in terms of respective negotiating power, that Anna has the most and Paul the least. In other words, in order to get what they want, Anna is less dependent on Paul than Paul is on Anna. She is also less dependent on Emma than Emma is on her, but Emma is also less dependent on Paul than Paul is on Emma. Further assume, however, that when Paul and Emma act together, Anna is more dependent on them than they on her. We can symbolize these power or dependency relationships as follows:

Anna > Emma, Anna > Paul, Emma > Paul

(Paul & Emma) > Anna

---

[10] *See generally*, RAIFFA, *supra* note 4, at 257–274.

[11] The term "alliance agreement" is here used quite loosely. The only agreement required is parallel action. Many coalitions form tacitly when parties informally coordinate their actions toward common ends. For example, when organizations face critical decisions, such as budget allocations, mid- and upper-level managers sometimes form alliances to protect budget shares. These alliances can arise even without face-to-face ally communication. The perception of shared interests will often lead to parallel action, e.g., similar voting.

[12] The vignette and scenario were suggested by the pure coalition game, and discussion of it, found in RAIFFA, *supra* note 4, at 262–267.

In this situation, aside from a grand coalition of all, there are three possible coalitions, as follows:

Emma & Paul (against Anna)

Anna & Emma (against Paul)

Anna & Paul (against Emma)

Paul, knowing he is the weakest of the three, might reason as follows. "If all three of us act solely for ourselves, I will come out worst in this negotiation because I am the weakest. Depending on what either of them will give me to join them, I may be better off joining Anna or Emma to form a coalition against the other. Emma is likely to ally with me because she too is weaker than Anna.

"But wait! I see another possibility that may result in an even greater gain for me. If Anna knows I'm thinking of allying with Emma, she will realize she is overpowered in this negotiation. She therefore may be willing to offer me more to join her against Emma than Emma offers me to join her against Anna. Amazing, although I'm the weakest of the three, I gain considerable strength from my ability to enter an alliance, and I can maximize my gains by playing Emma against Anna!"

Paul hasn't quite thought this through well enough yet, for Emma and Anna can play the same game. If Paul seeks to exact too much from Emma as a price for allying with her, Emma can approach Anna to see whether she can maximize her results by allying with Anna rather than Paul. In other words, when faced with a coalition, the noncoalition party may seek to weaken or break the coalition apart by changing the terms of its offers to one or more of the coalition parties.

4. Coalition and countercoalition processes; share allocation

Coalition formation thus may lead to countercoalition processes. Based solely on a rational calculation of maximal gains, and leaving aside matters such as loyalty, coalition partner skills, and other such considerations, a party will defect from a coalition if it gets a greater payoff from an alternative coalition. The possibility that a coalition member will defect from a coalition enhances the bargaining power of that member both *within* and *without* the coalition. The possibility that the member can join another coalition gives her an alternative to not dealing with the coalition in which she initially finds herself. The possibility of remaining with the coalition gives her an alternative to joining the coalition that seeks to entice her away from her initial alliance. Consequently, a coalition formed solely to maximize its members' gains, narrowly conceived, will be stable only if its members cannot get a greater payoff outside the coalition than within it. Of course, in real life, social factors such as loyalty, moral pressures, the possibility of future dealings with coalition-mates, and the like, can override the temptation to seek gain single-mindedly and opportunistically.

Nonetheless, the general point is valid. Practically speaking, parties can exact a price for agreeing to join a coalition, and exact an additional price for agreeing to stay with a coalition. Consider again the negotiation among Anna, Emma, and Paul described above. Assume, for illustrative purposes, that the parties have the following respective negotiating power: Anna–40, Emma–30, Paul–20. Assume also that the total available payoff from the negotiation is 90, and that the parties can, through their negotiation processes, divide whatever points they collectively control. If they don't agree on a division of points, no one gets any.[13] Consequently, if there is a grand coalition of the three, they can divide 90 points among them as they wish. If Anna and Emma ally, but Paul does not join them, Anna and Emma can divide 70 points as they wish, and Paul gets nothing. If Emma and Paul ally, but Anna does not join them, Emma and Paul can divide 50 points as they wish, and Anna gets nothing. If they don't agree, they all come away with nothing.

The negotiation might go something like this. Anna, Emma, and Paul begin negotiating as separate parties. Paul initially proposes that the three of them agree to divide the 90 points equally. Anna rejects this immediately and demands 40 points of the possible 90 points available for division. She proposes that Emma gets 30 and Paul 20, basing her position on the fact that 40 points is what she contributes to the overall total, in other words, an equity argument.

Emma responds, "No, wait a minute! I won't agree to that. I can get 30 points if I enter an agreement with Paul and leave you out. I'm not going to enter any agreement with you unless I can get more than 30 points. In fact, since if you and I enter an agreement together we can split 70 points, I want half of that, that is, 35 points, to join you."

Paul then enters the negotiation. "Hey, I don't want to get left out of this! If you two enter that agreement, I won't get any points! Anna, I propose that you ally with me, and of the 60 points we have to divide, I'll let you have 36 and I'll take 24. That way you get one more than you get by joining Emma."

"Well, Emma," says Anna, "it looks like I can do better by joining Paul than by joining you. Can you better your offer?"

"Perhaps I was hasty," says Emma. "I can see that you can play me off against Paul. I'll agree to give you 39 points and I'll take 31."

"Oh, boy," Paul interjects, "that'll leave me with nothing. Emma, if you agree to ally with me, I'll let you take 32 points, and I'll take 18."

---

[13] *Id.*

"Wait," says Anna, "I'm frozen out that way. Emma, I'll give you 33 points if you ally with me. No. No. Wait! Paul, I'll give you 22 points to ally with me. That'll leave me with 38."

"Then I'd get nothing," Emma jumps in. "Let's do it this way. "Let's have a three way agreement. You take your 38 points. I'll take 30, and Paul can have his 22."

"Oh, no!," responds Anna. " I'll agree to give Paul 22 points if you're not in the picture. After all, I only need him because you won't give me a better deal. I'm not going to allow you in unless I get something more for it. I want at least 50 points. I'll continue to agree that Paul gets 22. That leaves you with 18 points. That's a good deal considering that we could freeze you out and leave you with nothing."

"Wait just a minute! I'm not going to let you get away with that, Anna! Look: between us Paul and I command 50 points. I'll offer him at least 23 points to join me; that's one better than you're giving him. And for me, I get 27 points, and that's 9 points better than your proposed deal."

"I can do better for you than that, Emma," Anna responds. "If you ally with me, I'll let you have 28 points and I'll take 42."

And so on. As is evident from this example, parties proposing to enter coalitions somehow have to determine their share allocation of whatever results the coalition is able to obtain.[14] More importantly, however, the share allocation between prospective coalition partners is a negotiation like other negotiations. Forming a coalition is a problem-solving response to perceived weakness, and,

---

[14] In reality, this is often unstated. Indeed, parties may calculate, or speculate about, possible gains privately, without open bidding. In the example, however, the effort turned into a prolonged bidding without an equilibrium point. This occurred simply because each party's only stake was maximizing its individual gain. In realistic circumstances, prospective coalition partners apparently intuitively realize they face the prospect of interminable, inconclusive bidding, and therefore resort to some more principled basis of share division. THEODORE CAPLOW, TWO AGAINST ONE 26 (1968). The most likely ideas they would use to allocate shares would be either equity, that is, shares proportional to the resources the respective parties contributed to the coalition's success; or equality, that is, equal shares; or a midpoint solution lying between equitable and equal shares. On the equity principle, *see*, William A. Gamson, *A Theory of Coalition Formation*, 26 AM. SOCIOLOGICAL REV. 373, 376 (1961); on the equality and mid-point principles, *see* S.S. Komorita & Jerome M. Chertkoff, *A Bargaining Theory of Coalition Formation*, 80 PSYCHOLOGICAL REV. 149 (1973). *See generally*, BACHARACH & LAWLER, *supra* note 4, at 48–61.

Interestingly, the share allocation principle which the parties ultimately use also affects just exactly what coalition will form. This is easiest to see from considering the example again. In the Anna-Paul coalition, Anna commands twice the resources that Paul does, 40 points to 20 points. If equity is the basis of share division, then, on success of the coalition, Anna should receive twice what Paul does. If, however, Paul joins Emma in a coalition, and that coalition also uses equity to divide gains, then Paul will receive two-thirds of what Emma receives, for Emma contributes 30 points to his 20. All other things being equal, this should incline both Paul and Emma to enter a coalition with each other rather than with Anna, for they will each get a larger share of what is to be divided. In terms of actual receipts, neither are better off than they would be in a coalition with Emma, but they might prefer it because they feel less dominated. BACHARACH & LAWLER, *supra* note 4, at 63–66.

if the coalition succeeds in its aims, the parties to it in effect create value through alliance. Nevertheless, they still face a value-claiming problem—that is, dividing the value created.[15] Coalition members will share in whatever gains the coalition obtained, and they must decide their respective shares. The bargaining on that point can be distributive, a hard-bargaining contest as in the example. Alternatively, it can be problem solving in that the parties stumble on or resort to an agreed on principle to decide what each of them shall receive.[16]

The way coalition members solve the share allocation problem has important consequences for the maintenance and stability of the coalition. In the example, the possible coalition members were all acting opportunistically, being interested only in the size of their returns from cooperation. The single interest holding any proposed alliance together was individual gain. Such opportunistic coalitions are unstable. Where the base of shared interest is not strong, coalition partners may defect when offered more by an external party. In such circumstances, coalitions must both be vigilant and prepared to respond to possible or threatened defections by renegotiating the original terms of coalition formation.

Furthermore, although all coalitions will in some way distribute gain following success,[17] the example suggests it is not always wise for coalition members to attempt to allocate shares in advance. The bargaining process involved in allocating shares may divide the parties rather than bring them together. This seems particularly likely when all the coalition members seek the same kind of gain, for example, a share of money or a portion of a contract.

Where coalition members have different aims, however, by respectively seeking different kinds of gain, they can collaborate more readily. Consider, for example, the situation where an environmental group allies with a developer of large-acreage luxury homesites to oppose the development plan of a high-density home-builder. The gain the environmental group seeks is lower population density to limit adverse environmental impacts. The gain the luxury home-builder seeks is profit through exclusivity. These parties can ally readily, and probably even without a discussion of share allocation. Their success as a coalition will give each of them what they want.

B. Real coalitions

Matters are rarely as simple and unambiguous in real life as they are in the stick figure, cartoon scenarios of hypothetical cases or the rationality games of

---

[15] On the distinction between value creation and value claiming, *see* DAVID A. LAX & JAMES K. SEBENIUS, THE MANAGER AS NEGOTIATOR 30–32 (1986).

[16] On the use of objective principles to distribute negotiation gain, *see* ROGER FISHER & WILLIAM URY, GETTING TO YES: NEGOTIATING AGREEMENT WITHOUT GIVING IN 84–86 (1981).

[17] Perhaps it would be better to say that, in some way, all coalition members will realize some kind of gain on coalition success.

game theorists. While the example demonstrates some of the dynamics underlying coalition formation, it oversimplifies, and certainly does not capture all dynamics. It leaves out of consideration such obvious factors as personal interaction, investment in coalition-building, information availability and costs, the skill, loyalty, and ideological compatibility of the participants, and possible future uses of the developed relationship.

In real negotiations, parties may not be completely clear about their dependencies on one another. When they form coalitions, they may have uncertainties about how their joined forces will change the configuration of their dependencies on the other parties to the negotiation. This is particularly true where the other parties may also ally as a responsive move. Furthermore, negotiating parties often value the same things differently and weigh items traded among them differently. Parties' respective valuations may clarify only after they trade. Consequently, in forming an alliance to coordinate action to obtain a gain, the alliance partners may not be able to determine in advance their respective shares of the distribution realizable on alliance success. This uncertainty is greater when the gains or receipts of coordinated action are uncertain, variable, or differentially attractive to coalition members.

To illustrate the point, take a grand example. Consider the coalition of nations that formed to fight the Persian Gulf war. At the initiation of the war, its outcome was uncertain. Even if the alliance partners expected victory, none could predict how substantial a victory, its overall costs on all scales of imaginable cost, nor the costs partners individually would experience. Coalition members also had quite different stakes in a successful outcome. The security of oil resources was a concern to many, but not all, of the coalition members. Saudi Arabia hoped to retain its sovereignty and territorial integrity. Arab world political considerations partly motivated Egypt and Syria. Egypt had an additional motivation, as the United States proposed a loan-forgiveness side deal with it.[18] Japan, while not a military member of the coalition, agreed to help pay for the war, perhaps out of long-term strategic alliance considerations, even though it did not have significant oil security concerns.[19]

II. BUILDING AND SHAPING COALITIONS

A. Internal coalition negotiations

By joining a coalition, a party gains something it could not otherwise obtain, but also pays a price. The ability of a potential coalition member to extract gain

[18] Michael Ross & Melissa Healy, *Cheney, Baker Silent on Attack Iraq*, L.A. TIMES, Oct. 15, 1990, at A9.

[19] James Sterngold, *Tokyo Agrees to Pay Off Shortfall in Gulf War Aid*, N.Y. TIMES, May 22, 1991, at A15.

for joining a coalition depends on how much the coalition needs that party to add to its own bargaining power. What a party gains and what it pays therefore depends on its relative value to the coalition. That is partly a matter of what the other parties to a coalition bring to it. A party's value may also depend on what noncoalition members do. For example, if a countercoalition begins to form, an uncommitted party may find itself the object of a bidding war, and therefore in effect highly valued. On the other hand, competing coalitions might leave a party out altogether as they maneuver to enlist other players.

Coalition-building may be even more complicated, however, as coalition-builders may not fully know exactly what resources potential members might bring to the negotiation. As builders acquire information, they may shift their focus to other potential partners or change the proposed terms of the coalition. A coalition's external negotiation may provide information that causes its members to revalue their positions and the value of coalition membership. Furthermore, potential members of a tentative coalition may not be able to finalize their shares of any coalition gains until the coalition concludes its external bargain. Members' shares will depend on what the coalition gains in the overall bargain, and that may depend on what the allies contribute at the very end of the bargaining. In other words, no one may know the contribution that any given coalition member makes to the overall result until the end of play. For example, the single vote that creates the majority necessary to pass legislation loses its determinative value when others join the majority just before the vote.

Coalitions can also impede efficient bargaining.[20] Coalition partners may, in their internal bargaining, agree that any final external bargain must meet certain conditions. They may impose such conditions to ensure that each partner gets what it wants out of the external negotiation. In doing so, they may impose such constraints on their negotiator that he is unable to make the best possible trade-offs.[21]

B. Coalitional stability

If coalition members are merely self-interested and opportunistic, coalitions would appear to be volatile and unstable. Nonetheless, many coalitions, once formed, remain intact for the duration of a negotiation and, sometimes, even

---

[20] On efficiency in bargaining, *see* RAIFFA, *supra* note 4, at 138–142, 148–165.

[21] To avoid the situation where the negotiator is unable to reach gains that may be on the table, it would be better to link the coalition's internal and external negotiations. Rather than having individual coalition members constrain the negotiator to insure they don't suffer a loss, they could agree to compensate one another. That is, if the coalition's external negotiation should produce winners and losers within the coalition, the winners would agree to compensate the losers. Ralph L. Keeney & Howard Raiffa, *Structuring and Analyzing Values for Multiple-Issue Negotiations*, in NEGOTIATION ANALYSIS 140 (H. PEYTON YOUNG, ED., 1991).

longer. This would occur, of course, if coalition members have shared or compatible interests, ideologies, or affectional or other loyalty ties. Coalitions would also be stable where members see potential future advantage from the present relationship. Thus, even though a particular member might realize it does not presently gain from its participation in a negotiating coalition, it could conclude it will gain in the future. It foregoes short-term gain, or even suffers a loss, as a price of maintaining a relationship in anticipation of a possible long-term gain.

Even where such factors are not important, however, there are additional reasons for coalitional stability. Parties invest time, effort, and resources in creating coalitions, creating expectations as they do, and often changing their positions or making other commitments because of the alliance. Thus there are costs involved in forming coalitions, in breaking them up, and in creating new ones. Such costs impede coalition restructuring.

Furthermore, coalitions often form in conditions of uncertainty, and under circumstances of continuing uncertainty about results, the members' relative interests, and possible shares in results.[22] Beyond this, coalitions, in adding parties to a side, complicate even further the predictions, evaluations, assessments, calculations about others' calculations, and guesses that form the bases of judgments during negotiation. These factors of uncertainty, investment, commitment, information, and the added costs incurred in shifting alliances, will all tend to make coalitions, once formed, more, rather than less, stable.[23]

Where coalition parties are represented organizations rather than individuals, coalition restructuring may be even less likely, for it is notoriously difficult to get organizations to change course. Depending on the organization's structure, the costs of providing information to relevant actors and getting their approvals can be quite high. For example, trade associations or unions cannot convene their memberships for each shift in coalition politics. One moves mountains, if at all, only every so often.

Depending on the nature of the coalition, therefore, and on the character of the negotiations, there may be some tendency toward what we might call "coalitional inertia." Even when coalition members have no payoff reasons for staying in a coalition, other forces may incline them to remain. Note further, however, that although such a coalition member might not, at the end of the day, leave the coalition, it can certainly threaten to do so. In other words, it can still use its position to bluff for a greater share of the coalition's bargaining payoff. Whether other coalition members will call the bluff or pay depends on how well they analyze the threatening member's actual position and alternatives.

---

[22] *See infra* text accompanying notes 24–25.

[23] *See supra* note 14.

C. Bringing parties on board

In many situations, it may be fairly easy to determine which parties are likely to form a coalition. A coalition-founder will have a sense of whose support it needs to develop sufficient power to create a winning coalition. Knowing which parties to approach, however, doesn't mean that one can approach them. Indeed, a coalition-founder may not even have a relationship with a party deemed essential to create a winning team. In such cases, founders often build support by persuading critical players—those influential with others, to whom others listen—to join a coalition early. Once they have done so, their participation in the coalition becomes a resource the coalition can use to persuade others to join. Similarly, a coalition-builder could follow a strategy of using intermediaries, hopefully influential intermediaries, who could approach the essential party and persuade it to join the coalition. Indeed, even aside from the process of coalition-building, any party needing others' approvals to get something done can follow this "backward-mapping"[24] strategy of lining up parties to ensure support.

> Starting with the party whose agreement is ultimately needed . . . one then works backward, asking whose prior assent would maximize the probability of agreement from the parties ultimately needed. Then, from that prior group of parties, ask who is most likely to agree and whose assent prior to approaching this group would be most helpful. By this logic, one can work backward from an ultimate target to a present situation.[25]

D. Internal winners and losers; side deals

Sometimes, in order to create a winning coalition, founding members will have to recruit parties who stand to lose more from the alliance than they may gain. Alternatively, a coalition's potential gains and losses, and partners' respective shares of them, may not be clear until the overall negotiation concludes. In either case, fashioning and maintaining a coalition may require the allies to redistribute possible gains and losses among themselves in ways differently than they actually fall out in the negotiation. To maintain a coalition, winners may have to compensate losers for losses incurred from the alliance by making side deals with them.

A clear example of a side deal on the international level occurred in connection with the formation of the coalition that successfully conducted the Persian Gulf war. To isolate Iraq from other Muslim countries, the United States believed

---

[24] Lax & Sebenius, *supra* note 4, at 180.

[25] *Id.*

it was essential to enlist Egypt's support. In joining the allies against Iraq, Egypt risked losing standing and influence in the Muslim world and also ran risks of economic loss. The United States gained Egypt's support for, and participation in, the war by forgiving a $6.7 billion military aid debt Egypt owed the United States.[26] As a Muslim state, Egypt may have had little to gain directly from participating in a war against Iraq. The United States made a side deal with Egypt to compensate it for any losses it incurred in joining the alliance.

E. Adding or subtracting issues

Another way to form or solidify a coalition is to add or subtract issues to a prospective negotiation.[27] The parties to a negotiation themselves define the issues they will negotiate. Thus it is always open to a party to attempt to widen or narrow a negotiation. In order to bring a party into a coalition, a builder may have to either add or subtract issues that concern that party. Rather than make a side deal to gain the allegiance of a prospective negotiation member, the coalition reconfigures the negotiation in order to provide a prospective gain for an otherwise reluctant prospective coalition partner. If parties add an issue, it is equivalent to a side payment. If they subtract an issue, it alleviates a potential loss.

The tactic of adding or subtracting issues to shape a coalition seems common, as the following easily imaginable examples suggest. One of an employer's two unions wants to renegotiate a wage contract; the other wants changes in working conditions. The two ally to present a common front on wages and working conditions. A group of faculty wants to revise a school's curriculum, but other faculty oppose this because the revisions threaten to increase faculty workload. The parties agree to make teaching workloads an explicit issue. A Supreme Court Justice, assigned to write a majority opinion, has difficulty gaining support for the narrow opinion she has drafted. She revises it to satisfactorily address issues other potential members of the majority want raised.

F. Adding or subtracting parties

Adding parties to, or subtracting parties from, a tentative coalition has effects similar to adding or subtracting issues. Indeed, adding or subtracting parties may be a way to add or subtract issues. This arithmetic may have other effects as well.

---

[26] *See* source cited *supra* note 18.

[27] SEBENIUS, *supra* note 1, at 203.

> [A]ddition of parties is likely when they (1) have a tangible interest in or influence on the substance of the negotiation; (2) may strengthen an existing coalition directly or by leverage from unrelated issues; or (3) enable more binding commitments to be made. Subtraction of parties may take place for opposite reasons, as well as to reduce complexity and information costs and to provide focal points for larger settlements.[28]

Three organizations jointly apply for and receive a grant, but they are thereafter unable to agree on specific ways to spend the money. The granting agency enters the dispute and helps the parties renegotiate the terms of the grant. Two rural counties, adjoining a heavily populated county containing a major city, refuse to join a public regional planning organization for fear of domination by the populous county. Other county members of the planning organization call in federal authorities, who have regional planning moneys to dispense, to persuade the rural counties to join.

In these situations, the outside party, not originally involved in the negotiations, is nonetheless interested in, and perhaps affected by, potential negotiation outcomes. The outside party intervenes, either on its own or by request, to protect and advance its interest, and changes the bargaining configuration. In these examples, the entry of the outside party changes the original constraints of the situation, either adding issues or changing the alternatives available to the parties in the negotiation.

G. Intercoalition bargaining

Parties form negotiating coalitions to improve their power positions in a negotiation: weaker parties and parties sharing other perceived common interests are most likely to enter coalitions.[29] As parties enter coalitions to increase their bargaining power, coalitions may stimulate countercoalition efforts to break up the coalition or, if there are enough remaining parties, the formation of countercoalitions. A countercoalition, too, is likely to form around a set of common interests, but these are interests likely to conflict with those which were the ground of the initial coalition's formation. If countercoalition members actually shared a significant number of interests with countercoalition members, they would likely ally with them rather than the countercoalition.

What this suggests is that while the intracoalition negotiation involved in forming coalitions is a problem-solving activity, once coalitions form, intercoalition bargaining is more likely to be competitive or distributive in character.[30]

---

[28] *Id.* at 210.

[29] Gamson, *supra* note 14, at 374, 382.

[30] Bacharach & Lawler, *supra* note 4, at 110–111.

This is not to say that intercoalition bargaining inevitably will be distributive. It is merely to point out that where coalitions form around respectively conflicting sets of shared interests, the underlying conflict of interest, and psychological investment in coalitions, will incline coalitions to competitive bargaining.

Interestingly, however, because coalitions form in response to power imbalances, coalitions can also induce integrative bargaining. This is simply because negotiating parties are more likely to bargain integratively when they are at least roughly equivalent in bargaining power, when one party or another cannot in effect dictate the outcomes it wants.

III. NEGOTIATING AGAINST COALITIONS

A. Exploiting differential interests within coalitions

In multiparty negotiations, different parties may appear to have compatible or allied interests and therefore to be natural allies likely to form a coalition. For example, when the government proposes to build a new dam, developers, real estate brokers, bankers, and farmers often support the proposal while environmentalists, river rafters, and local residents often fight it. When several unions bargain with an employer, the unions generally appear willing to support each other. In such situations, there appear to be natural and predictable alliances.

Nevertheless, seemingly natural alliances may not be what they seem to be. Apparent coalitions, while often presenting a common front at first approach, usually consist of different stakeholders having different interests and priorities. Some apparent coalitions are only nominally coalitions. Confronting a coalition with choices emphasizing the differences between its members can split it apart or cause it, through its internal negotiation processes, to moderate its demands.

B. Splitting coalitions

Only an apparent or assumed commonality of interest among members holds many coalitions together. In some circumstances, it may be possible to split such a coalition by defining an upcoming negotiation with it in a way that exploits the different interests and priorities of coalition members. David A. Lax and James K. Sebenius give a good example of this involving the National Football League (NFL) and the Players' Association.[31] The Association, negotiating for the players, proposed salary schedules dependent on position and seniority. The NFL resisted, and there was a strike. The NFL then made an offer

---

[31] Lax & Sebenius, *supra* note 4, at 158–159.

of limited free agency, an offer attractive to some of the star players, who then crossed the picket line. The free agency offer meant more money for them, and the offer was in the interest of the NFL as well, as it is the stars who help fill the stadiums. The NFL offer thus drew the star players from the player coalition and weakened it.[32]

Redefining a negotiation issue—by making a new offer invoking interests shared by some opposing parties but not others—is a common tactic used to split or weaken coalitions. To take another recent example, the coalition that fought the Persian Gulf war against Iraq also imposed reparations sanctions on Iraq following the war.[33] One sanction was United Nations' control of Iraq's oil sales and revenues, which was to be used to compensate Iraq's victims. Iraq has always resisted and attempted to defy these requirements. To counter this resistance, some of the allies threatened to seize $1 billion worth of oil payments due Iraq as well as undelivered Iraqi crude oil. Iraq then made an offer to reopen talks and stated it would donate 5 percent of its proposed oil sale proceeds to buy relief supplies for famine-ridden Somalia and war-torn Bosnia.[34] This offer was a fairly obvious effort to appeal to those members of the UN deeply concerned with the suffering in Somalia and Bosnia. Iraq's evident strategy was to attempt to weaken the UN coalition opposing it by adding an issue that it hoped would split the coalition.

Another way to divide and weaken a coalition is to ally with a party with ties, or similar interests, to a coalition member. As the benefits or payoffs of belonging to a particular coalition are not always clear, this move may cause the target member of the coalition—that member whose interests are similar to those of the party with whom the countercoalition allies—to reassess its allegiance to the coalition. If parties it identifies as having interests similar to its own are on the other side, it may reason it has misjudged the situation and the ways it might best serve its interests.

There is a general lesson here. When negotiating against a coalition, it is essential to attempt to analyze the disparate interests of each coalition member affected by the negotiation. When a party negotiating against a coalition discovers it has interests common to, or compatible with, those of one or more opposing coalition members, it can attempt to frame an offer advancing those interests. This can have effects of either splitting the coalition or creating a *de facto* ally within the other coalition's camp.

On the other side, in maintaining a coalition, a coalition-builder must anticipate splitting moves and be prepared to meet them. This too requires a knowledge and analysis of coalition members' interests. It is, however, a knowledge

---

[32] *Id.*

[33] Nora Boustany, *Jordanian King Shifting to Criticism of Saddam*, WASH. POST, Sept. 29, 1992, at A16.

[34] They did not succeed. The UN Security Council ordered the seizure of Iraqi oil assets. Stanley Meisler, *Council Orders Frozen Iraqi Assets Seized*, L.A. TIMES, Oct. 3, 1992, at A13.

different from that used to identify and form the coalition in the first place. A coalition-builder must also understand and analyze the possible interests of opposing parties, for it is these that are the impetus for coalition-splitting offers.

IV. INCREASING ONE'S OWN GAIN WITHIN A COALITION

A. Using crosscutting *de facto* alliances

There is a complex interplay between a coalition's external bargaining and the bargaining internal to it, that is, the negotiation among its members. A natural alliance of interests may cut across coalitions, but coalitions will not necessarily decompose or fracture when their members share interests with opposing parties or with members of opposing coalitions. What may occur instead is that each coalition moderates its demands or reshapes its positions so that those members who have a *de facto* natural alliance with members of the opposing coalition will not defect. Parties who are members of a coalition thus can exploit their community of interest with their opponents in order to move their coalition in a direction that better serves their own interests. In other words, coalition members can sometimes use the coalition's external bargaining situation to give them leverage in their internal bargaining within the coalition.

B. Using external negotiations to obtain internal concessions

Strategically placed coalition members, usually those who effectively control the coalition's bargaining representative, can sometimes use the pressures created by the external negotiation to persuade other coalition members to make concessions within the coalition. A good example of this arose in international trade negotiations.

> Trade negotiations require a balancing of many interests, both within and across national lines. The main lines of cleavage are the differences between those industries seeking access to foreign markets and who are free traders versus those competing against foreign imports and who are protectionists. In this internationalized brokering of interests, access to the external negotiation increased the capacity to balance interests internally. The greater the access that government agencies dealing with constituency groups had to the external negotiation, the greater the likelihood that they could trade off internally to reduce the more extreme demands of some groups. Extreme demands on other countries in trade negotiations almost always invoke a "payment" in return. Because the STR [State Trade Representative], working through the SAC [Private Sector Advisory Committee] system, could transmit back to the internal constituency what the costs

might be of taking certain extreme positions, it helped to keep such positions from being taken in the first place.[35]

C. Manipulating coalitions

Coalitions are not monolithic. Nevertheless, in bargaining involving coalitions, someone must speak for the coalition. Put otherwise, all coalition members do not necessarily participate in the bargaining. Indeed, there may even be communication protocols, formal or informal, within coalitions, so that only certain parties speak with other parties. Thus not all members of a coalition necessarily have the same information. Instead, some will often have only the information the coalition's bargaining representative gives them. Consequently, a coalition's bargaining representative is in a strategic position; it can use its access to, and control of, information to solidify or manipulate its own coalition. It can do this to facilitate an agreement between negotiating coalitions, and it can also sometimes cleverly manage information for its own gain. Obviously, a coalition's selection of its bargaining agent is a critical act; and its relationship with its agent is crucial.

V. THE NEGOTIATOR AS AGENT OR REPRESENTATIVE

A. Negotiating for others

Negotiating, not for oneself, but as an agent or representative of another—a client or a constituency of some kind, such as a union, a management group, an agency, or an interest group or association—places potentially significant constraints on both the substance and manner of bargaining. Parties represented will usually have both substantive expectations regarding negotiation outcomes and behavioral expectations about how the negotiator should conduct the negotiation. Indeed, even in cases where the negotiation doesn't involve additional parties, and nonnegotiators merely form an observing audience or a psychological presence—''phantom'' players at the table—a negotiator may feel pressures and restrictions on the way he bargains.[36]

There is a range of possible ways in which a negotiator can carry out the role of representing another party in a negotiation. In any given negotiation, of course, the nature of the representation depends very much on the relationship between the negotiator and the party represented. Quite obviously, some represented parties are more directive, involved, demanding, and communicative than

[35] Gilbert R. Winham, International Trade and the Tokyo Round Negotiation 315–316 (1986).

[36] Jeffrey Z. Rubin & Bert Brown, Social Psychology of Bargaining and Negotiation 44–45 (1975).

others. In some cases, the parties may place significant trust and authority in their negotiators, supervising them little. Beyond these evident matters, however, there is good evidence that the very fact of representation introduces particular psychological dynamics into a negotiation that would not otherwise be there.

In particular, it appears that bargaining as a representative inclines negotiators to bargain adversarially or competitively, or at least with a limited ability to consider options that the represented party hasn't endorsed. This is simply because the represented party will demand loyalty, commitment, and advocacy of its positions or points of view.[37] In such circumstances, the situation will motivate the negotiator to perform for his principal, to attain its approbation. When a negotiator is accountable to another, whether a client or a constituency, that can evaluate and sanction his bargaining performance, he must be responsive to it. This is particularly true where the negotiation is carried out in public or in the presence of the client or constituency, allowing them to monitor or surveil the actual conduct of the negotiation.[38] In short, negotiators who represent others seek the approval of those they represent, looking for validations of competency, ability, and strength, and will take the actions thought necessary to earn the client's favor.

These "representative capacity," "loyalty over logic," accountability, and face-saving effects are probably even stronger when the negotiator is a member of the group represented, for then group influence and loyalty pressures are stronger. "[A] representative of a group, having a strong commitment to the group's position, may not merely be handicapped in accepting an opposing position, but, on a more fundamental level, may be impeded from being able to even recognize superior elements in that opposing position."[39] In other words, bargaining as a representative may entail a "narrowing" of a negotiator's vision, capacities, and aims. This, of course, will also affect the way in which the negotiator bargains. Similarly, negotiators who represent others may make certain negotiation moves, not because the moves make substantive sense, but in order to protect or enhance their image and reputation with their principal.

In some cases, these effects may operate even more strongly where the negotiator is not a member or regular employee of the group represented, but is an independent professional. This would appear particularly true for negotiators, such as lawyers, whose normal role is that of professional advocate. The lawyer's ethic requires the lawyer to be a vigorous and zealous advocate for his client, and the lawyer's general ethos, at least in the American legal system, is

---

[37] *Id.* at 51–54.

[38] *Id.*

[39] *Id.* at 51.

adversarial.[40] Lawyers battle for their clients and aim at winning contests with other parties. Those who hire lawyers often have the same understanding and hire them for that very reason. Ethos and expectations thus mutually reinforce one another, and this can powerfully shape negotiating behavior. This is not to say that all lawyers always view their role this way, nor that all those who use lawyers to represent them in negotiations have such expectations. It does suggest, however, that many lawyers, and perhaps other "hired gun" negotiators, will *naturally* incline toward, and their clients will expect them to, bargain adversarially and competitively.

Bargaining competitively is not always the best way to maximize one's gains from bargaining.[41] Indeed, competitive bargaining may cause parties to lose potential gains and opportunities for creative joint action. It's therefore important for focal negotiators acting in representative capacities, or dealing with other negotiators acting as representatives, to understand the possible pressures on that role. In particular, if such a negotiator perceives problem-solving negotiation as a viable and beneficial option, she will have to take some action to secure her ability and authority to undertake it.

B. Representing groups and constituencies

All negotiators who represent other parties in a negotiation must face conflicts between the principal's expectations and the realities of the actual negotiation. Additional problems, however, arise when the principal is a group or a constituency of some kind. When the negotiator represents a group, conflicts within the group may further complicate her task. The group may lack consensus on bargaining goals. Different persons or coalitions within it may have different priorities regarding goals or issues. Group members may disagree not only about goals, but also about strategy, tactics, and bargaining styles, and about the significance of developing particular kinds of relationships with the other side.

Indeed, the larger and more heterogeneous the group represented, the more likely the group itself will be in conflict. Individuals comprising the group will have different positions in life, different interests and needs, and different perceptions of the bargaining situation. Subgroups, coalitions, or factions may also form. Relatively independent individuals, subgroups, or some combination of these may compose the larger group. These different actors will likely operate from different information bases, with different levels of intelligence and experience, and will differently interpret, assess, and value what's involved in the

---

[40] Disciplinary Rule 7–101, Ethical Consideration 7–1, ABA Model Rules of Professional Conduct (1983); *see* CHARLES WOLFRAM, MODERN LEGAL ETHICS §10.3 (1986).

[41] *See generally*, FISHER & URY, *supra* note 16; LAX & SEBENIUS, *supra* note 15; Carrie Menkel-Meadow, *Toward Another View of Legal Negotiation: The Structure of Problem Solving*, 31 UCLA L. REV. 754 (1984).

negotiation. In addition, the negotiable issues, as well as varying possible outcomes regarding them, may have a differential impact on different individuals or subgroups. These actors are therefore likely to respond differently to various proposed negotiation outcomes.

Even where a group unifies in consensus on some issues when a negotiation begins, consensus may dissolve as the negotiation progresses and group members' perceptions of the issues and bargaining situation change. The group may continue to lack consensus on issues unresolved within the group prior to negotiation. Other, unexpected issues, on which the group has not deliberated at all, may also arise during the course of the negotiation. Indeed, the very process of negotiation may provide the material that raises group members' awareness of such issues and creates incentives to resolve them. Thus, even while engaged in negotiations with others, a group may have to engage in its own internal negotiations. These will impact the agent at the table, and the agent may, as well—indeed, in some circumstances, will be likely to—participate in or even manage the internal negotiations.

The negotiator who represents a group is in a critical position. It is useful to think of the negotiator in such a situation as a political actor having to respond to the demands and expectations of a constituency. Where there is group consensus, the group will subject him to its substantive expectations regarding negotiation outcomes and its behavioral expectations regarding the manner in which he negotiates. The group will likely enforce its expectations through surveillance. Where there are conflicts within the group, group members will target or focus their influence attempts on the negotiator, as the individual in a critical position. On the other hand, the negotiator develops information during bargaining and can assess bargaining possibilities. He is in a privileged position vis-à-vis the group and can influence its decisions.

Evidently, there is a group politics that can arise in representative bargaining. If it does, it will inevitably involve the negotiator. The negotiator in such a situation is in a delicate political position, for he occupies two potentially conflicting roles. As a group representative, the group expects his loyalty and demands that he act either according to instructions or only in ways that always further its defined interests. As a negotiator, however, he has the functional role of working with the negotiator for the other side to craft a settlement.[42] Because he is at the bargaining table, he will have a much more realistic sense both of what is possible in the negotiation and how best to achieve it. His assessment, however, may be at odds with that of his constituency. If the group he represents takes a hard-bargaining approach and expects him to demonstrate his toughness and ability to deliver the results it expects, it limits his flexibility to overtly

---

[42] RICHARD E. WALTON & ROBERT B. MCKERSIE, A BEHAVIORAL THEORY OF LABOR NEGOTIATIONS 283–289 (1965).

undertake problem-solving bargaining. Indeed, the need to impress his constituency, at least if it oversees his bargaining, may even constrain his ability to develop a cooperative, friendly, and trusting relationship with the negotiator on the other side. In such a situation, the negotiator is quite aware of the audience for which he must perform, even if it is not present. His performance for that audience may interfere with what his considered judgment tells him constitutes the best way to bargain under the circumstances.

C. Working with clients and constituencies

Negotiators caught in such "boundary"[43] role conflicts have a number of options regarding ways to proceed. Indeed, whether the negotiator represents a single client or a constituency, the problems her representative role presents are similar. The only significant difference arises from the fact of constituency politics. Plainly, the politics within the constituency, and the politics of working with, or on behalf of, a constituency, deeply affect the ways in which a negotiator goes about her work for it. Nevertheless, because the two kinds of representation involve similar problems, I will treat them together, noting, where necessary, unique problems involved in constituency representation.

Ideally, the negotiator working for a client or constituency needs its trust and confidence and its authority to operate freely and flexibly to craft the best possible agreement. A negotiator will not always have that freedom of action, however. Her client or constituency may have its own confirmed views of what it wants and how it wants to get it. Within a constituency, there may be factions or coalitions, and the reigning power may need to deliver in certain ways to retain its position. The constituency may view the negotiator as a mere agent of its will and not as an active player in determining what to seek in the negotiation.

What a negotiator can do in such circumstances is highly contingent on the character, unity, and sophistication of her client or constituency. Her freedom of action also depends on her skill and sophistication and the nature of her working relationship with her principal. There are a number of general possibilities. When the principal's substantive expectations appear to be greater than the negotiator's considered judgment of what is possible from the negotiation, she can work, in advance of settlement, to shape those expectations. In effect, the negotiator takes an active role in working with her client or constituency to create the substantive flexibility she believes she needs to negotiate effectively.

To maximize negotiating room, the negotiator needs to educate her principal about the advantages and disadvantages of various ways of negotiating. She should also seek authority from the client to negotiate flexibly. If the principal

[43] *Id.* at 284.

gives the negotiator broad authority to negotiate as she deems appropriate, she obviously will have to work with it to discover its true interests in the negotiation. She will also have to work with it to anticipate the other side's interests, and to develop possible alternative solutions to the bargaining problems presented.

She can do this by working with the client or constituency as it develops its substantive bargaining expectations and aspirations. If a party has settled views, she may have to educate it regarding bargaining possibilities and attempt to persuade it to revise its expectations. Obviously, working with a group is more difficult than working with an individual client because there are more persons involved, and group consensus is often hard to achieve and, once achieved, even harder to revise. Factions or coalitions within the group will also complicate the negotiator's task, and the negotiator may even have to negotiate alliances within the group that will enable the group to be effective in external negotiations.

The client or constituency, however, may have settled substantive expectations that the negotiator cannot alter prior to negotiation. If negotiation will not lead to results that satisfy these expectations, the negotiator may have to act in some way to alter her principal's expectations. If she can do so, perhaps it will both accept the results and not blame her for failure. But that may be quite difficult: "[T]he negotiator is most vulnerable to censure by his principals if he attempts to alter their assumptions and attitudes about the opponent *during* negotiations."[44] Depending on the trust vested in her, she might succeed in direct efforts to educate the principal about the realities of the situation. If it is not educable in this way, she could possibly manipulate the bargaining so that the represented party has to confront the apparent realities of bargaining itself. In this way, she might force it to revise its expectations.[45]

A negotiator's client or constituency is likely to have not only expectations about substantive negotiation results, but also about the way in which the negotiator negotiates, that is, as a hard-bargainer, compromiser, or problem solver. If a constituency has no representatives at the table other than the negotiator, and does not surveil her bargaining activities, she may retain flexibility to bargain in whatever way she deems most useful. If the resulting proposed agreement, however, does not better or meet her client's substantive expectations concerning outcomes, she will have the problem of justifying or explaining the discrepancy. She will be in trouble if she bargained in unexpected ways. To gain flexibility in the way she bargains, the negotiator can work to shape her principal's behavioral expectations about how she will bargain. The ideal way to do this would be to educate the principal regarding all the different bargaining strategies, particularly problem solving, for it is the least understood bargaining strategy.

---

[44] *Id.* at 305 (emphasis added).

[45] *Id.* at 310.

The latter may be a difficult task, particularly where the principal is a group without a defined authority structure. Even if the represented party does understand problem-solving bargaining in principle, it may not accept it in practice. For example, one study has reported that "[c]onstituents . . . resisted mutual gains bargaining because it generated innovative options that they had not foreseen or approved."[46] The result was angry confrontation and increased constituent monitoring of the negotiator. The study further concluded that when attempting to bargain integratively, a negotiator representing others may encounter severe communication and coordination problems.[47]

> [N]egotiators are caught between constituent expectations that they will be kept informed on every aspect of negotiations, and the need for open, innovative discussions. Constituents could be informed of every new idea, but this would greatly restrict the brainstorming phase and tie negotiators up in constant meetings with constituents. Yet, if negotiators eventually bring back ideas to constituents that are too radical or too difficult to understand without bringing them along gradually, the new ideas will not be accepted. And since radically new ideas are apt to be generated in mutual gains bargaining, constituent management problems are heightened considerably.[48]

If the negotiator cannot educate her principal in integrative bargaining, or concludes she will be unable to manage relations with it when she openly attempts to bargain integratively, she has the following choices. She can ignore, at least selectively, her principal's expectations, taking the risk that the results she obtains will justify her actions or that they will not be observed or otherwise discovered. Alternatively, she can simply satisfy her principal's expectations—carry out its wishes about the way in which she should bargain—and let the results fall as they will. Even if the outcome results are unsatisfactory, her principal cannot blame her as she expressly carried out its wishes. Most likely, the principal will blame the other side, not realizing that some other way of bargaining might have led to better results.

Finally, negotiators sometimes, at least to a certain degree, collude or work with the other side in ways that will help them with their own clients or constituencies. The negotiator may, for example, pretend to hard-bargain, as her principal wishes, while signaling[49] to the other side that she is in fact more flexible

[46] Deborah G. Ancona, Raymond A. Friedman, & Deborah M. Kolb, *The Group and What Happens on the Way to "Yes,"* 7 Negotiation J. 155 (1991).

[47] *Id.* at 167.

[48] *Id.*

[49] Negotiators "signal" by using language or demeanor that gives at least two, sometimes inconsistent, messages. Taken superficially, the message indicates the negotiator is not flexible. The subtext of the message, however, is that the issue is in fact negotiable. For example, suppose the negotiator says, "That's a pretty solid condition." Listening superficially, one might conclude that the negotiator was talking about a "must have." But the language is qualified. "Pretty solid" is not solid. An acute listener and experienced negotiator would realize the negotiator making the statement was indicating the matter was actually negotiable.

Negotiators use signaling when they do not feel free to disclose openly what matters are negotiable or

and open than she appears to be. If the other side reads the signals correctly, it will realize that, to reach some satisfactory bargain, it will have to cooperate with the negotiator in allowing her to maintain the appearance of hard-bargaining. It can, for example, adopt a reciprocal hard-bargaining stance to convince the negotiator's principal of its toughness. It may thereby make the principal more receptive to conciliatory moves. Similarly, it can overinflate the value of some particular issue or concession, bargain hard on it, and then finally concede. This provides the negotiator a win she needs to help her with her principal and her efforts to move it.

D. Constituencies on the other side

Until this point, I've considered agency or representative bargaining from the point of view of a negotiator representing others. In most cases of representative bargaining, however, there will be a represented party on each side of the bargaining. In the case of multiple-party bargaining, there may be many represented parties, individual clients or constituencies. It's easy to imagine how complex such bargaining situations can be. For example, suppose a negotiator succeeds in gaining flexibility from the constituency he represents and persuades it to permit him to engage in problem-solving bargaining. The negotiator representing a constituency on the other side may not agree, or not know how, to problem solve. Alternatively, the latter constituency could be factionalized in a way that so constrains its negotiator that he must negotiate only for particular positions or results and in particular ways.

Consequently, when a negotiator represents another party, he must attend not only the needs and possible politics of his own client or constituency. To be effective in the negotiation, he must also have a good sense of the pressures and problems that the other negotiator's client or constituency imports into the actual negotiation. Additionally, he needs to understand the other negotiator's relationship to his own principal. Finally, he may even have to take actions that, while not alienating his own principal, will assist the other negotiator in managing his principal.

VI. SUMMARY

Coalitions, collective actors in many complex bargaining situations, are fluid and dynamic alliances of parties having the aim of securing gains through joint action. Coalitions complicate negotiations not only by adding parties, but also by multiplying the negotiations taking place. At the least, coalition bargaining

---

whether there is more room to bargain on certain issues. This usually occurs when there is some audience the negotiator must impress, i.e., the negotiator's principal.

involves a double negotiation game, an internal and external negotiation. Coalitions, however, can reconfigure kaleidoscopically as the bargaining situation changes and as parties responsively renegotiate the terms of their alliance, defect, or re-ally. Coalition bargaining may thus entail many negotiation plays and games as individual actors change positions before the final accounting. In this sense, coalition action is political action and crosses any conceptual divide between negotiation and politics.

Coalition action is an inescapable element of collective decision making. Anyone who seeks to influence the latter, or who essays to help groups reach negotiated decisions, or acts as an agent for a negotiating collective, needs to understand the interplays and possibilities of coalition dynamics. Further, much of coalition bargaining is agented bargaining. Introducing an agent who represents a group brings new elements and dynamics into a negotiation. The fact and constraints of representation shape the agent's behavior and moves both at and away from the table. They also open to the agent possibilities of shaping, even manipulating, the party who placed her there. When the party is a coalition, matters can become complicated in interesting ways and raise questions of who is the servant of whom. A wise appreciation of these factors—of coalition actions and actors—helps the focal negotiator to navigate and, if necessary, manage coalitions.

CHAPTER 11

NEGOTIATION PREPARATION AND PLANNING

Success in negotiation comes from preparation, and the best way to prepare for a negotiation is to plan for it. In negotiations, as in life, decision opportunities arise all the time, but we cannot use them if we are unaware they are there. Preparation opens you to those kinds of possibilities, and while the future is unpredictable, you can maximize your ability to deal with it, whatever it turns out to be.

Preparing for a negotiation is like getting ready for an expedition through territory not yet completely explored. Having a certain ultimate objective in mind, you want as good a map of the terrain as you can get and local knowledge of what you are likely to encounter. If the map has gaps or lacks details, you would seek further information. Examining the characteristics of the terrain from the map and from whatever other intelligence you could get, and considering your capabilities, you anticipate what you might encounter on various routes through the territory. This gives you a sense of what resources and personal preparation you need to navigate safely and successfully. You are likely to select certain routes in advance, yet also prepare to take alternate routes if you meet with unexpected obstacles or hardships—"facts on the ground"—that require you to change your approach.

Negotiation planning is contingency planning, seeking to settle goals, gain clarity of purpose, and examine alternative and preferred means of reaching those goals. It is an anticipatory problem solving undertaken to insure that one is ready to, and capable of, engaging an unfolding situation in order to advance one's aims. Contingency planning involves setting a goal or objective, and generating and evaluating ideas about how to reach that goal. It also involves analyzing the factors both leading to and standing in the way of the objective, including one's own resources, strengths, and weaknesses. Along with analysis and assessment, planning requires choices regarding possible courses of action. When reaching the objective involves dynamic interaction with others, planning also requires analyzing the aims and capabilities of other actors, as they are either part of the problem or its solution. This too includes developing, as well as possible, the information necessary to assess others' goals and how those relate to realizing one's own.

Negotiation planning and preparation call for systematically thinking through decisions the negotiation may involve. This may require investigating and analyzing all significant negotiation variables, obtaining the information useful for making negotiation decisions, and taking action to enhance negotiation success. The second part of this chapter sets out an extended negotiation planning and preparation worksheet to help you do just that. There are, however, some orienting considerations.

I. RELATIONSHIP BETWEEN NEGOTIATION PLAN AND STRATEGY

As it is not possible to plan without having an objective, the first task in negotiation planning is to determine exactly what you want from the negotiation. Of course, both how you plan to bargain and how you anticipate the other side will bargain affect your consideration of objectives. This in turn determines tactics and other details of your bargaining approach.

Competitive, compromise, and integrative bargaining are different approaches to bargaining, and planning for them differs correspondingly, primarily in the way in which one executes negotiation goals. For example, interest-bargaining focuses on satisfying general ends. As its processes are cooperative, open-ended, creative, and involve a relatively free flow of information, it may employ extremely flexible means of reaching those ends. By contrast, competitive bargaining focuses on realizing quite specific aims. Its basic process is adversarial, involves information-control and manipulation, and uses tactical means to achieve those ends. It is clear therefore that selecting one approach over the other will also entail a decision about goals and means.

Notwithstanding these major differences, all negotiations can benefit from planning analysis involving clarifying negotiation aims or goals. Such analysis should also assess the relative bargaining power of the parties, determine what alternatives there are to negotiation, and look closely at the factual predicates for the bargaining. Finally, it should consider how the other side is likely to bargain and devise methods for dealing with that.

II. BARGAINING POWER AND ALTERNATIVES TO NEGOTIATION

Negotiators use their perceptions and assessments of relative bargaining power both to evaluate what kind of bargaining approach to take and where to settle. Consequently, while relative bargaining power may not always determine the outcome in a negotiation, it often does so. As a potentially critical element in negotiation success, therefore, negotiators prepare most intelligently when they examine the power, or dependency, relationship in a particular negotiation carefully. In other words, the negotiator needs to analyze, quite specifically, whether, why, and in what respects each party needs the other.

Interest analysis provides the first step, for comparing the parties' interests will show how the parties may depend on one another to satisfy their respective interests. Simply comparing interests may not be enough, however, because at least one of the parties may be able to satisfy its interests in ways other than the pending negotiation between them. Consequently, in determining how dependent one party is on another, it's necessary to take into account that party's alternative ways of getting what it wants. Furthermore, a party may work to improve or change its alternatives, improving what it can get outside of the negotiation. Therefore, negotiators must consider the realistic ways parties may enhance their alternatives to negotiation.

A. Working on actual alternatives

Negotiating with others is not always the best way to gain one's ends, and a party should negotiate an agreement only when the negotiation brings better results than those obtainable without negotiation. Prior to negotiation, a party should determine what its best alternatives to negotiation are. In other words, it should decide what it will do if there is no negotiation or if the negotiation fails to reach results that satisfy its interests.[1] The party should be very specific and state exactly what it will do if the negotiation fails, for the only reason to negotiate is to realize a gain or benefit unattainable without agreement. If it appears that the negotiation will not produce a better result than one realizable without negotiation, there is no point in continuing it. Thus a party's alternatives to negotiation give it a way to measure success in negotiation and to determine whether it should accept a negotiated agreement.

III. FACTS[2]

Negotiation results sometimes turn on contested facts: how and where the parties decide to settle may depend on what facts they accept as a foundation

[1]When a party doesn't have or can't devise good alternatives to a negotiated settlement, circumstances effectively force it to negotiate. It may nonetheless be able to improve those alternatives it has and thereby enhance its bargaining power.

[2]*See* Chapter 14, Other Negotiated Dispute Resolution Processes, for a more complete discussion of factual conflicts.

for bargaining. It is therefore important to know whether the parties will contest facts during the negotiation, what facts they will contest, and how to settle the factual contest.

In some cases, settling the facts may simply require getting more, or more accurate, information, and it's obviously valuable to have such information available when the negotiation begins. However, the source of such information may also be important, for a negotiating party may not trust the information if it comes from an interested party negotiating on the other side. Consequently, in preparing for a negotiation, it's important to consider not only what information is necessary and useful, but how to present the information in a manner most acceptable to the other side—for example, by using a trusted expert or a neutral source.

There will be other cases, however, in which no amount of additional information will help settle the facts. For example, consider the kinds of factual disputes typical in lawsuit negotiations, say a tort suit over an alleged product failure or a performance suit over an alleged contract. In these kinds of cases, the facts of what actually happened are usually in dispute. Did the product fail when used as intended, or did the user use the product improperly? Did a party actually agree to enter a contract or did she not? Furthermore, even if no party disputes facts, parties may dispute what those facts mean, that is, how to interpret them. When the alleged contracting party said, "Yeah, I'd like to see another order like that," did she actually order or was she just hypothecating?

Arguing about facts in such cases is likely to result in an endless go-around, neither side convincing the other because so much turns on what the facts are. When parties cannot accept each other's versions of the facts and cannot agree on a common version, they need some acceptable method or process for settling them. Anticipating that a negotiation will raise a factual problem, a party should attempt to think through alternative ways of settling facts that the other parties might accept, for example, binding or nonbinding neutral fact-finding.

IV. NEGOTIATION PLANNING WORKSHEET[3]

A. General considerations

1. Parties' Interests

It is important to think through why you are negotiating with this particular party, why you need it, and why it needs you.

What are your needs or interests in this negotiation? Be expansive in creating this list and include economic, relationship, reputation, face-saving, social, and psychological interests.

Interests

1.

2.

3.

4.

In what ways can the other side advance or threaten your interests? What will you lose if you do not come to an agreement with the other side? What ways do you have of protecting or furthering your interests if you do not come to agreement with the other side?

1.

2.

3.

4.

What are the other side's (OS) needs or interests in this negotiation? Again be expansive in creating your list. In considering this question, it is useful to role-play, or pretend, that you are the other side, and from that position, ask yourself what your goals are. In this regard, you will want to take into account the general nature of its business and the particular reason it is entering this negotiation. Include in your consideration strengths and weaknesses, advantages, disadvantages, problems, and weaknesses.

---

[3]Although this form may provide all of the relevant questions to ask in preparing for the average negotiation, it should not be considered complete for all situations. There may be times when, due to the complexity of the negotiation, there are additional questions which need to be asked, or when some of the questions in this form do not apply to a particular situation. This form should be considered a guideline, and a tool for negotiators to use in developing their own planning materials as they become more experienced in the processes.

OS's Interests

1.

2.

3.

4.

Compare the interests of the parties as you now perceive them. What issues do you think the parties will negotiate about?

Issues

1.

2.

3.

4.

2. Bargaining power

In what ways are you dependent on the other side to get what you want from this negotiation?

In concluding you are dependent in those ways, what assumptions have you made?

Are these assumptions correct? How would you affirm or disconfirm them?

What alternative ways do you have to get what you want other than through negotiating with the OS?

What are your negotiating costs? How can you reduce them?

In what ways, practically speaking, can you reduce your dependency on the other side? In other words, in what ways can you improve your alternatives to a negotiated settlement or create new ones?

What can you do to cause the other side to think you are less dependent on it than you actually are?

In what ways is the OS dependent on you?

In what ways can you increase its dependency on you?

What are the OS's investments in dealing with you?

What additional costs will the OS experience if it continues to negotiate with you?

What alternative ways does the OS have of getting what it wants other than through negotiating with you?

What can you do to cause the other side to think it is more dependent on you than it may actually be?

In drawing these conclusions about the OS, what assumptions have you made?

How can you confirm or disconfirm these assumptions? What information do you need?

How can you get that information before negotiation?

What questions will you ask during negotiation either to confirm or disconfirm information that you have or assumptions you have articulated?

1.

2.

3.

4.

What questions will you ask during negotiation to get further information that you believe you need to make decisions about whether to make concessions or where to settle?

1.

2.

3.

4.

3. Fact-finding and valuation

What are the important facts in the negotiation?

1.

2.

3.

4.

Do you have any factual uncertainties? What are they?

Is the OS likely to have any factual uncertainties? What are they?

Which issues depend on which facts?

Issues	*Facts*
1.	1. a.
	b.
2.	2. a
	b.
3.	3. a.
	b.
4.	4. a.
	b.

Which of these facts, or its interpretation, is likely to be disputed?

1.

2.

3.

4.

In what ways can you strengthen the facts on which you wish to rely? If you need further information, state where and how you will get it.

In what ways can you weaken the factual case on which the OS is likely to rely?

If there is a factual dispute, how will the parties settle the facts? Can you propose a fact-finding method which the OS will accept?

If your negotiation involves valuation or items of contested value, how do you propose to settle value? Is the OS likely to accept your proposal? Why or why not?

4. Negotiation pressures and politics

Consider the role of the negotiator for the OS. Is he negotiating for himself or as an agent for another? If he is an agent, what is his relationship to his principal?

To whom is the negotiator directly answerable? Who is the negotiator's client, employer, or constituency?

What is its business and how is it organized?

What is its external operating environment, that is, what are the economic conditions affecting it? What competitors, other market forces, or legal or political pressures does it face?

What is its internal operating environment and politics? How does this particular negotiation play into that?

What kinds of substantive and behavioral expectations is the client or constituency likely to place on its negotiator? Are there any client or constituency politics likely to be involved? If so, what do you think they will be?

How can you meet, or give the appearance of meeting, his perceived needs?

B. Bargaining strategies

1. Competitive negotiation—single issue

What is your bottom line?

What is your aspiration point?

What is your starting point or position?

What plausible reasons or arguments do you have to advance that position?

What counterarguments is the OS likely to raise?

How can you effectively respond to these arguments?

Considering your starting point and your aspiration point, what natural, or plausible, concessions can you make in moving from your starting point to your aspiration point? List them and assign reasons for making or not making the concession. Can you make your reasons more plausible?

Concession	*Reason*
1.	
2.	
3.	
4.	

What is the incremental progression of concessions? If you were the OS attempting to read one of your concessions, or a series of them, what would you conclude was your bottom line?

As a part of your concession strategy, can you use false issues? What issues do you think you can use and what arguments can you make for them?

Are there any small concessions, either informational or substantive, which you can make early in the negotiation, without significant cost to yourself, to induce the OS to cooperate or to test its bargaining strategy?

What bargaining tactics can you use to help you succeed?

How will you make them plausible?

Is there a negotiation deadline or can you set one? How will you time your bargaining moves? Can you use the pressure of a deadline to your advantage?

2. Competitive or cooperative bargaining—multiple issues

Fill out the following chart:

Figure 11–1

Issues	Bottom Lines	Maximal Positions	Intermediate Positions

In what ways are these issues related?

How will you sequence the discussion of issues? Should you discuss some issues before others? Are some issues more difficult than others?

Is it to your advantage to bargain these issues separately, as a package, or as several packages? Why?

Multiple-issue negotiations raise the possibility of trade-offs among issues. You will need some way to assess the value, to you, of the various packages that may be proposed in trading. Examine your chart of issues and positions. Determine which package of positions, across the issues, is minimally acceptable to you and which package is the best possible for you. Using the former as a baseline and the latter as a ceiling, compare other possible packages and attempt to value, prioritize, or quantify them.

3. Integrative bargaining

Compare your interests and those of the OS as you perceive them.

What are your shared interests?

1.

2.

3.

4.

What are your compatible interests?

1.

2.

3.

4.

What interests appear to conflict?

1.

2.

3.

4.

Objectively speaking, what would you define as the common problem or problems you and the OS must solve if you are both to satisfy or advance your respective interests?

Explore the differences between the your side and the OS, as appropriate, according to the following schedule:[4]

---

[4]This item in the form is based on the list of differences found in DAVID A. LAX & JAMES K. SEBENIUS, THE MANAGER AS NEGOTIATOR 115 (1986).

Your Side *Other Side*

1. Relative evaluation of items
2. Forecasts or predictions
3. Willingness to take risks
4. Time preferences
5. Capabilities
6. Attitudes toward precedent
7. Criteria for evaluating the goodness or fairness of the deal

Considering the foregoing analysis of needs, interests, concerns, and differences, brainstorm and list as many possible solutions as you can to the problems you have defined.

1.
2.
3.
4.
5.

Which of these solutions do you favor? Why?

Specifically how do these solutions meet the needs or interests of the OS? In answering this question it is useful to consider your proposal from the OS's point of view. Assume now that you are the OS and are presented with the proposals or solutions you plan to offer.

If the OS says yes to your proposal, what favorable *and* unfavorable consequences follow for him? In listing these, estimate the weight or priority the OS will give to these consequences. In drawing up this list, be sure to include considerations the OS's critical audience will likely raise if apprised that the OS has accepted your proposal.[5]

Consequences

Favorable *Unfavorable*

[5]This portion of the form is based on ideas found in HARVARD NEGOTIATION PROJECT, CURRENTLY PERCEIVED CHOICE TOOL (1987).

If the OS says no to your proposal, what favorable and unfavorable consequences follow for him? Again, in listing these, estimate the weight or priority the OS will give to these consequences. In drawing up this list, be sure to include considerations the OS's critical audience will likely raise if apprised that the OS has refused your proposal.

Consequences

Favorable	*Unfavorable*

Comparing consequences, do you think it likely that the OS will accept or reject your proposal? Why?

In what ways can you amend your proposal, without injuring your own interests, to change the ratio and weight of favorable and unfavorable consequences for the OS so that it is more likely to accept your proposal?

If the OS has a critical audience for its decision, what can you do to alleviate the concerns of that critical audience about the decision that you wish the OS to make? In other words, how can you amend or shape your proposal so that if the OS accepts it, it can persuade or satisfy its critical audience that accepting your proposal was the best decision possible under the circumstances?

Given what you know or can reasonably conclude regarding the OS's needs and interests, what proposals do you think that the OS is likely to make to you?

Proposal 1:

Proposal 2:

Proposal 3:

If you agree to the OS's proposal(s), what favorable and unfavorable consequences would follow for you? Assign weights or priorities to them as they advance or impair your interests. Include in your list reactions or criticisms from your critical audience.

Consequences

Favorable *Unfavorable*

If you refuse to agree to the OS's proposals, what favorable or unfavorable consequences will follow for you? Assign weights or priorities as they advance or impair your interests. Again, include in your list the reactions or criticisms from your critical audience.

Consequences

Favorable *Unfavorable*

Compare your lists and evaluate the OS's likely proposals. If you conclude that you should reject the OS's proposals, are there ways the OS can amend them to meet your objections? What are they?

Considering the foregoing analysis, what proposals do you think you should make to the OS?

What principled arguments can you make for your proposals?

How do the principled arguments you advance apportion shares of any gain your proposals, if accepted, would create? Is the OS likely to object to the particular share allocation?

CHAPTER 12
LAWSUITS AS NEGOTIATIONS

Lawsuits are adversary competitions or contests, and lawsuit negotiations often reflect these sharply adversarial origins. In short, many lawsuit negotiations are basically highly competitive, hard-bargaining negotiations. Nothing requires that they be so. Yet the process and culture of adversary litigation, the reasons people choose to litigate, the investments they make in winning, the rewards litigators receive for their work, and other features of the economic and social structure of litigation make many lawsuit negotiations competitive. It is as though, once the two sides of a dispute enter the lawsuit factory, they cannot leave until a final product has been delivered to the shipping door, transformed from the raw material of the dispute into highly crafted offensive and defensive weapons.

I. LITIGATION AS TWO-TRACK DISPUTE RESOLUTION

Litigating a dispute is both a major alternative to negotiating it and a way to force its negotiation. Litigation arises when the parties to a "mature" dispute have attempted to negotiate it and failed, or have ignored, or refused, the possibility of negotiating it. If the dispute goes to trial, the parties will, through the cases they present, importantly influence the result. Nevertheless, a judge or jury, rather than the parties, will decide the outcome. On the other hand, parties settle most lawsuits rather than try them to verdict. Indeed, it is the deadline that a pending trial imposes on the possibilities of a negotiated settlement, the risk of loss at trial, and possibly the added expense of trial, that motivates these settlements.

Since most lawsuits settle before trial, it is useful to look upon litigation not solely as a way to reach an adjudicated result. It can also be a highly structured negotiation game, a refined, and constrained version of competitive bargaining.[1]

[1] There is a certain irony in viewing settlement as the basic aim of most litigation, for conventional wisdom is, at least superficially, otherwise. The great national lament over litigation and the call for alternative

In effect, litigation is a branched-track mode of dispute resolution. Although apparently heading for an adjudicated result, the parties can, and usually do, shunt their dispute away from trial station onto a negotiation siding. It's important therefore to consider how and why parties progress toward a litigated result while at the same time moving toward settlement and to understand why the process works as it does.

A. Why parties litigate

There are many reasons why parties choose to litigate rather than negotiate. Indeed, while the parties in all cases theoretically could negotiate their dispute rather than litigate it, there is often no effort to negotiate before a party files a lawsuit. As most lawsuits do settle, however, we should look on the filing of a lawsuit, and subsequent litigation steps seemingly headed toward trial, as steps in a probable negotiation. Why do parties invoke this means of entering negotiations?

1. Refusals to deal

Parties sometimes litigate rather than negotiate because they lack bargaining power. This occurs when one party is dependent on another to get something it wants, but the other has, or perceives, no need on its part to deal with the dependent party. For example, the mere existence of a dispute or claim between parties cannot normally force an unwilling respondent to deal with the claimant. Some adverse consequences must fall on the respondent for failure or refusal to deal. Absent compulsion, it has no obligation to respond to a claim. Absent virtue or business necessity, it may have little other reason to do so. An unwilling respondent may not even acknowledge that there is a legitimate claim or dispute. In its view, it has no need to negotiate. Practically, it also might not think it wise. On a failure to respond, the claimant may become discouraged or lack resources to continue to press the claim, and the claim will disappear. In other words, the very conditions necessary to enter negotiations are not there. At least one party doesn't perceive that it needs the deal with the other.

Filing a lawsuit, however, forces the initially nonresponding party to attend to the claim. In bargaining power terms, the filing confronts the nonresponding party with a markedly different set of alternatives than existed before. It can no longer ignore or dismiss the claim. It may even be disabled from negotiating it,

---

dispute resolution as the remedy is in reality not so much a complaint about trying cases as it is about the widespread use of the litigation system as a means to work toward, and gain leverage in, an ultimate negotiated settlement.

for a negotiated settlement depends on the opponent's agreement. Given a possible adverse outcome of the litigation, filing a lawsuit creates a new situation in which the parties need each other to escape an adjudicated outcome.

2. *Refusals to deal and claim discounting*

An important subclass of lawsuits involves business or other parties seeking to minimize settlement losses. Parties include repeat players such as insurance companies or other businesses handling or facing a large number of claims. For them, whether to resist claims to the point of suit, when claims go to suit, and when and how to settle them become, in large part, business questions.

Where the guiding rule is profit, it is rational to treat claim resolution, including trial, as just another aspect of business. There are many strategies, and mixes of strategies, such parties could follow in treating claim resolution. One obvious and commonly adopted strategy is hardballing. Hardballing involves resisting a claim until there is a credible threat of suit, or even a continuing refusal to negotiate in spite of a pending litigation. A party can impose significant financial, psychological, and opportunity costs on a claimant by forcing it to pursue litigation. Hardballing, or ignoring or resisting claims, requires the claimant to bear all the costs of filing and prosecuting a lawsuit to force the respondent into a position where it must address the claim. Many claimants won't cross that threshold, and their claims will either fade away or the respondent can negotiate them quite advantageously. By forcing claimants to resort to law, the nonresponder creates a claims clearing-and-discount system.

Even when a claimant files a lawsuit, however, continued hardballing can bring discount benefits. Prosecuting a lawsuit involves additional expense, delay, uncertainty, and perhaps anxiety. Any or all of these may either cause a claimant to give up or to compromise its demands. Thus, even when a resisting party knows the claimant is in the right and can succeed, it may nonetheless use litigation to impose litigation transaction costs on the claimant and erode the asserted value of the claim.

Particularly where a business faces repetitive "garden variety" claims, business judgment might follow this kind of claim resolution policy. That policy, while perhaps occasionally costly in those cases where the strategy results in a trial that the business loses, might be least costly in the aggregate of all cases. Thus, parties sometimes ignore or resist even meritorious individual cases because they treat them as instances of a class of cases to be hardballed to ensure they are discounted. Similarly, in some cases a party will prefer trial to negotiation because settling the claim may encourage similar claims by others.

In more unusual cases, business calculation will take into account the possible precedential value of the case. Then the decision whether to settle or litigate will turn partly on an assessment of which process in that case will lead to the best prospects for future cases. For example, cigarette companies generally choose to litigate rather than settle cancer-from-smoking claims. They do so because the cases are not clear cases of liability, because plaintiffs demand large settlements, and because the companies can afford expensive litigation. More important, however, notwithstanding the great expense of these trials, the company's investment in winning the trial has a large potential payoff for its possible future liabilities.

3. Negotiation failures

Even where parties attempt to work with one another without resorting to litigation, they may change their dispute into a lawsuit when other efforts to resolve it have failed. The parties may be unable to deal with one another in productive ways or may even suffer a complete breakdown of relationship. No longer trusting one another, nor feeling capable of working together, one or both parties may view a lawsuit as the only way to get a resolution.

The parties' ways of interacting, their possible lack of negotiation skills, and the demands of their constituencies could all cause negotiation to fail. Negotiation could also fail because a party believes it has a legal right or advantage which the other will not acknowledge. It may think a lawsuit will give it leverage, or that it will get a better result from trial than from negotiation. Finally, it may prefer litigation because it wants to establish a precedent.

4. Zero-sum situations

Many lawsuits arise in situations that the parties view, or are persuaded to view, as zero-sum. That is, the parties are in absolute conflict over what is at issue so that what one party gets, the other party necessarily loses. The suit concerns some perceived or claimed injury or liability arising from past actions. The parties define redress in exclusive terms, such as damage awards, ownership or authority rights, or the parties' respective freedom of action regarding one another. Thus, in a tort or contract action, one party demands money damages from another. In a property action, a party claims exclusive possession of some item. In an injunction action, one party seeks to prevent another from doing something. Even in less conventional actions, such as a toxic chemical cleanup action, the aim is to force the defendant to bear certain costs and to do something that it doesn't want to do.

Some of these situations are not inherently zero-sum. Suppose the parties considered the full potential range of their relationships and possibilities of future joint action. They might then perceive an immediate dispute in a broader context and redefine it in a non-zero-sum fashion.

Nonetheless, in many cases the parties neither have nor contemplate an ongoing or future relationship, nor do they perceive benefits from nonlitigation-induced cooperation. The dispute arises out of a one-time past transaction or event, the parties are competitors, adversaries, or hostiles, the asserted claim is unalterably zero-sum, or litigation appears to offer better results than negotiation.

II. LITIGATION AS A NEGOTIATION PROCESS

A. Legalizing disputes

Lawsuits shape the substance and conduct of settlement negotiations. When disputes arise, the parties have two major ways to resolve them: by negotiation or by adjudication. When a party elects to sue, however, it places the dispute into a framework and context significantly affecting the process and substance of any negotiated settlement. This not only limits the scope of the dispute but also determines what is relevant to its litigated resolution, no matter what the parties may think or what other considerations they would ordinarily deploy.

The elements that adversarial trial process uses to reach an adjudicated decision also become highly important in settlement discussions. These elements are: proof of facts using relevant and admissible evidence and witness credibility assessments; substantive and procedural rules; precedent; and legal and other persuasive argumentation aimed at a neutral trier of issues. Litigators evaluate these elements, as well as the skill and resources of the lawyer on the other side, to estimate likely success at trial. They will carry their conclusions, confidence, and arguments to settlement discussions. In any event, settlement discussions will be law- and proof-based. In other words, after a dispute becomes a lawsuit, legal assessments and arguments about the law, about proofs, and about rights will dominate settlement discussions.

One major reason disputing parties turn to litigation is their need for a neutral process to settle contested issues of fact, law, and the applicability of law to facts. Theoretically, if the parties trusted one another to deal fairly as between themselves, they would not have this need. Realistically speaking, however, parties in many disputes are untrusting. Indeed, the incidents or events that gave rise to their dispute often also create, or exacerbate, distrust between them.[2] As we shall see, however, what many litigating parties really need in order to settle

---

[2] Litigation, of course, is not a trusting process; indeed, exquisite suspicion and mistrust of the opponent provides the basic premise for its procedures and structure.

is neither neutral fact-finding, neutral applications, nor interpretation of law, *but rather the threat of them.*

Filing a lawsuit begins a process of translating the actual dispute the parties have into an adversarial contest the judicial system can resolve. In other words, the litigation process formally "legalizes" the dispute, that is, frames it in terms of legal concepts, proofs, and argumentation that the judicial system can process. This limits the scope of the dispute and makes it amenable to third-party resolution. In many cases, however, this transformation, once well along, also enables the parties to predict what the outcome of the third-party adjudication would be. Once the parties can reasonably predict the outcome, they no longer need the neutral third party. In many cases, they will settle. In unpredictable cases, and in predictable cases where at least one party gambles that a realistic trial threat will increase its gain in any final settlement, the parties will continue on the trial path.

B. Trial as process remedy

A trial is both a fact-finding process and a neutral third-party decisional process determining rights and obligations as between litigating parties. While trial, in large measure, integrates these processes, it is useful to consider them separately. It is the combination of the distinct features of each process that helps explain some of litigation's attractiveness as a way of resolving disputes.

Disputing parties often disagree about critical facts, or about the interpretation or meaning of facts. Where parties cannot verify disputed facts or cannot agree on ways to verify them, they must settle them in some other way. Even if the parties wish to negotiate a settlement, the factual disagreement may disable them from moving forward. They must first agree on a process to settle the facts before they can turn to using those facts as a basis to make other decisions between them.

However, a great deal may turn on which facts the parties accept as true. They will not agree to accept any fact-finding process that they suspect may be biased against them or which otherwise appears to disadvantage them in settling facts. Where there are important stakes, each party has a great incentive to advance its version and interpretation of the facts. Without significant pre-existing trust no party will trust the other's version of facts nor permit the other solely to settle them. In such cases, each party has a strong interest in contesting facts and in winning that contest.

When parties contest facts solely between themselves, neither can prevail. In such circumstances, a readily available fact-finding process, neutral as between the parties, is highly attractive. Trials, either in a court or before an arbitrator, may provide exactly the neutral fact-finding that parties both want and need.

The litigation process provides specific ways of proving and finding facts. Much of trial preparation, discovery in particular, aims at proof of facts. In many cases, just before trial, completed discovery will clarify the trial-provable facts. To the degree therefore that the parties' dispute was fact-based, the discovery process may resolve the problem. The discovery process can thus position the parties either to negotiate, or try, the case.

Of course, litigation discovery does not always resolve factual disputes; indeed, it may intensify them. Facts may remain contested even after thorough discovery. This is not only because the provable facts may conflict and require a choice as between them, but also because important facts at issue may be matters of inferential, as opposed to direct, proof. Assessments of witness credibility may also play an important role in fact determination. In such cases, the factual contest remains in play after discovery, and each party may want to exercise its opportunity to persuade the fact-finder. Opposing litigators may believe they can "impression manage" trial proofs to persuade the fact-finder that their respective versions of the facts are true.

Even where there is no initial factual dispute, or where the parties successfully settle facts, they may yet contest what rights and obligations those facts generate at law. A negligence case provides a typical example. A party is negligent when he fails to meet a duty of care the law imposes and thereby injures another. The law defines that duty of care by reference to the reasonable person standard. If a reasonable person would not have done what the defendant did, then the defendant is at least negligent. If a reasonable person would have acted as the defendant did, then the defendant is not negligent. While there are many clear cases of negligence, there are also borderline cases. In a borderline case, what a reasonable person would have done may be debatable or contestable. If it is, the parties may want a neutral decision maker to apply the legal standard, which involves a determination of community expectations regarding conduct, to the facts.

Of course, in some cases where the issue is application of law to facts, experienced legal professionals, such as litigators and judges, may with some confidence predict how a normal jury would resolve the question. The unpredictable cases in this category, however, remain as prime candidates for trial resolution. Additionally, there are cases involving contested facts, legal standards, and applications of those legal standards to the facts which are prime trial candidates.

Where parties settle their lawsuits, the litigation process works in one of two ways. First, it shapes the dispute to make it amenable to court resolution. In many cases, even well before adjudication, this means the parties can predict the outcome of the suit if adjudicated. Once the parties can predict the outcome, they no longer need a neutral adjudicator. In other cases, however, the outcome remains doubtful, even after litigation processing, and the parties continue to move toward trial. Finally, in some cases, which may or may not have predictable outcomes, at least one party uses the litigation process and the threat of trial as tools to induce bargaining and maximize gain.

C. Litigation as bargaining-power equalizer

Litigation is combative, expensive, and—compared with some other ways of reaching agreements or decisions—highly inefficient, distracting, time intensive, and resource consumptive. Viewed simply as a form of competitive bargaining, those are some of its virtues. The power to litigate is the power to force the situation, the power to require another party to attend to one's claims seriously. Further, the litigation dynamic creates situations of perceived stalemate and deadlock, but under substantial threats of impending loss of adverse decision and consequent externally imposed loss. Litigation, therefore, does not necessarily result from a failure to seek negotiated resolutions of problems; it is, instead, also a way—a potent, albeit painful way—of initiating a process leading to a negotiated agreement.

Filing a lawsuit invokes the intervention of a court that has the power to compel disclosure of information and to adjudicate the issues between the parties. It is also a way to impose costs—time, money, administrative, psychological, and reputational costs—on another. The ability to impose costs, through forcing a need for legal services, requiring responses to discovery requests and appearances at hearings and depositions, changes the bargaining power relationships between the parties.

Unless parties refuse to settle, it is generally the unusual, rather than the ordinary, case that proceeds to trial. Where the facts of a case appear to fall within some established norm of resolution for similar kinds of cases, it is predictable and likely to settle, eventually. Where a case is unusual, or an attorney can make it appear so, it poses the serious prospect there will be a trial. If the case is even marginally triable, that prospect can introduce major uncertainties about possible outcomes. The adjudication will turn on many variables that, try as they might, the parties cannot control. These variables include the respective skills of the parties' attorneys, the state of the provable evidence, the availability and credibility of witnesses, and the composition of the jury. Yet other variables, such as the trial judge, the character of the complaint, the causes of action, the state of the law, who the parties are, how they present themselves, and the resources they have available for discovery and trial preparation can also affect the trial outcome. All these uncertainties serve, to a certain degree, to equalize the parties' bargaining power because neither can predict who is likely to prevail, thus placing a party's alternative to negotiation in doubt.[3]

1. Two-track discovery

In a lawsuit, lawyers and parties are partisan. As partisans, they are often not in a good position to assess their cases objectively, at least not until they complete major discovery.

As parties progress through the litigation process toward trial, they constantly assess their case. Their perceptions of the value of their case changes as they gather further information, assess probable witnesses, and receive favorable and unfavorable court rulings on motions and requests. Because of these changes, the parties may not have strong incentives to consider settlement discussions until faced with the prospect of immediate trial.

In the discovery process available in American litigation, the litigating parties can force one another to disclose information. This imposes a cost, but also could facilitate settlement negotiations. It may be a lack of information or a misperception of provable facts that causes parties to make unrealistic claims or have unrealistic expectations. Nevertheless, because discovery takes time and is the subject of adversarial combat, the process usually works against settlement efforts. Obtaining full discovery may take years, and many lawyers, hoping to find some valuable information or simply acting cautiously, will defer serious settlement discussion until discovery is complete. This is particularly true when the lawyer is also busy with other cases and doesn't have, or take, the time to assess the settlement suitability of pending litigation. Additionally, because parties usually contest discovery adversarially, it psychologically reinforces adversariness as a dispute resolution mode. The costs that discovery imposes on the parties also constitute an increased investment in a litigated solution.

Of course, at the end of the discovery process each party should have fairly full information about the other's case. This information is most useful to lawyers in assessing the viability and value of a case. Such information can stimulate productive settlement discussions, but can also limit settlements. This is because lawyers have shaped the case adversarially. The information they have acquired is, for the most part, only information relevant to the issues framed in the suit. Other information that might be useful for fashioning a creative settlement, for example, information regarding party interests not directly or immediately implicated in the suit, are usually unavailable. Unless all concerned make special efforts, this means that lawsuit settlement negotiations, whenever they occur,

---

[3]The basis of a trial decision is legal right, rather than superior negotiating position or resources. A lawsuit thus also tends to equalize bargaining power by neutralizing nonfinancial advantages an opposing party may have, for example, superior nonlegal knowledge, negotiating skill, or psychological strength.

will tend to follow competitive-compromise, rather than problem-solving, bargaining models.

In some, but not all cases, the driving forces in litigation vector litigating parties away from early settlement and toward a tense equilibrium of deadlock as trial approaches. Nonetheless, most cases do settle; relatively few go to trial.

Of course, parties or litigators sometimes settle their suits well before then. These are cases in which either the predictable outcome is fairly clear or the parties' needs make the further delay, expense, and risk of trial unacceptable. Nonetheless, as many lawsuits close on trial, the opposing parties remain fixed in standoff postures, the litigation having become a competitive negotiation contest of relative firmness.

On the eve of trial, while the parties may have clarified and sharpened their theories and proofs, many of the reasons they took the trial path continue, often intensified. Principal among these is the absence of a neutral fact-finder and decision maker. While settling does not require the parties to agree on facts nor the applicability of law to facts, their differing predictions of what a trial would produce regarding these matters may create sharply conflicted settlement positions. Neither party will accept the other's assessment of the case or its value. They remain in need of a neutral party to intervene.

Many jurisdictions introduced mandatory settlement conferences in order to resolve this impasse problem. The requirement may be either that the litigants get together to discuss possible settlement or that the litigants appear before a judge, or other neutral evaluator, who will host a settlement conference.[4]

Mandatory settlement conferences between the parties only do no more than mandate that the parties get together before trial and attempt to discuss settlement. Other than providing an opportunity to settle, nothing in this requirement meets the important need litigating parties have for a neutral intervenor. While they may be talking, and at least exploring the possibility of settlement, they remain unrefereed opponents.

Mandatory settlement conferences before a judge, either the judge who will try the case or another not associated with it, are another matter. The judge can provide the neutral assessment the parties need. But the judge can also do more. She can pressure the parties, recommend compromises, and provide the litigators

---

[4] In addition some jurisdictions attempt to introduce additional incentives to settle, principally in the form of a penalty assessment scheme. Under this system, each party must lay its best offer on the table. If they cannot agree and the case goes to trial, the winning party may, in the discretion of the trial judge, tax its costs to the losing party if the winning party's verdict is less than its best final settlement offer. In other words, the loser, in choosing to go to trial, rejected an opportunity to do better than it ended up doing at trial. *See, e.g.*, CAL. CIV. PROC. CODE §998. The aim of such a statute is to "punish a party who fails to accept a reasonable offer from another party." Hurlbut v. Sonora Community Hospital, 207 Cal. App.3d 388, 408 (1989). Such a provision is an obvious attempt to make the parties closely and carefully estimate possible trial success and the reasonable value of their case.

and parties with ways to save face, for example, by offering rationales for agreements. In effect, what was a two-party standoff becomes a three-party negotiation, with the judge, an authority figure, playing the role of intermediary or activist mediator. This often works.

A simple example shows how. Parties heading for a trial competition will not willingly disclose or admit weaknesses in their case to their opponents. They will not do so because their opponent might utilize it and because it suggests less than complete confidence in victory. Just as in competitive bargaining, each litigant will have some reservation price, or settlement figure, he is willing to accept, yet is unwilling to disclose, for fear of losing possible gain. The litigants' reservation prices may overlap or be close, but they will not know it. Instead, they will have postured with large, possibly extreme, demands.

In each of these circumstances, if a trusted judge caucuses privately with the litigants, she can obtain the private information and discover where the give is. Using that information from both sides, she may then be able to craft a settlement acceptable to all. In doing this, she would not necessarily disclose the private information, but simply offer as her own proposal a position she realizes the parties can live with but cannot directly communicate to one another.

In addition, by discussing the case with each party privately, the judge discovers each party's view of its own case. She can also discover its assessments of proofs and witnesses and its assessments of the other side's case. The judge then has a view of the case as a whole and can, using her experience, arrive at her own view of probable result if tried. The situation positions the judge to provide each party privately with an "objective" assessment of its case. While a party will not accept an opponent's assessment of the case because it would assume it to be self-serving, distorted, and biased, it will far more likely accept the judge's assessment.

In sum, as an experienced neutral nonlitigating party with authority, a judge's pronounced assessment of the case, and other interventions, will carry substantial weight with the litigants. Just that kind of intervention is often necessary to shunt the parties from their litigation track to a negotiated settlement. Of course, whether or not a judge-hosted mandatory settlement conference succeeds in inducing settlement depends on various factors. These include the judge, her legal, negotiation, and persuasion skills, and her interest in trying to craft a settlement rather than permitting the case go to trial.

D. Settling lawsuits: theory and empirical evidence

There are so many subject matter categories of lawsuits, involving different substantive rule regimes and different forces at play, that efforts to devise a single, comprehensive theory of lawsuit settlement and trial seem futile. Nonetheless, we know that some factors are particularly important in influencing litigants to settle or try their cases. Two notable theories, selection theory[5] and strategic bargaining theory,[6] examine and explore decisions to settle or try a case. Empirical researchers have tested some predictions these theories make and have found some support for them, at least in certain classes of cases.[7] Together, these studies identify variables that illumine lawsuit bargaining dynamics and influence the decision whether or not to try a case.

The most important of these variables are:

- predictability of trial outcome;
- settlement and litigation costs relative to possible trial gain or loss;
- the differential relative stakes the parties have in the litigation, sometimes called "asymmetric" stakes;
- litigation financing, that is, who bears the litigation costs and the risk of litigation loss;
- whether the parties are one-time or "repeat player" litigants; and
- "ally effects."

1. Predictability

Selection theory asserts that trials take place in close cases. By implication, this theory would hold that litigants are likely to try cases for reasons related to their perceptions of the merits of the cases. In this view, litigating parties assess their cases before trial and predict their likelihood of success. Their bargaining behavior depends on their estimates. Both parties predict the verdict and the award. The plaintiff deducts litigation costs from the predicted award and uses this figure to set his minimum settlement demand. The defendant adds litigation costs to its predicted award, and this figure becomes the defendant's maximum settlement figure. If these two figures overlap, there is a bargaining range, or contract zone, and the parties will settle. If the parties' predictions of trial outcomes are quite different, however, there may be no overlap of offer and demand. Lacking any potential contract zone, the parties will not settle.

---

[5] George L. Priest & Benjamin Klein, *The Selection of Disputes for Litigation*, 13 J. OF LEGAL STUD. 1, 6-12 (1984).

[6] Robert Cooter, Stephen Marks, & Robert Mnookin, *Bargaining in the Shadow of the Law: A Testable Model of Strategic Behavior*, 11 J. OF LEGAL STUD. 225, 238 (1982).

[7] *See, e.g.*, Priest & Klein, *supra* note 5; Cooter, Marks, & Mnookin, *supra* note 6; Samuel R. Gross & Kent D. Syverud, *Getting to No: A Study of Settlement Negotiations and the Selection of Cases for Trial*, 90 MICH. L. REV. 319 (1991).

This will occur in cases where the parties cannot reasonably predict outcomes, that is, in close cases.

There are problems with selection theory. The relatively few empirical studies attempting to test it do not provide strong support for its predictions, at least not across all kinds of cases. Further, the model makes unrealistic assumptions. It assumes that the litigants are equally informed and skilled. This is certainly not the case in many lawsuits. It also apparently assumes that the parties do not attempt to gain bargaining advantages through misrepresentations of positions, imposition of costs, and litigation tools. Whatever its predictive ability and limited case assumptions, however, selection theory succeeds in focusing on predictability of trial outcome as one important variable in lawsuit negotiation and trial behavior.

2. Strategic bargaining

There are, however, lawsuits whose outcomes are easy to predict, yet which do not settle, ending instead in trial. This is an anomaly in selection theory. Strategic bargaining offers an explanation, however, and a richer model of litigation bargaining.

Strategic bargaining theory asserts that litigants strategically misrepresent their willingness to settle, maneuver for advantage, and adopt bargaining strategies to help them increase their settlement gain. In this view, even if there is in actuality a bargaining contract zone, the parties might not settle. This would occur because one or both parties engaged in hard-bargaining. Here, at least one side, in order to increase gain, misleads the other about where it would actually agree to settle. Even in a case where a party could predict he would lose, he might take a risk and mislead the other side into thinking he preferred trial to settlement. He might calculate that the other party would concede further under realistic threat of trial. He might also hope that the imposition of additional litigation costs might flush out a risk-averse opponent and give her another reason to settle.

3. Bargaining variables: incentives to settle or try

The bargaining model proposes variables in addition to predictability of outcome that help explain whether the parties will settle or go to trial. For example, a litigant's need for a quick resolution or an increase in likely trial costs incline a litigant to settle. Similarly, if the litigants are familiar with one another, they are better able to assess one another and thus are less likely to make the kind of strategic miscalculations that result in trial. If the parties must negotiate, the costs of negotiating will incline them toward settlement to reduce those costs.[8]

As parties must take litigation costs into account in deciding whether to settle, the method of financing litigation becomes important.[9] Where a party must pay its own costs, it has an incentive to settle to avoid costs. Where a lawyer or insurer subsidizes party costs, as occurs in some cases, she has less incentive to settle.

Other factors move litigating parties toward trial rather than settlement. If delay benefits a party, it is more likely to resist bargaining until absolutely required to do so—on the eve of trial. By then, however, there may no longer be a bargaining opportunity. A tenant remaining in possession following an eviction notice might pose just such a case. Similarly, a litigant who finds some unusual value in trial resolution—for example, a party suing to establish some legal principle or suing from spite—will likely increase her settlement demands and thereby make settlement less likely. In general, a risk-neutral litigant—one who for some reason is willing to accept the risk of trial loss—will resist settling and demand more to settle.[10]

A recent empirical study testing selection and strategic bargaining theories found strong support for the bargaining view.[11] The work also finds that the economic and social structure of litigation, particularly litigation-financing and insurance arrangements, are important determinants of settlement and trial behavior.

4. Risk-aversion and lawsuit bargaining strategies

Lawsuits are win-lose competitions. That fact can make them not only initially difficult to settle, but at the same time can conversely contribute to a settlement, usually at the last moment. Psychologically speaking, this is exactly how one would expect parties in such situations to act.

---

[8] Of course, if the parties can refuse to negotiate and thereby avoid negotiation costs, the possibility of higher negotiation costs might cause them to prefer trial to negotiation.

[9] In the United States, litigants are responsible for their own trial costs. In England, the loser as a general rule pays costs for both sides. Relatively speaking, the American system should lead to a higher number of trials; the cost of losing a trial is less.

[10] In the strategic bargaining model, litigants, such as insurance companies, who are "repeat" players, are clearly likely to engage in hard-bargaining against one-time litigants. This strategy is likely to dampen the expectations of future claimants. As a hard-bargaining strategy is risky, however, it will also occasionally result in trials from miscalculation. On the other hand, where repeat players litigate against other repeat players, settlement is more likely as they are familiar with one another.

[11] Gross & Syverud, *supra* note 7, at 381.

Persons act conservatively when faced with the prospect of significant loss or gain. They have a risk-averse orientation toward seeking gains and a loss-averse or risk-positive orientation in taking action to prevent losses.[12] In other words, persons will take a risk to prevent a loss but will not take equal risks to secure a gain. In the context of a lawsuit, this conservative strategy dictates a strong preference for not going to trial. All trials, where there is any uncertainty of outcome at all, carry a significant risk of loss. Repeat players, such as insurance companies, however, are relatively risk-neutral. They have a present interest in the impact of settlement on future cases—the message settlement sends to future claimants. Therefore they factor potential future loss into their bargaining equation and have an incentive to hard-bargain.

Parallel logic suggests that a party suffers the least loss from a negotiated settlement when it negotiates from a position of maximum power. A litigating party's power is maximal when it convincingly appears it will elect its alternative to try the case rather than negotiate a settlement, in other words, close to the eve of trial.[13] Consequently, litigators often follow a combined strategy of doing everything possible to appear committed to trial while secretly preferring and looking for settlement. Of course, it is exceptionally difficult for a litigator to *pretend* she is going to try a case, for she may actually *have* to try it. The litigator therefore has no real alternative than to prepare for trial. Of course, this conveys the right message to the other side, yet also may increase the risk of going to trial.

"Sunk cost" psychology and nonrational processes of escalation also play a role in this phenomenon of trial eve settlement. Parties who have already invested significantly in a particular course of action are likely to invest more when faced with a choice of investing more or changing course. Similarly, when a party faces losses stemming from a lack of agreement, which is always the case in an ongoing lawsuit, it is likely to *increase* rather than *decrease* its commitment to its position. Thus, the parties will incline toward pursuing the lawsuit rather than seeking a negotiated settlement—at least until the threat of impending loss forces them to seriously reconsider negotiation.

Experienced lawsuit-settlement observers draw the same conclusions:

> As time passes and the parties pay more fees to their attorneys, their positions tend to harden somewhat. If what was considered a fair offer has been rejected, the offeror may become antagonistic. As investment in the litigation increases and a party develops a good rapport with counsel, that party may become less reluctant to litigate; after all, considering the investment to date, the balance,

---

[12] Daniel Kahneman & Amos Tversky, *Prospect Theory: An Analysis of Decision Under Risk*, 47 ECONOMETRICA 263, 288 (1979).

[13] The same reasoning suggests that a party will be willing to try a case when the loss it contemplates from settlement approximates the loss it might experience if it goes to trial.

relatively speaking, may not appear to be particularly significant to him. As a result, leverage is lost in many cases with the passage of time. In other words, as the cost of litigation rises, there is not necessarily a commensurate increase in motivation to settle. As a matter of fact, protracted negotiation, coupled with extensive preparation for trial, may have the opposite effect.[14]

5. Litigation fee and financing arrangements

Another variable that may affect how a litigating lawyer acts as a negotiator is the lawyer's fee arrangement. Depending on the way in which the litigation is financed, the lawyer may have a personal stake in both litigated and negotiated outcomes. This is perhaps most obvious when the lawyer uses a contingent-fee arrangement.[15] That personal stake may affect the lawyer's assessments of trial or settlement prospects and may also induce a lawyer to shape his client's perceptions in ways that favor the lawyer's, rather than the client's, interests. For example, a lawyer who receives the same fee whether the case settles or goes to trial and who prefers to settle rather than undertake a three-week trial may persuade his client to settle although it may not be in her best interest to do so.

A lawyer representing a client on a contingent-fee basis, and perhaps financing the litigation, has a direct personal interest in the litigation and any possible settlements. Notwithstanding rules of professional ethics, one would expect contingent-fee attorneys to exert a greater say in litigation and settlement decisions than attorneys lacking such an interest. The lawsuit is, effectively, a joint venture.

Attorneys hired on an hourly basis also have incentives that may affect their judgments regarding negotiated settlements. It is not, of course, always a question of extending, or complicating, a litigation because that means more billable hours. It is rather a question of judgments affected by combined calculations of fee, client satisfaction, and prospect of future business.

Other lawyer interests, not necessarily coincident with those of a client, may also factor into the lawyer's attitudes toward settlement. These include the lawyer's reputation, the publicity or other-business generating value of the case, and the lawyer's relationship with attorneys on the other side.[16]

---

[14] ROBERT A. WENKE, THE ART OF NEGOTIATION FOR LAWYERS 186 (1985).

[15] An attorney handling a case on a contingent-fee basis receives a percentage, usually a third but sometimes more, of the settlement or trial recovery. In addition, contingent-fee attorneys usually finance the litigation, that is, they advance the costs necessary to move the case to litigation.

[16] This, of course, may also be true of other nonparty players in lawsuits, for example, the insurance company which finances it and which may be liable for any damage award.

A party who can, without risk, shift trial costs onto someone else is more likely to litigate than to settle. When a litigant has a litigation sponsor, such as occurs in attorney-financed contingent-fee cases or cases where insurance companies bear defense costs, the litigants can afford to hard-bargain. On the other hand, where the litigant pays her own litigation costs, she may incline toward settling, except in those cases where she is reasonably certain of trial victory.

Sponsored litigation does not by any means always result in hard-bargaining. Whether a sponsored litigant will force a case to trial depends on the litigant's relationship to its sponsor and who controls the decision whether to litigate. For example, in ordinary litigation involving relatively small sums, neither hard-bargaining, nor integrative bargaining, nor trial makes much sense. Negotiation and trial transaction costs are high relative to stakes, and the lawyer needs to monetize the claim, rather than engage in creative problem solving in order to collect a fee. When the case is relatively small, the lawyer's interest is to invest relatively little and settle cases rapidly.

Empirical evidence indicates this is what occurs. Most small, ordinary litigation cases settle in only one or two rounds of bargaining, and the lawyers do not engage in strategic bargaining to maximize gains.[17] Indeed, in these cases, the lawyer's predominant bargaining aim apparently is "to locate a case within a set of norms and expectations"[18] and to settle it for the "going-rate" for that kind of case.[19] Attempting to maximize results for individual clients would impose additional costs on the attorney and might lead to trials with a risk of no gain at all. Turning over many small cases rapidly, however, makes for a steady income with minimal investment. Thus in small and relatively situable cases, attorneys apparently deal both to obtain satisfactory results for clients in individual cases and maximize their own aggregate gain or effective hourly rate over all their cases.[20]

In high-stakes contingent-fee cases, the pattern is different. The contingent-fee attorney may gamble on going to trial in the hopes of obtaining a large judgment. Viewed as financial investors in litigation, contingent-fee attorneys actually carry a portfolio of cases in which they have invested. If they win some big cases, they can afford to lose others, for it is the overall return on the overall investment that counts.[21] Thus in high-stakes cases, contingent-fee lawyers are

---

[17] HERBERT M. KRITZER, LET'S MAKE A DEAL 132-133 (1991).

[18] *Id.* at 71.

[19] *Id.* at 121, 199.

[20] *Id.* at 105, 124.

[21] Gross & Syverud, *supra* note 7, at 349. A contingent-fee lawyer with an investment portfolio of cases is really a repeat player, and in that sense, relatively risk-neutral in individual cases.

both more likely to engage in hard-bargaining and to go to trial. Trial may result either from a gamble on trial results or a bargaining miscalculation.

6. Relative or asymmetric stakes

Opposing parties in lawsuits sometimes have different stakes in a litigation. For example, suppose a single plaintiff, disturbed by the noise level coming from a factory near his home, sues to enjoin the factory from producing noise above a certain level. If the factory had to curtail manufacturing to comply, it might lose far more from the suit than the plaintiff gains from a lowered noise level. Similarly, a defendant might worry that a particular lawsuit, if litigated through appeal, might establish an adverse precedent that would damage his position in future cases. The plaintiff, however, might want a recovery, and care nothing about making law.

In these examples, the defendant would want to settle. On the other hand, a doctor sued for medical malpractice might wish to go to trial, having a concern about the effect of settlement on her reputation and future career. In other words, one litigating party's greater relative stake in a litigation could incline it either to hard-bargain or to compromise. Which it elects to do depends on which strategy best serves its overall set of interests, as implicated in the litigation.

7. Lawyer-client relationships in lawsuits

Filing a lawsuit takes away much of the parties' power to decide the shape and content of their dispute. Instead, it devolves that power to legal professionals who, using system resources, translate that dispute into a strictly enforced adversary contest. Over time, the demands of the adversary trial process, the advocacy ethos that encourages and justifies taking extreme positions,[22] and the momentum of invested emotion and contest may work progressively to polarize the parties' attitudes. They certainly shape the parties' perceptions of the situation. Finally, the adversary contest itself excludes the principals from a continued active role in resolving their own dispute.

Clients vary in their degree of sophistication in dealing with lawyers and handling involvements in lawsuits. Lawyers differ in their approaches to clients

---

[22] "[A] lawyer should represent a client zealously within the bounds of law." Canon 7, American Bar Association Model Code of Professional Responsibility. See also Ethical Consideration 7-1 and Disciplinary Rules 7-101(A)(1) and 7-101(A)(3). The Canon does not quite express the actual strength of the obligation, or lawyers' devotion to it, in American legal culture, but that has been captured in scholarly commentary on the Canon: "[The Code and Model Rules of Professional Responsibility] require lawyers . . . to seek every lawful objective for a client *regardless of its morality.*" CHARLES W. WOLFRAM, MODERN LEGAL ETHICS 583 (1986) (emphasis added). For an extended discussion, *see id.* at 578-585.

and in the ways in which they manage or relate to them. In a lawsuit, the lawyer is a representative or agent who occupies the boundary role position. That is, while nominally only a client's agent, the lawyer is the major actor in advancing and managing the litigation. The lawyer is in a position to assess it, to make predictions regarding it, and to compare litigated, as against negotiated, result potentials. The roles lawyers have in shaping, managing, and assessing the possible outcomes of lawsuits, and their ability to shape their clients' perceptions of the litigation, give them considerable situational power. One might even say, depending on the client, that they virtually dominate their clients regarding settlement matters.[23]

8. *The litigator-negotiator's bias*

The lawyer's status as legal representative will also predispose her in her approach to dispute resolution. Often, accountability to another leads one to greater advocacy than when acting for oneself. The lawyer who represents a client is accountable to the client, and the client will evaluate the lawyer's performance.[24] Strengthening this effect in the lawyer-client relationship is the lawyer's ethical obligation to devote herself single-mindedly to her client's interests.[25] Furthermore, lawyer-client meetings, where the parties discuss lawsuit progress, likely increase pressure for lawyer loyalty, commitment, and advocacy. Finally, litigation is itself a competitive contest. As a lawsuit progresses, the other side presents its point of view oppositionally. Inevitably, this inclines all parties, clients as well as lawyers, to view themselves as engaged in a combat or battle. Thus aside from the parties' possible initial competitive stances, the

[23] Depending on the specific lawyer-client relationship in a particular case, the lawyer may or may not have what is called "client-control." In the sense familiar to lawyers, client-control simply means the ability of the lawyer to persuade the client to do whatever the lawyer concludes it is in the best interests of her client to do. Thus in a lawsuit a lawyer has good client-control when the client agrees either to go to trial or to settle, as the lawyer thinks best.

Lawyers sometimes mismanage clients by causing them to have expectations which, in the event, cannot be fulfilled. This would occur, for example, where a lawyer persuades a client to litigate, encourages inflated expectations regarding the results of a lawsuit, but then either has to backtrack when it appears the suit will not succeed or to go forward with the lawsuit because of the client's settled expectations.

[24] When lawyers enter lawsuit negotiations, they do so as representatives, but they are not necessarily subject to all the constraints and pressures that negotiators who act as representatives may feel. For example, the particular lawsuit may be the only occasion the lawyer has to negotiate for a particular client, having no other business relationship with her, as would likely be the case in a plaintiff's tort suit. In that circumstance, the prospect of future negotiation employment, from the same client, is not significant, and the lawyer as negotiator can afford to be less responsive to client pressures and expectations.

Contrast, however, the relative position of an insurance plaintiff or defense lawyer who has repeat business from an insurance company. Because the company can withdraw future business, the lawyer may have to negotiate a particular case in ways that meet her client's expectations both about the manner of negotiating and about substance.

[25] *See* sources cited *supra* note 22.

litigation process generates additional, and increasing, competitive impetus, or competitive "lock-in" effects.

9. The litigator-negotiator's role

Lawyers obviously play an important role in transforming grievances, claims, or disputes into lawsuits and in channeling clients into litigated, as opposed to negotiated, dispute resolution. This is not to say that lawyers will inevitably advise clients to sue, even when they appear to have a good and litigable claim. Lawyers often do move clients toward litigation. A lawyer may assess the situation as one requiring litigation, not seeing nonlitigation ways to get good results. In a good many cases, lawyers instinctively or calculatedly advise litigation as a way to get, and leverage, an ultimate negotiated solution.

Consider, in this respect, the character of some of the advice a trial judge offers lawyers regarding the negotiation of lawsuits.

> There are cases that should not be tried because the risk of loss is too great. Nevertheless, it is essential in such cases to project an image of willingness to go to trial.
>
> * * *
>
> Obtaining an interim advantage, such as a preliminary injunction or a writ of attachment, tends to give the successful litigant added power.
>
> * * *
>
> A cross-complaint or counterclaim should be filed whenever there is any basis for it. Defense counsel ought to pursue the matter vigorously, standing firm and talking about receiving payment from the plaintiff rather than offering anything. This is an excellent tactic for placing the other side on the defensive.
>
> * * *
>
> Tactics commonly employed to intimidate the opposition follow: 1) a display of preference for trial rather than settlement, 2) a threat to contest intensively every stage of the proceedings, 3) a threat to withdraw an offer or demand because of the prospective cost of preparation, 4) an allusion to the experience and formidable reputation of trial counsel, and 5) a reference to the precarious financial condition of the defendant-offeror.
>
> * * *
>
> Some business litigators are inexperienced in jury trial work. They are comfortable with court trials, but they lack confidence in their ability to persuade juries. Against this type of adversary, a demand for a jury trial coupled with projection

of an image of steadfast determination to submit as many issues as possible to the jury can be intimidating.[26]

* * *

The best offers in [substantial] cases are almost always made near trial dates. An early offer generally reflects a hope that personal considerations, extraneous to the merits of a case, will induce a plaintiff to accept less than the reasonable value of his case. A truly adequate offer rarely comes unless an opponent is persuaded the negotiator is ready, able, and willing to try the case. Many excellent trial lawyers believe that maximum offers are tendered only at or during the start of trial.[27]

Indeed it is often the pressure of an impending trial date that finally forces a lawyer to evaluate his case possibilities carefully. In this regard, the chicken-game factor sometimes operates as well. In an attempt to gain maximum advantage for a possible settlement, each lawyer, while pretending to wish to go to trial, chooses to defer entering settlement negotiations until the last possible minute. In such showdowns, lawyers test the resolve of their opponents to litigate, hoping to pressure them into favorable settlements. Indeed, this is an endemic attitude among lawyers. Many of them assume that the lawyer who first raises the issue of settlement discussions thereby discloses that his case is weak or that, for some other reason, he lacks confidence in his ability to win it.

10. Ally effects

While most lawsuits have only two sides, represented by the plaintiff and the defendant, lawsuit negotiations are only superficially two-party negotiations. The parties themselves are not unitary, but litigating teams composed of client and attorney. The litigating team may involve other participants as well. For example, as in the sponsored litigation mentioned above, an insurance company may stand in the background in a defendant's case, sometimes supplying and controlling the defendant's lawyer, sometimes not. In any case, allies compose litigating teams, and this means that lawsuit negotiations are multiparty negotiations. It also means that a lawsuit team has its own internal negotiations—regarding relationships, decision making, and control—to conduct.

The allies on each side in a lawsuit negotiation do not always have completely congruent interests. Instead, they have some interests that are compatible and some which are divergent. This is particularly true in contingent-fee and insurance-defense cases where the litigant's ally is the litigation sponsor. For

---

[26]WENKE, *supra* note 14, at 79-80.

[27]*Id.* at 195.

example, a contingent-fee attorney in a high-stakes case sometimes has a greater interest in gambling on a trial than does her client, who may be more risk-averse. Similarly, an insurance company might prefer to settle a libel case in which going to trial risks a high award. In the same case the named defendant might prefer trial for vindication that he had done nothing wrong. As a further complication in the same case, the defense attorney, usually paid on an hourly basis by the insurance company, may have an interest in drawing out the litigation to enhance his fee.

There is no rule to use to determine how litigation allies will sort out their relationship and litigation control issues. It is reasonable to claim that where litigation ally interests diverge, the interests of the ally having practical control of the litigation will determine whether the parties settle or try the case.[28] As there is evidence of lawyer domination in litigation, that's most likely to be the lawyer except in cases involving sophisticated business or corporate clients.

[28] This analysis locates some of the bargaining problems in lawsuit negotiations in the divergent interests of allies on the same side. Interestingly, it also suggests a complicating factor. Lawsuit negotiations may involve bargaining between parties on opposite sides, and bargaining between allies on the same side.

CHAPTER 13
MEDIATION

Mediation[1] is a problem-solving negotiation process in which an outside, impartial, neutral party works with disputants to assist them to reach a satisfactory negotiated agreement. Unlike judges or arbitrators, mediators have no authority to decide the dispute between the parties; instead, the parties empower

[1] The term "mediation" is generally used to refer to any nonlitigious dispute resolution process in which a nonparty to a dispute intervenes in it to bring about a settlement. This is unfortunate, because the emphasis on outside-party induced settlement as the defining characteristic of mediation makes it impossible to associate any single process with mediation. Instead, any method a mediator uses to bring about a settlement becomes a method and technique of mediation.

Defining mediation by the dominant aim of settlement rather than by specific processes designed to facilitate settlement creates confusion. For example, if we look at mediation as a process in which the disputing parties, with outside help, themselves finally fashion a voluntary agreement, our focus is primarily on how mediators go about facilitating problem-solving negotiation between the parties. If, however, we are more concerned with whether the parties settle, we are more indifferent to just exactly how the parties reached the settlement.

To understand the difference, consider contrasting cases. In the first case, a mediator assists the parties to understand their real interests, teaches them how to engage in problem-solving negotiation, and helps them generate creative options to maximize their gain. In the second case, the mediator uses his position to pressure one party to compromise her interests in order to reach a settlement. If our chief concern is settlement, then we will not care much that the mediator pressured a party to settle. If, however, we believe that the way a result is achieved matters as much as, or more than, the result, we would seriously question a settlement reached under pressure.

This may seem a rather academic question, but actually there is a great deal at stake, ranging from fundamental questions regarding the mediator's role, the training of mediators, assessment of the success of mediation, the desirability of using mediation as an alternative to other dispute resolution processes, to the determination of just which cases are suitable for mediation. How active should mediators be in fashioning agreements? Is it merely the mediator's role to provide an impetus and neutral forum for the parties to work out an agreement? Should a mediator instead take charge, dictate the best settlement for the parties, and do whatever is necessary to get them to accept it? Otherwise put, should a mediator simply orchestrate an agreement between parties, or should a mediator be the deal-maker, devising solutions and imposing them on parties. Should a mediator impose substantive or public policy constraints on agreements, for example, refusing to facilitate any agreement which the mediator believes is not in the public interest even if the public is not a party to the negotiation? Should a mediator take an activist role and try to insure that any agreements further policy aims in which the mediator believes? Should a mediator intervene to rectify power imbalances between negotiating parties or does the requirement of impartiality and neutrality preclude such action, even

the mediator to help *them* resolve the issues between them. "The assumption . . . is that a third party will be able to alter the power and social dynamics of the conflict relationship by influencing the beliefs and behaviors of individual parties, by providing knowledge or information, or by using a more effective negotiation process and thereby helping the participants to settle contested issues."[2]

Mediation, a dispute resolution device long associated with labor-management conflicts, is now an important alternative to the adjudicated resolution of disputes. Increasingly, in recent years, courts, communities, and industries have turned to mediation as a preferred method of resolving certain kinds of disputes. Court-mandated meditation in divorce, family relations, landlord-tenant, and consumer cases is common. Many communities have created mediation services to handle low-level disputes or small cases that might otherwise tie up courts. The insurance industry and large merchandising companies have also instituted mediation as a means of handling consumer claims.

The expense, delay, and inefficiency of litigation have also prompted parties to use mediation. Increasingly, parties in ordinary lawsuits attempt some form of mediated settlement prior to trial. Finally, parties in "polycentric" disputes, that is, those involving many parties and issues, or those involving complex public policy choices—environmental disputes, for example—have also resorted to mediated rather than litigated solutions. Even some major regulatory agencies, traditionally steeped in adversary procedures, have begun to use some form of mediated or facilitated dispute resolution, as, for example, in negotiated regulatory rule-making.

I. ADJUDICATION COMPARED

Adjudication, either by court trial or arbitration, is formal, coercive, backward-looking, adversarial, and rights-based. That is, when parties litigate a dispute, strict rules govern adjudicatory procedures; and a third party's conclusions regarding past events and the parties' respective legal rights and obligations will determine the result. By contrast, mediation is informal, voluntary, forward-looking, cooperative, and interest-based. A mediator helps willing parties craft an agreement that looks to the future, satisfies their needs, and meets their own standards of fairness. Like judges and arbitrators, mediators must be impartial and neutral, but they do not intervene to decide and impose any particular

---

if an unjust agreement results?

The view we take of what mediation is or should be helps decide many of these questions. If we think of mediation primarily as a facilitated problem-solving process, where the parties are the principal players, we would say the mediator is not the primary deal-maker.

[2] Christopher W. Moore, The Mediation Process 16 (1996).

substantive outcome; the parties themselves decide whether or not they will agree.

II. WHEN MEDIATION IS USEFUL

Sometimes parties who must deal with one another are in dispute or conflict, but are unwilling or unable to negotiate an agreeable resolution. This occurs in many different situations. The parties may have differences of view based on misunderstandings. They may have a dysfunctional pattern of relating, perhaps involving serious mistrust, hostility, misperception, stereotyping, and poor communication. Resentments over the past may rule the present. The parties may have conscious or unconscious psychological needs to seek revenge or sate anger. These perhaps arise from their prior relationship or events occurring between them, and therefore act to block, thwart, or punish the other side.

The parties may perceive themselves as having opposing or conflicting interests or needs. They may have incompatible values, and each tries to impose its value structure on possible settlements. They may incorrectly assess the situation involving them, have unrealistic expectations, or do not understand the real nature of their interdependency. If locked in a power struggle or an escalating conflict spiral, they may believe they can win a test of strength.

Parties may lack necessary information and not know how to get it, may not agree about facts nor information relevant to the dispute, have conflicting information, or interpret or assess data differently. They may even disagree on the methods they should use to resolve the dispute or not know how to negotiate effectively.

The dispute may have many facets and there may be many parties to it. Indeed, the number of issues and parties may be so great that the parties themselves cannot organize and manage information flow and party interactions. The parties may have inflexible constituencies, difficult to educate or manage, having high and apparently nonnegotiable expectations. Finally, in the most complex disputes, some or all of these problems appear, and the resulting snarl is so great the parties cannot even begin to focus on their difficulties. Indeed, they may not even be able to identify any barriers to agreement except other parties.

Some of these seemingly intractable conflicts are in fact negotiable, but the parties are unable to negotiate successfully without outside assistance. They need a trusted outside party, without a stake in any particular outcome, who can comprehend the whole dispute impartially. Such a party could analyze the sources of conflict and the barriers to negotiation, and intervene as necessary to assist the parties to overcome their dispute resolution problems. They need a trusted diagnostician, counselor, teacher, moderator, and facilitator. In short, they need a mediator.

III. HOW MEDIATION WORKS: A FANCIFUL EXAMPLE

When parties negotiate competitively, they seek to maximize their gain. In order to do this, they withhold from the other side information regarding their minimal settlement points or reservation prices. A party's fear is that once the other side knows its bottom line, the other side will not settle at a point above it. Of course, the other side reasons in the same fashion. Consequently, each side seeks to hide or disguise its settlement points while at the same time attempting to discover the other side's actual settlement points. Each side mistrusts the other. They may be so mistrusting, so fearful of being taken advantage of, that their bargaining places seem so far apart that no settlement appears possible. They may become locked in a struggle where each side is afraid or unwilling to make concessions. This strategy, as it plays out, however, also prevents the parties from knowing whether and where they could agree.

Let's complicate the picture somewhat and suppose that the parties are bargaining over a range of issues, but adopt the same competitive stance regarding each issue. Then, not only will they not realize that their possible ranges of agreement on single issues may overlap, they will also fail to see and exploit possible trade-offs between issues. Because each party hides or dissimulates its true position on each issue, none can determine how the other really values it. Furthermore, even if the parties manage to make some trades, they are unlikely to make the maximally best trades. They will settle for the best they think they can get, not the best they could actually get if they each had full knowledge.

Introduce now into this scenario a remarkable negotiation computer called *Optimus*. The function of *Optimus* is simply to calculate whether, in any hypothetical negotiation, settlements are possible. Where there is a range of possible gains over a range of issues, the computer examines the various possible combinations of settlement points and trades over the issues and determines the respective gain for each party. Our computer has a lot of "what if" capacity, and can quickly determine how every shift of any party's position on any issue will affect results over the array of issues. It calculates the pareto-optimal curve or the efficient frontier and shows whether particular settlements leave gains on the table. When we look at the computer printout, we can determine what moves the parties can make to insure that they distribute all possible gain. We can also determine various ways to distribute gain between the parties and decide whether particular ways distribute gain fairly.

We can even make our computer more sophisticated, however. We have a program called *Solomon* that has maximizing and fairness equations. When we input through *Solomon* all available negotiation information, *Optimus* produces a single best possible result. Consequently, all our negotiating parties have to do to have the most successful possible negotiation is to drop their full information packets into a slot in *Optimus*. In a few minutes, *Optimus* tells them where to settle.

Unfortunately, there is no *Optimus* or *Solomon*. Mediators, however, can approximate those roles and do even more. When parties are untrusting, posturing, and nondisclosing to one another, they cannot themselves arrive at efficient and productive settlements. If, however, they each trust the same third party to take their private information to see whether and what trades and settlements are possible, they have made their own *Quasi Optimus*. There are differences, of course. *Quasi* is completely interactive. *Quasi* can offer the parties considerations they had not taken into account. *Quasi* can provide them additional information. *Quasi* can work with them to help them clarify what is really important to them. *Quasi* can suggest settlements and explore their possible consequences with each side. Knowing each of them, *Quasi* can even figure out whether some nonsubstantive matter, such as hostility, emotion, or miscommunication forms an impediment to settlement, and can help them devise means to work around it. Finally, in using *Quasi*, unlike *Solomon*, the parties themselves get to decide what is best. They provide their own fairness equation.

IV. OVERVIEW OF MEDIATION PROCESS

In any given dispute, a mediator tailors her interventions to the particular context and content. Her specific work depends on the nature of the dispute, the power relations and interaction dynamics between the parties, and the parties' openness to the moves the mediator can make. There are, however, mediator activities common to all mediations, and it is useful to consider them to understand how mediations work.

Mediations proceed through four stages[3] roughly defined by the major activity or focus of activities during the stage. These stages are:

- creating the forum or bargaining framework;
- information gathering and sharing;
- problem-solving bargaining;
- decision making.

A. Forum creation

At the initiation of the mediation, the forum-creation stage, the mediator informs the parties about the nature of the process. He also sets out ground

[3]There are many ways to look at mediation, and some commentators describe a three-stage process, e.g., setting the stage, problem solving, and achieving a workable agreement. Some describe more stages,

rules, works on developing rapport with the parties and gaining trust as a neutral, and negotiates his authority with the parties.

1. Negotiating a role and authority

There are many reasons why parties in dispute may be unable to reach agreement. What is common to them all is the fact that the parties view the dispute, or essential elements making it up, in one-sided and predominantly self-interested ways. Each party has a perspective on the dispute, or its component parts, that conflicts in some significant way with the perspective of other parties. Often there is mistrust, and the parties do not cooperate in sharing information—at least not in ways nor to the degree helpful in moving toward settlement. No party trusts any other party sufficiently to allow it to take the lead in fashioning an agreement.

If the parties invite a mediator to assist them, they, to some degree, acknowledge they cannot proceed on their own and that third-party intervention may be useful. Nonetheless, unless experienced with mediation, the parties may not know how mediation works or exactly what to expect of a mediator. The mediator's first task then is to establish a role with the parties that will enable him to be effective in assisting them to come to agreement. The mediator must negotiate his role in the dispute and with the parties.

The initial stages of a mediation comprise a teaching and learning process. In it, the mediator informs the parties about mediation and discusses the ways they should relate to one another as well as to the mediator. Note however that mediation is a fluid and contingent process. A mediator custom-tailors his interactions to the parties and the particular features of their dispute, as appears useful at any particular time, in order to help bring about agreement. Depending on the circumstances and the length and requirements of the mediation, the mediator's role will likely evolve during its course. Consequently, at the beginning stage of a mediation, the mediator works with the parties to gain their initial trust and cooperation, and, more generally, to gain the authority to manage the process and party interactions.

The mediator needs to establish credibility with the parties, both for the process and for himself. If the parties have themselves initiated the mediation, there will already be some credibility, and the mediator should act to secure and deepen it. If it is a mandated mediation, the mediator may have a greater burden of informing parties about the process and establishing his own role. In any case, it is essential that the mediator persuade the parties that he, and the process, are neutral. In particular, the mediator is neutral as between the parties

as many as seven, e.g., introduction, problem-determination, summarizing, issue identification, alternatives generation, alternative selection, and closure.

and impartial as to the mediation results, at least as long as the parties find their agreement fair between themselves.

2. Joint meeting and opening

The mediator generally opens the mediation session by introducing himself and the parties and then making an opening statement explaining the mediation process, his role as a neutral facilitator, and rules for party interaction. This usually entails explaining that mediation is a negotiation process in which the parties, with the mediator's facilitation, themselves determine the terms of any settlement. The statement may also involve distinguishing mediation from adjudication, arbitration, counseling, and therapy. The mediator makes clear to the parties that he has a neutral role and that he will not act as an advocate for any party. He has a role of ensuring that the parties deal with each other civilly and fairly. He will enforce certain rules of decorum, but he is not a decision maker who will impose a particular settlement on them. If confidentiality is important for the particular mediation, he further explains the rules of confidentiality applying to him and the parties, as well as any limits on confidentiality. The mediator then gives the parties an opportunity to ask questions or raise concerns they may have about the process. If the parties agree to proceed, the mediator obtains a commitment from them that they will abide by the rules of the mediation, including confidentiality.

B. Information stage

In the information stage, the parties share information with each other and the mediator in joint sessions, and privately share information with the mediator in caucus sessions.[4] Assuming the parties agree to continue the mediation, the mediator then has each party present its version of the facts and the position it takes in the dispute. The mediator may ask questions to develop further information, but does not permit the other party to ask questions nor to interrupt in any way. The mediator gives each side a hearing on its version of the dispute. The mediator uses ''active listening'' techniques with the aim of gaining a clear understanding of a party's perspective and position. The parties' respective presentations enable the mediator to understand and clarify the dispute for himself and may also enlighten each party about the other's views.

To ensure that he has understood the parties, and to let them know he has heard and understood them, the mediator neutrally summarizes each party's

---

[4] *See supra* Chapter 7, Section II (A).

presentation. He restates essential facts, fairly relating each party's perspective or position regarding the dispute.

1. Caucus

Following opening statements and the mediator's summary, mediators sometimes caucus separately with each side in the mediation. In a mediation, a caucus is a private meeting of parties on one side or a private meeting between parties on one side and the mediator. Parties caucus in order to confer, permit communication between team members, develop information, reassess positions, explore options, and seek agreement among themselves. As parties may not be completely forthcoming in joint meetings—for example, they may not disclose full information for fear the other side will use it adversely—it is sometimes helpful for a mediator to caucus with a party. In caucusing with a party, a mediator can obtain information not revealed at joint mediation sessions. She can also help a party determine its alternatives to settlement, and explore and evaluate options, interests, and settlement possibilities more openly and readily than in joint sessions. Consequently, many mediators find that calling a caucus with a party is a useful tool for finding possible grounds for agreement.

When a mediator caucuses with a party, she meets privately with it, and this may raise a concern about mediator neutrality. To avoid this problem, mediators who use the caucus tool explain the exploratory purpose of caucusing to the parties, state that they will caucus with both sides, and also set out rules for mediator conduct relative to caucusing. Those rules include confidentiality—the mediator will not, unless authorized, disclose to the other side anything confidentially revealed during a caucus. A second rule is equal treatment—the mediator will caucus with each party and remain impartial and neutral notwithstanding private communications. Finally, there is notice—the mediator will notify parties when she is caucusing with another party. After explaining these matters, the mediator then seeks the parties' approval of her use of the caucus.

2. Controlling party interactions and communications

One of the mediator's most important tools is controlling the parties' interactions and communications. The structural form of mediation reinforces the mediator's ability to control the parties. Note that the mediator asserts the authority of neutrality and dispute resolution expertise. Through his demeanor and actions, the mediator effectively claims the right to act as a director of activities. He is a procedural referee, a coach for each side, and, on occasion, a roving player who temporarily allies himself with one side or the other in the interests of all.

> Mediators control the communication flow between the parties by determining the extent to which they speak directly to each other rather than through the mediators. They can control who speaks, allow or disallow interruptions, and encourage and regulate the amount of participation by all parties. The mediators can interrupt and cut off discussion in order to focus it on grounds of settlement. Quite simply, mediators determine when public and private sessions begin and end, the types of information to be exchanged, and the point at which it will be cut off. With more extensive caucusing, the parties speak most often with the mediators. . . . Thus control over the flow of information creates extended control over the substance of communication as well since the mediators decide what information to pass between the parties.[5]

3. Rephrasing a dispute

Mediators control not only the flow of information, but its substantive content as well. Working with the parties, the mediator attempts to move them from their individual conceptions and accounts of the dispute to a reconstructed account acceptable to all parties. In other words, starting with the individual narratives of the dispute that the parties present in the opening session, and using information gained in caucuses, the mediator ''rephrases'' the dispute in ways that facilitate negotiation.[6] Mediators commonly do this by describing the dispute in the language and framework of interest-based bargaining. Once the parties accept this new understanding of their dispute, the mediator applies the tools of interest-based and cooperative bargaining models to broaden or narrow the dispute. She defines specific problems, creates options, locates and evaluates trade-offs, and helps the parties in specific joint problem solving.

C. Problem-solving stage

During the problem-solving bargaining stage, the mediator works with the parties jointly and separately, as necessary, to help them define common issues or problems. She also sets an agenda for working through issues, and devises and evaluates solutions.

1. Issue and problem identification

Following the mediator's summaries and caucusing, if any, the mediator helps the parties identify the issues between them. Here the mediator uses the

---

[5] Susan S. Sibley & Sally E. Merry, *Mediator Settlement Strategies*, 8 LAW & POL'Y 7, 14–15 (1986).

[6] *Id.* at 15; Lynn Mather & Barbara Yngvesson, *Language, Audience, and the Transformation of Disputes* 15 LAW & SOC'Y REV. 775, 778 (1981).

problem-solving model of negotiation as a guide. Indeed, the mediator may give the parties some instruction on problem-solving bargaining.

The first effort, undertaken either in caucus or in joint session, is to move the parties from positions to interests. Once the parties identify their respective interests, the mediator helps them define their common problems. In doing so, he effectively reframes the dispute and helps the parties understand one another's views in terms of the new frame. He points out their shared interests, where and in what respect they have compatible interests, and where interests conflict.

Identifying and valuing interests, as we have seen before,[7] is sometimes quite difficult. The mediator helps parties by serving as a sounding board, raising considerations that a party does not perceive, and adding perspectives. She can also invoke interests that a party, narrowly focused on the dispute, perhaps hasn't considered.[8]

Once the parties have identified the issues, the mediation turns to an effort to generate alternative solutions to the identified problems. The mediator prompts the parties themselves to propose options and may propose them himself. To the degree that the mediator has private information from both sides, and knows how the parties value or prioritize their respective interests, she may be in a position to suggest options which the parties themselves do not perceive.

2. Decision making

In the decision-making stage, the mediator works with the parties to help them select mutually agreeable or, at least, acceptable solutions to the problems identified.

After the parties identify possible solutions, they must evaluate them and select options, or combinations of options, as a basis for agreement, if there is to be any. While the parties themselves must decide what they will agree to, the mediator may have a large role in helping parties evaluate options and in tailoring or combining them. At the decision-making stage, the parties must always face the value-claiming issue—how to distribute or allocate between themselves the shares of whatever they have jointly created or found. In evaluating options, the mediator assists the parties in finding a fair basis for satisfactorily distributing gains, and helps insure the agreement lasts. The mediator may also help the parties fashion the terms of the agreement to make the bargain as efficient as possible, that is, so that the parties leave little or no gains on the table.

---

[7] *See supra* Chapter 8, Section I (A–F).

[8] Because this exploration and weighing of interests may invoke sensitive information that parties are not, at least initially, openly willing to disclose to other parties, this effort is best done in caucus.

Of course, this description is idealistic. While mediators strive to help the parties negotiate win-win bargains, it is not always possible to do so. Instead, the parties may have to compromise some of what they want in order to find any agreement. Nonetheless, compromise is a solution in disputes, and a mediator can help parties realize that their only available solution is compromise. Parties are more likely to draw this conclusion if they have fully and fairly explored every other alternative, including nonagreement alternatives. Working through options with a trusted neutral may aid parties in coming to this realization.

Parties sometimes resist compromise because of high or unrealistic aspirations. Mediators often obtain settlement notwithstanding such impediments. They may provide a needed reality check or pressure parties to settle. They pressure parties by enhancing the perceived benefits of settling, by stressing the costs and disadvantages of nonagreement, and by magnifying parties' doubts or uncertainties about their alternatives to settlement. Mediators also help devise face-saving formulas and, where necessary, help parties with any constituency problems they may have.

D. Graphic overview

Figure 13–1 outlines the mediation process, and the mediator's activities in it.

E. Mediator roles and activities

It is useful to view a mediator as a kind of negotiation "therapist." This therapist analyzes and diagnoses a particular dispute, and then designs and manages process and other interventions aimed at bringing the parties to a healthy agreement. The major mediator roles thus are:

- diagnosing the conflict;
- identifying issues and critical interests;
- setting the agenda;
- facilitating and managing communication;
- educating the parties in bargaining processes and skills;
- helping the parties gather essential information;
- problem solving to generate options.

1. Diagnosing disputes to facilitate problem solving

To know exactly what interventions to make to help parties reach agreement, the mediator must diagnose the dispute. Christopher Moore, in his book, *The*

Figure 13–1

Stage	*Mediator Activities*
Creating the Forum	Joint Meeting Mediator Opening Statement Educate the parties Set out ground rules Develop rapport and trust Parties' Statements Give a "hearing" Develop and clarify information Model and discipline interactions
Information gathering and sharing	Separate caucuses Develop further information Explore parties' interests Help parties assess and value interests Educate parties on problem-solving bargaining
Problem solving	Joint sessions and additional separate caucuses Agenda setting Problem-solving activities Facilitate Cooperation Identify and clarify the issues or problems Generate alternatives or options Assess options Help parties assess, value, and prioritize their interests
Decision making	Caucuses and joint sessions Locate tradeoffs, pose and help parties evaluate packages Help parties narrow differences Confirm and clarify agreement Help parties compare settlement proposals with non agreement alternatives Pressure parties Devise face-saving formulas Help parties deal with constituencies Help parties memorialize agreement

Mediation Process, sets out a useful taxonomy of different sources or kinds of conflict and interventions appropriate to them. These kinds of conflict are essentially: conflicts of interests, data or information conflicts, relationship conflicts, structural conflicts, and values conflicts.[9]

Interest conflicts clearly call for interest-based bargaining interventions. Data or information conflicts can result from the parties' differing information, differing interpretations or evaluations of information, differing views of information relevance or importance, lack of information, or any combination of these. Such sources of conflict prompt interventions aimed at insuring that parties have the same information base and that they interpret and evaluate it similarly. In more difficult cases, eliminating this source of conflict may require devising some process, acceptable to the parties, for settling contested facts.[10]

Relationship conflicts potentially arise from grievances, offensive behavior, dysfunctional patterns of relating and communicating, misperceptions, faulty assumptions, and stereotyping. For example, a party may engage in dominating or intimidating behavior, emotional outbursts, insults, or threats; contrarily, a party may be indecisive or engage in avoidance or withdrawal. Mediators attempt to deal with such conflicts in various ways. They assert and enforce rules of civility in party interaction, make explicit the objectionable behavior that occurs, draw out parties, and clarify and insure the parties' respective understandings of one another's communications. Using caucuses, they allow parties to vent emotion. They may point out and help parties correct dysfunctional behavioral or communication patterns.

Structural conflicts include more general situational factors, such as the parties' unequal power, status, constituency pressures, time problems, geographical distance, and the like. These factors make it difficult for them to bargain openly, productively, or conveniently. To help remove such sources of conflict, a mediator might attempt, in some appropriate way, to equalize the parties' bargaining power. She could also assist parties in educating and handling their constituencies, lengthen mediation time, impose deadlines, or convene meetings at mutually convenient places.

Value conflicts arise from differing ideologies, belief systems, fundamental goals, and different evaluation standards. Conflicts over fundamental values, for example, theist versus atheist values, may be intractable. Where there are value conflicts like this, the mediator attempts to define the dispute so that it doesn't implicate fundamental values. She usually does this by focusing on immediate and concrete problems rather than global and ideological ones.

---

[9] MOORE, *supra* note 2, at 58–63.

[10] *See* Chapter 14, Other Negotiated Dispute Resolution Processes.

For example, there was a deep and fundamental ideological conflict between the United States and Iran involved in Iran's seizure of the American Embassy in Teheran and holding Americans hostage. Initially, the dispute was ideologized, at least on one side, as a conflict between fundamentalist Islamic religious values and Godless Satan, as represented by the United States. Eventually, the parties redefined the conflict as a set of more practical questions relating to hostage release and unfreezing Iranian assets held in the United States, and thereafter resolved the conflict.

In other value conflict cases, a mediator may help the parties by focusing on values the parties share rather than on those which divide them. Sometimes this involves invoking a more fundamental value than those which the parties assert are at issue. For example, in a dispute over a physician-director's handling of a private hospital emergency room, the parties had a conflict over who had the right of control. The hospital hired the physician as an independent contractor to provide all emergency room services, but didn't like the way the physician provided those services. Initially, the parties defined the dispute as a conflict over the physician's independence and the hospital's right of control. The mediator suggested an overriding value of excellent patient care within the context of a profit-making hospital, and the parties used this common value as a guide to devise ways to work together cooperatively.

F. Mediator tactics

Mediators use a variety of tactics to help parties reach settlement. As disputes and parties differ, mediators use these tactics contingently, as appears necessary or useful. Many mediator tactics, however, have multiple purposes and effects, and this makes them difficult to categorize. Thus, for example, a tactic such as "clarifying the needs of one party to another" may serve substantively to insure accurate communication and also serve emotionally or attitudinally to reinforce trust in the process. Similarly, the tactic of "discussing other settlements or settlement patterns" may open unconsidered options to the parties, suggest evaluative norms, comprise a subtle form of pressure, or have some combination of these effects.

Particular mediator tactics may have multiple uses, and the same tactic, used in different contexts or with different parties, may have different effects. Nonetheless, it is useful to get a sense of how mediators achieve their results, and we can roughly group some of the more common mediator tactics as follows.[11]

---

[11] This list, with additions, changes of expression, and reorganization is based on a list of mediator tactics found in Peter J.D. Carnevale, Rodney G. Lim, & Mary E. McLaughlin, *Contingent Mediator Behavior and Its Effectiveness*, in MEDIATION RESEARCH 221–222 (KENNETH KRESSEL AND DEAN G. PRUITT, EDS., 1990). The authors of this article, reflecting prior research, categorize mediator tactics as reflexive, substantive, and contextual. "Reflexive tactics are designed to orient mediators to the dispute and to create a foundation for their future activities; substantive tactics deal directly with the issues in the dispute, such as suggestions for

1. *Decision-framing tactics*

- Setting the agenda
- Attempting to simplify the agenda by eliminating or combining matters
- Developing a framework for negotiations
- Keeping negotiation focused
- Attempting to settle simple issues first
- Attempting to settle key, or more productive, issues first
- Trying to change the parties' expectations

2. *Tactics to gain authority and elicit cooperation*

- Trying to gain the parties' trust and confidence
- Avoiding taking sides on issues
- Attempting to speak the parties' language
- Assuring each party about the other's honesty and good faith
- Developing rapport
- Engaging in active listening
- Emphasizing potential gains rather than potential losses
- Emphasizing similarities and commonalities; minimizing or ignoring differences
- Avoiding contentious issues

3. *Tactics to control emotion*

- Setting ground rules for party interaction
- Controlling the expression of hostility
- Using humor to lighten the atmosphere

---

settlement; and contextual tactics involve facilitating the dispute resolution process so that the parties themselves are able to discover an acceptable solution." *Id.* at 215.

It is also possible to divide these categories somewhat further. Thus we can divide substantive tactics between those which facilitate a party's movement, those which bring pressure to bear on a party, and those which help a party save face. Similarly, we can divide contextual tactics into those aimed at building trust and those aimed at controlling the agenda and the process. *Id.* at 220.

- Letting everyone vent or blow off steam
- Expressing pleasure or displeasure at the progress of the negotiation
- Expressing optimism that solution is possible
- Modeling appropriate behavior
- Pulling deeply contentious issues off the table

4. Informational and problem-solving tactics

- Calling for caucuses
- Drawing the parties out, discovering exactly what motivates their particular proposals and positions
- Noting parties' factual bases, interpretations, valuations, assumptions, and priorities (and reasons for them)
- Teaching the bargaining process
- Delegalizing the dispute by focusing on the future and on existing or possible relationships rather than on the past and legal rights
- Gathering information on, and understanding, the parties' realistic alternatives to settlement
- Exploring and clarifying the parties' needs, both separately and together
- Expanding the set of interests each party is considering and bringing the new interests into play in the discussion
- Helping the parties prioritize issues
- Reducing the number of issues
- Arguing one side's case to the other side
- Posing hypothetical or contingent agreements
- Stating issues as concrete, practical matters rather than as matters of principle
- Making substantive suggestions for compromise
- Suggesting trade-offs among issues
- Showing the parties how their alternatives to settlement are worse than proposed settlements
- Taking responsibility for concessions
- Discussing other settlements or patterns of agreements
- Pointing out the costs of continued disagreement

- Suggesting particular settlements
- Suggesting a review of needs with the parties' constituencies
- Helping parties deal with constituency problems or with their superiors

5. Face-saving tactics

- Suggesting proposals that help avoid the appearance of defeat on an issue
- Helping individuals save face through devising acceptable formulas or joint statements

6. Pressuring tactics

- Controlling the timing and pace of negotiations
- Setting deadlines
- Keeping the parties at the table and negotiating
- Warning that the next impasse step is not better
- Telling parties that their position is unrealistic
- Using late hours or long sessions to facilitate compromise
- Enhancing the perceived benefits of settling by:
    - emphasizing the costs of nonsettlement
    - amplifying parties doubts about alternatives to settlement
- Pressing the parties hard to compromise
- Conducting a relative bargaining power analysis and pressing the parties to accept an outcome that their relative strength warrants

G. Dispute suitability for mediation

Mediation is not suitable for all disputes or conflicts. In mediation, parties generally represent themselves rather than use attorneys. Mediations also lack the formal, rule-based protections of trial or arbitration. Furthermore, mediators, although committed to neutrality, do control and manipulate parties, and the parties' perceptions of the situation, in the interests of settlement. In cases where the parties have significantly unequal bargaining power, there is a danger that a truly neutral mediator will simply facilitate the wishes of the party with dominant bargaining power. On the other hand, if the mediator intervenes in some way to equalize the parties' bargaining power, there is a risk that the parties will perceive her as taking sides, thus losing the neutrality and impartiality essential to the process. If, to solve the unequal bargaining power problem, the mediator intervenes to ensure that any settlement is fair to both sides, the mediator risks imposing her notions of fairness on the parties. Yet in mediation, it is supposedly the parties, not the mediator, who decide whether to accept any particular settlement. Mediators who are too activist, in the sense of pressing for a particular negotiated resolution, become closet judges.

Beyond the problem of party power imbalances, there are situations where parties should have an adversary, adjudicated resolution of their dispute, or at least some portion of it. Where the situation is zero-sum and the parties will have no future dealings, nor otherwise need one another's cooperation or goodwill, adjudication may be a better choice. Similarly, if a party wishes to make law, either for itself in future cases or for itself and others, neither mediation nor arbitration (as it is private and nonbinding on nonparticipants) makes sense.

These considerations, and others of a similar kind, suggest that mediation is a negotiated dispute resolution process best utilized for disputes having certain features. The general question then is: What disputes are amenable to a negotiated resolution? The following list sets out the factors to consider.

- The parties have equal bargaining power or have the perception that they do. The filing of a lawsuit, or the pendency of a hearing, tends to equalize bargaining power by changing a party's alternatives to a negotiated agreement.
- No party has a significant interest in establishing a legal precedent.
- The parties have relatively poor alternatives to agreement with one another, or, assuming at least one good alternative, some possible settlement is better.
- The parties have a concern for, or can be taught or persuaded to take into account, their future relationships. Put otherwise, perhaps the parties can frame the dispute in a forward-looking, as opposed to a backward-looking, perspective.
- If the parties have constituencies, the constituencies are educable, manageable, or controllable. If allies comprise parties, the interests of the allies are congruent. If there are coalitions, the coalitions are opportunist rather than loyalist or disciplined.
- All the major players (deal-breaking players) are at, or can be brought to, the table.
- There are multiple issues having a range of possible outcomes and there are useful differences in the parties' relative assessments of the situation. These features permit trade-offs and packaging.

- There is a need to make a decision—for example, an impending deadline of some sort—or the intervenor can persuade the parties to make a decision to improve the situation. The prospect, and imminence, of third-party decision making creates a deadline.
- There is no intractable factual dispute between the parties. If there are important factual issues, there is some means or process, agreeable to the parties, to settle those facts on which agreements turn.
- The parties initiate, or voluntarily acquiesce, in negotiated dispute resolution. The parties are educable. The parties do not have a long history of antagonism nor heavy emotional investments in beating or dominating the other side. There are no insurmountable personality conflicts. There do not appear to be any hidden agendas.

CHAPTER 14

OTHER NEGOTIATED DISPUTE RESOLUTION PROCESSES

Sometimes, parties, either when negotiating on their own or negotiating with assistance, fail to reach a negotiated settlement. There are a variety of reasons why this might be so. These include the use of competitive strategies, unrealistic expectations, fundamental ideological differences, hidden agendas, personality issues, the need for a precedent, issue complexity, the nature of the issue framing, third-party influence, the need to vent emotion, a desire for vindication of a perceived wrong, and the like.[1] Two large classes of reasons for possible negotiation failure, however, are of special interest. These are contested facts and structural barriers to agreement, particularly those arising from representative or surrogate bargaining.

It is a fair assumption, which only strong evidence should overturn, that people are not objective regarding their own interests. We expect people to frame their own judgments in their own favor. Countless legal rules, social customs, and social inferences make this assumption, and empirical evidence also strongly supports it.[2] In any controversy, when parties dispute facts, they will generally disbelieve another's factual claims that conflict with their own. They will both favor their own versions of the "facts" and also assume that the other side has a biased, or, at least, uninformed view. In most cases, this means that parties having a serious factual dispute have no way, without using extraordinary procedures, to work through the factual dispute themselves.

There is also another kind of standoff that negotiating parties can experience that may preclude them from negotiating an agreement without some kind of

---

[1] *See* KENNETH J. ARROW, ET AL., BARRIERS TO CONFLICT RESOLUTION 7–21 (1995); Frank E.A. Sander & Stephen B. Goldberg, *Fitting the Forum to the Fuss,* 10 NEGOTIATION J. 49, 53 (1994).

[2] *See* THOMAS GILOVICH, HOW WE KNOW WHAT ISN'T SO (1991).

outside assistance or intervention. This is easiest to understand through an example. Suppose disputing parties publicly lock themselves into severely conflicting bargaining positions and that each party has a constituency. Suppose further that there is a public audience for the dispute. This has been the case for unions and management in major industries, e.g., the professional baseball players' union and the professional baseball team owners. The conflict may implicate serious factual or quasi-factual issues, and the parties may have no way to back away from their public positions and assertions: in an extended sense, the dispute has become politicized. Although parties in this position conceivably can negotiate a settlement without resorting to extraordinary means in addition to negotiation, they may be unable to do so. Constituency and public pressures, as well as nonapparent factors, such as coalition or psychological commitments, may prevent them from working it out themselves. The parties find themselves in a sort of standoff equilibrium. In order to move, they need a way to reconfigure their situation without losing face, and all that it may entail.

When there is a factual contest that parties can't manage or a structural barrier that impedes parties in reaching agreement on their own, they can employ various devices to help the negotiation process. Before considering these devices, however, it's useful to review some of the ways in which factual and other problems may interfere with negotiation.

I. UNAVOIDABLE FACTUAL DISPUTES

Facts are important in many disputes, and usually involve questions of what actually happened in a given situation, who was responsible for it, or predictions about what will happen in the future. For example, factual claims regarding the occurrence or nonoccurrence of some event form the basis of most lawsuits. Did the lawnmower blade fail because of a design or manufacturing defect or because of operator misuse? Did a party actually agree to a contract term or reject it; was there reliance on the alleged agreement? Is the serious building leak, which causes great water damage in storms, attributable to the architect's design, the building contractor's work, a materials failure, or some other cause?

Factual contests are important even outside of lawsuits. Suppose a county proposes to authorize the use of sanitized and treated sewer sludge as fertilizer for properties within the county. Sewer sludge contains toxins of various sorts, often in trace amounts, that reasonably economical treatment cannot remove. When local citizens' groups protest the proposed action on the theory that the trace toxins in the sludge may prove harmful to humans, how does the county determine whether this is so?

In these and myriad similar cases, parties are unlikely to reach a negotiated resolution until they satisfactorily resolve the factual dispute. As long as the facts remain in doubt, the parties have neither a basis for allocating responsibility nor one on which to make a sound decision.

II. CONTESTS REGARDING APPLICATION OF NORMS TO FACTS; QUASI FACTS

Even when there are no factual disputes, parties may dispute the appropriate conclusions to draw from applying judgmental standards or norms. For example, a person who fails to exercise the standard of care a reasonable person would exercise in similar circumstances is legally negligent. Parties could agree that Amy was driving 40 miles-per-hour in a 50 mile-per-hour speed zone, that there was a storm, and that the road was slick and wet when Amy collided with another car. They might disagree, however, as to whether 40 miles-per-hour was a reasonable speed under the circumstances. To take another example, suppose citizens agree that it is necessary for the city to build another bridge over the river. The issue is location, and the standard to apply is "public convenience, safety, and necessity." Merchants want the bridge to align with a street that leads directly to the city's commercial district. Unfortunately, this runs through a residential district. How should the standard apply in this case?

Judgmental standards or norms such as "reasonableness" or "public convenience" appear to have two elements about which parties could dispute: a quasi-factual element and a normative element. The quasi-factual element seems to ask the decision maker using the standard to determine what is the case. That is, it asks, respectively in the examples used, what a reasonable person would actually do or what the public convenience actually requires. At the same time, however, the standard has an implicit normative and judgmental aspect, i.e., how *should* an ordinary reasonable person act, and what *is really* in the best interests of the whole public.

Applying standards or norms even to agreed-upon facts will generate disputes when differing interpretations of the standards or norms have substantially different consequences for different parties—the assumption of party bias. With so much riding on an interpretation, no party will likely accept another party's interpretation. They need an "objective," or independent and somehow legitimated, interpretation they can commonly accept and apply in order to continue negotiation. Courts and juries often fulfill that need, but submitting a matter to conclusive litigation takes the final decision away from the parties. If the parties want to retain control, they must find other ways to resolve such issues, ways which allow them to resolve the final matter themselves.

III. FACTUAL DISPUTES AS MASKS

Sometimes parties dispute facts, particularly what may seem to an outside observer to be trivial facts, as a way of expressing some nonfactual dispute, a kind of displacement. For example, in a child-custody dispute, the parties might argue endlessly about the time at which the husband returned the child to the mother after visitation. There could be some genuine issue of fact, but the intensity of the dispute suggests that there is more, perhaps an unstated relationship problem that is the real source of the controversy.[3]

Parties also sometimes contest facts as a form of strategic behavior to gain a negotiation advantage. Even where facts may appear reasonably clear, a party may not admit them, for to do so would undermine its position or interest. It therefore contests facts in order to put the other party in the position of proving them. The expense and difficulty of proof, as well as the delay occasioned, may then cause the party advancing the factual claim to back off or make concessions. The behavior is strategic in that the party contesting facts knows, or thinks it likely, they can be proven, yet is trying to extract an advantage or bargaining leverage from the proof process.[4] This, of course, is even more likely when each party believes it has a reasonable chance of persuading some decision maker about its version of the facts.

IV. FACTUAL BELIEFS AND DISPUTES AS TRAPS

Many seemingly fact-driven disputes are actually value-driven. When people make decisions about what they want, concerning matters in which it is impossible to have certainty, they often make choices based on values they hold rather than on some other basis. In other words, they make a choice that is both consistent with their values and appears to implement them. They then selectively use facts which support their choices, and attempt to diminish or undercut counterfacts.

Reconsider, in this connection, the bridge example. It's fairly obvious that the contending parties take a position on the facts that their aims, goals, values, and interests determine rather than arriving at their judgment after an "objective" determination of the facts. Merchants see their preferred bridge site as serving their financial interest. Residents see the same site as inimical to their interests in repose and as possibly threatening their health and safety. In such a situation, although the parties may argue vehemently about facts, or the application of standards to facts, facts are really not at issue. Resort to fact-finding might not help much, although clarifying underlying values or interests might. Parties could see what values and interests they shared, perhaps work through some value conflicts, or perhaps even find some other bridge solution that would satisfy their disparate values and interests. In this kind of decision making, facts

---

[3] KENNETH KRESSEL, DEAN G. PRUITT, AND ASSOCIATES, EDS., MEDIATION RESEARCH 335 (1989).

[4] *See* Chapter 12, Lawsuits as Negotiations.

play a subsidiary and supporting role. People use facts that support their decision and dismiss, explain away, or contest facts not supporting it.

In other cases, a party actually believes it can prove its factual claims, yet were a neutral party to examine the proofs, she would disagree. In this sense, a party's own beliefs trap it into refusing to accept contrary proofs or disconfirming evidence. This is not uncommon, and there is good empirical evidence that once someone commits himself to a belief, confronting him with even strongly conflicting evidence that negates the belief serves rather only to strengthen it.[5] People subject information that is inconsistent with their beliefs to much greater scrutiny than they do information that is consistent. They are much more likely to find flaws in it or to accord it a lesser weight than consistent evidence.[6] This is not the place to discuss the question of belief formation, but rather to note that a belief, once formed, powerfully restrains a party's ability to consider matters objectively. When we add to this consideration the fact that disputing parties are likely to be untrusting, it is clear that a factual dispute can preclude a negotiated agreement.

V. STRUCTURAL BARRIERS: THE ROLE OF NON-NEUTRAL THIRD PARTIES

The foreground or background presence of non-neutral third parties can exacerbate factual disputes, or any dispute for that matter. Third parties can have a direct or indirect interest in a dispute, and whether or not actually at the table, can have a substantial, even determinative, impact on whether parties can reach a negotiated agreement.[7] Disputants may involve allies or use advocates to assist them. In either case, as other parties take, or claim, a share of the dispute, their presence affects the parties' abilities, and inclinations, to settle. These third parties may reinforce factual beliefs or provide other kinds of support for positions taken, and thus have the effect of keeping negotiating parties apart. The effect may be even worse where the principals turn over negotiations to representatives, thereby distancing principals from their dispute. Finally, when there is a concerned audience or constituency for any side of a dispute, negotiating parties, whether principals or agents, may have to "perform" for the audience. When a party so situated stakes out a factual or bargaining position, it may find it difficult to retreat, even if persuaded it was wrong. There are simply too many explanations to make, and there is a substantial risk of loss of credibility, loss of face, and loss, or weakening, of authority.

---

[5] GILOVICH, *supra* note 2, at 53–54.

[6] *Id.*

[7] *See* Chapter 12, Lawsuits as Negotiations.

VI. NEGOTIATING FACTS

We generally think of facts as being nonnegotiable and do not normally use negotiation processes to resolve factual issues. Actually, there are circumstances in which decision makers "negotiate" facts, but these usually do not involve stakeholders with seemingly opposed interests. One might reasonably claim, for example, that trial juries, hearing tribunals, and other group "fact-finders" "negotiate" facts. What this claim means is that the fact-finders discuss and deliberate over their different perceptions of the evidence, the credibility of witnesses and testimony, and different inferences the evidence supports, to arrive at a mutually acceptable common understanding of the "facts." This sort of factual "negotiation" between nonstakeholding parties jointly responsible for a decision is not the same as a factual negotiation between stakeholders, each of whom stands to lose through factual "concessions." In interest-based terms, the interest of jurors is a supermajority or unanimous decision, and they may have to "negotiate" facts to reach it. Stakeholders, however, wish to maximize their own interests, whatever they may be, and conceding "facts" that may be important to securing one's interests doesn't make sense, except where substantial trade-offs are possible.

Where the resolution of facts, or application of norms to facts, is truly important to disputing parties, it is quite unlikely that they themselves will negotiate such issues. If the factual issue is whether the light was red or green, and one party has red facts while the other has green, no party is likely to concede the other's facts, nor will any party agree that the light was yellow after all. Where parties disagree about important facts, or the application of norms to facts, and the resolution of issues between them turns on an agreement on facts or norms, simple negotiation won't help. Give and take or compromise over facts is unlikely, and it would rarely be in a party's interest either to allow the other side to dictate facts or authoritatively interpret norms.[8]

Negotiating parties can, of course, engage in joint fact-finding and even agree on what the facts, or some of the facts, are. If parties are both reasonable and objective, and treat each other as such, they might agree to share and compare their respective factual proofs and then jointly decide which is correct. This is usually far from the case, but even in this ideal situation, many issues arise. How would they present proofs to one another? What standard of evidence relevancy and evaluation should they use? What are their sufficient evidence thresholds, and so on? The parties would be in the position of having to invent a process for deciding facts, a process that they thought was both fair and likely

---

[8] This makes sense in bargaining power terms. If my alternative to conceding the facts which establish your claim is to engage in a contest where I have the opportunity to prove my facts and establish my claim, I am better off with the latter.

to discover the actual facts as accurately as possible. This is a monumental task, however, and few negotiating parties can undertake it.

In some disputes, there are ways to limit the impact of factual contests. One might, for example, "bracket" facts. That is, to the degree possible, parties might settle those parts of the dispute that were not fact-sensitive, and then leave the factual contest for some sort of adjudication. They could then negotiate following that factual adjudication. Alternatively, negotiating parties might be able to arrive at factually contingent agreements. In such a situation, the parties agree that if the facts turn out to be X, then one solution applies, but if the facts turn out to be Y, then another solution applies.[9]

In many situations, however, parties will be unable to finesse the factual contest. Fortunately, in such cases, parties need not settle facts themselves, something they are in any case unlikely to be able to do. What they may be able to do, however, is to agree to a process for establishing facts. In other words, when there is a factual contest, parties can still reach a negotiated agreement by first agreeing to a process for finding facts and then by accepting the results of that process. Indeed, a negotiated resolution may be possible even where parties do not agree in advance to accept the results of a particular process. All that may be necessary is that they agree to reconsider or revisit their views following the process. If the process is fair and credible, then, even should the facts turn out adversely, the party will find it difficult not to reconsider.

VII. RESOLVING FACT AND NORM CONTESTS

For many of the foregoing reasons, parties having substantial factual disputes, or otherwise structurally constrained in their ability to reach a negotiated agreement, need ways to escape the situation in which they find themselves. The two prominent alternatives they have are litigation followed by adjudication or neutral fact-finding and evaluation, which may involve litigation-like processes, followed by negotiation. Neutral fact-finding and evaluation enable parties to resolve factual disputes and gain an "objective" view of their situation, things they cannot do themselves. In addition, and depending on the circumstances, neutral fact-finding and evaluation can relieve other constraints on reaching a negotiated agreement. They can provide a legitimate basis both for conceding factual claims and for reassessing previously taken negotiation positions. Neutral fact-finding and evaluation allow parties to test out a major alternative they have to reaching a negotiated agreement, i.e., third-party decision,

[9] Furthermore, not all factual quarrels are about facts, although on first impression they may appear to be. It's important, therefore, to identify when facts really count and when they don't, for one shouldn't, in the ordinary case, resort to fact-finding when it won't assist in solving any problem. There may be cases, however, where unnecessary fact-finding might be useful, e.g., to help parties understand that facts aren't really at issue or to save face, but that would be an alternative use of a fact-finding process.

without actually giving up their ability to negotiate. In this way, neutral fact-finding and evaluation can change the parties' perceptions of their alternatives to negotiation.

There are a variety of neutral fact-finding and evaluation processes, varying in their degree of elaboration, formality, and similarity to ordinary processes of litigation and adjudication. The key to understanding and using them in particular circumstances is the realization that a fact-finding or hearing process *needs only to be as good as the parties themselves need it to be* in order for them to accept its results. Thus, in some cases, a trusted mediator's opinion about factual findings or likely adjudicated results may satisfy the parties' needs and permit them to go forward and negotiate a settlement. In more complex cases, particularly those involving non-neutral third parties and audiences or constituencies, the process may have to be more elaborate and formal, perhaps even trial-like in character.

With these considerations in mind, let's look at the various devices there are to help negotiating parties resolve factual issues and overcome structural barriers to negotiation.

VIII. NON-BINDING FACT AND NORM-DETERMINATION PROCESSES[10]

The devices that I discuss are merely common frameworks for approaching fact-finding and evaluation. There are no set rules for implementing any of these processes, and it is up to the individuals involved in the negotiation to find the optimal solution to facilitate resolving their individual problems and eliminate the obstacles to a negotiated settlement. The parties may choose to adopt one or more of these processes in part or in whole. They must carefully consider the ground rules of whatever process they ultimately choose. There may be some hidden pitfalls in each of these processes, and although I have tried to present the most obvious and common ones, the individual conflict encountered may lead to other unforeseen problems. The parties must keep their eyes open for these potential pitfalls, and be open to changing the procedure, or abandoning it, as the need arises.

Parties should also pay considerable attention as to why they are using these processes in the first place. How the parties choose to define the problems they

[10] Each of these procedures is gaining in popularity and acceptance in more traditional settings. In the 1993 amendments to the Federal Rules of Civil Procedure, the advisory committee notes to Rule 16(c)(9) state that judges and attorneys may use "mini-trials, summary jury trials, mediation, [and] neutral evaluation" in order to resolve a dispute through consensus rather than a full trial.

are having will naturally lead to the set of available alternatives, and may ultimately dictate the eventual solution. Before the parties engage in any of these processes, they should examine why they are engaging in them. What do they hope to accomplish? What are their reasonable expectations? Understanding the problems facing them will help to narrow the issues that will arise as they go through the process they created, and will help facilitate an agreement.

Many of the alternative processes that I discuss are hybrid processes, that is, combinations of other processes commonly used either in negotiations or in other legal contexts such as trial. It is important to note that what the parties choose to adopt is entirely up to them and should be tailored to the specific problems arising in the context of their current negotiation. What worked well once may or may not work again. There is no such thing as a sure-fire method, and parties must be willing to be creative and flexible when working with these methods.

A. Neutral evaluation—neutral fact-finding

Where parties themselves can't resolve fact or norm interpretation disputes, the simplest way they could help themselves would be to resort to a neutral fact-finder or evaluator. All that is required is that the parties trust the neutral and that the neutral have sufficient credibility, expertise, and authority that the parties accept his or her judgment. In mediation, mediators often take on this role, even without specific request of the parties. Settlement judges in lawsuits also play this part, and some courts are now experimenting with using experienced attorneys with expertise in particular areas as neutral evaluators in lawsuit settlements. Undoubtedly, resort to this kind of assistance occurs informally in many low-level conflicts in various businesses and agencies, as employees agree to invoke the assistance of a trusted superior or co-worker. But it isn't necessary for negotiating parties to resort to mediation or litigation to take advantage of a neutral; they can hire one for the limited purpose of settling what they themselves can't settle.

Just to illustrate, take the simple example of the sale of a house. Assume that A wants to sell her house and B wishes to buy it. A's asking price is $450,000 and B's initial offer is $410,000. The parties could try to haggle over the price, and this may prove successful. However, they could also bring in a neutral third party who is an expert in his field and whom they both trust to appraise the value of the house. Assume that he appraises the house to be worth $432,500. This is within the bargaining range of the parties. The parties may then either accept his appraisal or use it as a focal point around which to continue bargaining.

In more complicated disputes, such as those involving complex causal chains, e.g., scientific disputes, parties may need to resort to a panel of neutral experts. In yet other such cases, it may be that there is no definitive factual resolution nor clear guidance on norm resolution. At a minimum, however, a neutral expert or panel of experts may be able to enlighten negotiation decision makers concerning the assumptions and methodologies involved in scientific tests or studies and thus to appreciate the limits of expert judgment. Knowing there is no definite answer is itself of value, and perhaps negotiation can go forward on that basis.

The significant issue in using a neutral "expert" as a fact-finder is whether all negotiating parties will accept the expert. This may pose a difficult problem. Not all experts are equally expert, some experts are biased, depending on the question, different experts may adopt different theories or use different assumptions or methodologies.[11] Thus, in using a neutral evaluator to find facts and help facilitate a settlement, the parties must not only decide what type of expert they would like to have deciding the issue, but must also pay attention to whom they are entrusting their fact-finding.

B. Mini-trials

Parties involved in litigation often fixate on winning, and lose perspective on what they are doing and on possible alternatives to litigation. In many cases, they simply turn their cases over to lawyers and thereafter play subsidiary, rather than principal, roles in resolving the dispute. The mini-trial is a tool developed to address these problems by returning control over dispute resolution to the executives or other principals whose dispute it is.

In the mini-trial process, after some limited discovery, lawyers for each side put together their best possible case and present it to a panel composed of high-ranking executives or principals of the disputants. The panel members have full authority to negotiate a binding settlement. There is also a neutral third-party facilitator, usually a retired judge or experienced and trusted lawyer, who moderates the proceedings. Along with panel members, the neutral third party may ask questions and, if requested by panel members at the conclusion of the case,

---

[11] There may be some "easier" cases; if one wants to find the value of a diamond, one goes to a jeweler for advice. It is not difficult, however, to come up with a myriad of situations in which there is no "easy" answer. For example, assume that two different parties, an individual and a corporation, have contracted to have a race car built and raced. A disagreement arises due to the lack of success they had on the race circuit, and they wish to terminate their contract. However, each blames the other for the failure of the car and insists the other should cover the losses. Whom should they call as a neutral evaluator? An engineer who designs these sorts of cars? A machinist who builds them? A mechanic who maintains them? The race car driver who uses them? All of these "experts" would probably be acceptable in a court of law. Each understands how the vehicle works, and potential problems. Each, however, also has his own understanding of the problem and looks at the problem from a different point of view. All of these "experts" might come up with the same answer, but it is also possible that each would arrive at a different solution because each had a different perspective.

give his or her own views of what the evidence shows and how liabilities might likely fall.[12] In other words, in a mini-trial, the neutral, as well as managing the proceedings, can play the role of neutral fact-finder or evaluator.

Mini-trial presentations are relatively short; even in complicated cases they take only a day or two. Lawyers for each side outline the cases they would make were the case to be tried in a court. They present evidence quite selectively and argue the merits of their cases. These presentations permit the principals in a dispute to see how the case would appear were it to be tried and how their own side's case compares with that of the other side.[13] After the lawyers conclude their presentations, the principals take the information and enter negotiations in an attempt to reach agreement. In the event that they are unable to come to an agreement, the executives may ask the neutral advisor to issue an advisory opinion to see how a judge or jury might rule on the case, and possibly provide a focal point for further discussions.

One example of a successful mini-trial occurred in a dispute between Texaco and Borden, involving both contract and antitrust claims amounting to more than $200 million.[14] The parties already had each spent millions of dollars on attorney fees, having completed about 30 percent of the discovery, a process that delivered more than half a million documents.[15] After mini-trial presentations, the respective executive vice-presidents of the corporations entered into discussions. Three weeks later, they came to an agreement that both sides regarded as win-win. In the agreement, no money actually exchanged hands. Instead, the parties restructured existing agreements that were never considered part of the agreement in controversy, and found a way to eliminate the issues that divided them.[16]

As mini-trials involve lawyers and take place after some discovery, they are expensive, albeit less expensive than trials, both in terms of actual trial costs and the costs of delay. More important, mini-trials provide litigating parties a way to retain control over their dispute, to have highly informed settlement discussions, and to bring to bear considerations and interests beyond those that would be addressed in litigation. The Texaco-Borden example demonstrates how the mini-trial can expedite dispute settlement, save money, and help reach a solution that is much more favorable and equitable than a court decision could have been.

---

[12] Eric Green, *Growth of the Mini-Trial*, 9 LITIG. J 12, 12 (1982).

[13] One of the most important features of the mini-trial is that it is completely confidential and nothing that is said in the mini-trial or during the following negotiations may be admitted as evidence in a court of law if the parties go to trial. This is so because it is considered a settlement discussion which is inadmissible under Federal Rule of Evidence 408.

[14] John F. Henry, *Mini-Trials*, 1 NEGOTIATION J. 13, 14–15 (1985).

[15] *Id.* at 14.

[16] *Id.*

C. Summary jury trials

The summary jury trial is similar to a mini-trial, except that the parties present their cases before a judge and an advisory jury. Once the jury is impaneled, the attorneys make summary presentations of their case, generally without direct testimony. These summaries usually last no more than a couple of hours. The jury then deliberates and makes an award based on the presentations made by the attorneys. The parties then undertake settlement negotiations in hopes of reaching an agreement. If the parties fail to reach an agreement they may hold a "real," binding trial.[17]

Although mini-trials and summary jury trials operate within a litigation context, their common procedure, that is, adversary presentations before disputing parties and a neutral, is one useful for negotiating parties. Parties who wish to negotiate, but who confront a seemingly intractable factual or quasi-factual dispute, could adopt a similar, and even less elaborate procedure. All that is really necessary is that the parties themselves find the procedure credible and enter it willingly.

IX. MIXED PROCESSES

A. Med-arb

As the name suggests, med-arb is a hybrid process involving elements from both mediation and arbitration. In this process, the parties engage in mediation as if they were not employing any other facilitative process. However, should the parties fail to come to an agreement within a certain time, they shift to

---

[17] There is disagreement whether the jury should be told that they are giving only an advisory opinion to aid in settlement discussions, and if so, when they should be told. Some argue that telling them before deliberation may reduce their effectiveness and cause the jury members to take their responsibility less seriously. Others argue that they must be told, otherwise the legitimacy of the jury system will be compromised. Generally, though, it is up to the individual judge as to whether the jury will be told and when.

There have also been concerns that the summary jury process may not be constitutional because it is using the court's power of conscription for jury service for private gain, and that the costs should be borne by the parties involved, not the public. The process, however, has been affirmed by several courts and was specifically mentioned in the Federal Rules of Civil Procedure as an acceptable and effective method for facilitating settlements. FED. R. CIV. P. 16(C)(9).

Additionally, the cost arguments are weak because the long-term costs of a trial, including all of the attorney time and preparation work, greatly outweigh the costs of a summary jury trial. Even if the case does not settle after the summary jury trial, the costs are not wasted because the attorneys will have done more thorough preparation for trial, and may have narrowed the issues such that trial will proceed more quickly. Thomas D. Lambros, *The Federal Rules of Civil Procedure: A New Adversarial Model For A New Era*, 50 U. PITT. L. REV. 789, 799 (1989). The reduced caseload and shorter trial will help the public as a whole by making the courts more efficient and reducing the overall amount spent on trials.

arbitration.[18] The arbitrator then renders a nonbinding or binding decision, in accordance with the parties' agreement.

There are several options available to the parties in the med-arb process. They can choose to have either the mediator act as an arbitrator or they can assign the arbitration task to someone else. The arbitrator, whoever it is, then evaluates the parties' respective cases and issues a ruling. The award then either becomes binding or establishes a basis for further negotiations and becomes binding only if the parties continue to deadlock on settlement.

In nonbinding arbitration, the parties may choose to have the arbitrator issue an advisory opinion to be used as a basis for further negotiations. The arbitrator may or may not sit in on any further negotiations between the parties. In the event that the parties fail to reach an agreement after the issuance of the advisory opinion, depending on the parties' med-arb agreement, the opinion may or may not be admissible in trial.

The parties must decide between these different options before they begin the med-arb process because each choice may have an impact on how the parties behave during the process and beyond. The first decision to be made is whether the same person will function as both mediator and arbitrator. Many commentators criticize the practice of using the same person as both a mediator and an arbitrator with potentially binding authority.[19] It may be argued that this dual role held by one person may confuse the process. Parties who perceive themselves to have less bargaining power may not be entirely forthcoming during the mediation phase for fear of giving something away that may hurt them during the arbitration phase. There may be things that come out during the mediation phase that should have no bearing on the arbitration, but it may be impossible for the arbitrator to put those things out of mind. Likewise, other parties may engage in strategic behavior in order to manipulate the mediator and the other parties in order to exact greater gains during the arbitration phase.

Having a fourth party act as arbitrator in the event of mediation failure would eliminate these concerns. Doing so, however, would lead to extra costs and to unnecessary redundancy, as the issues must be explained once again to an entirely new person. Using a separate arbitrator also may preclude better

---

[18] An arbitration is a process where the participants attempting to reach an agreement present their arguments to a neutral third party who evaluates their positions and issues a ruling. Similar to a court bench-trial, this decision is binding and may be enforced in a court of law. Unlike a mediation, the parties are presented with their solution, and are forced to live with it (appeal is generally not available). Although the arbitrator may try to find a mutually agreeable solution, more often than not he goes with the side that "feels" right or fair under the circumstances. Arbitration is less time intensive and cheaper than a trial, but it may lead to the same sort of inefficient results.

[19] For a good discussion on various viewpoints in the med-arb debate, *see* STEPHEN B. GOLDBERG, ERIC D. GREEN, & FRANK E.A. SANDER, DISPUTE RESOLUTION 247–255, 264–267 (1985).

solutions: the arbitration is an adjudicative proceeding and in the litigation the parties will focus on positions and rights rather than on interests.

Another important issue is whether the arbitrator's ruling will be a final binding decision or a mere suggestion for continuing negotiations. The advantage of having a binding final decision is that the issue is resolved, and the parties can move on. However, the solution might not be an optimal solution. It may be a win-lose, or even a lose-lose, solution leaving potential gains on the table. Similar to a court verdict, it may be ignored if another settlement is reached, but the "winner" will be in a much more powerful position to keep nearly all of the gain he "won." Additionally, if the parties use this binding process as a way to overcome one obstacle in a series of negotiations, and there is more work left to be done before a final agreement is reached, the "losing" party may be left with resentments that may affect further negotiations. Similar to a court verdict, this binding settlement may facilitate a quick and easy short-term solution, but it may severely harm long-term relations.

A nonbinding award has the potential to leave the parties in a better position for long-term relationships, for it is but a new "fact" that they can take into account in further negotiations. Depending on the parties' trust in the arbitrator, and the perceived fairness of the hearing, even the losing party may feel the award is good evidence of what would occur in a binding litigation. In such a case, he might think it better to forego further litigation and prefer to negotiate a settlement. Furthermore, having a better sense of how the case might come out, the parties can bring to bear interests other than those immediately involved in the litigation, and thus craft a better solution than a simple award would have been.

If parties choose to make an arbitral award nonbinding so they can continue negotiating if they wish, there is a further issue whether the arbitrator will participate in further negotiations between the parties. If the same person acted in both roles as mediator and arbitrator, there may be difficulties in her returning to "neutral" ground and attempting to facilitate an agreement. Now that the arbitrator has taken a public stand and expressed her opinion, the "losing" party may have concerns regarding the arbitrator's ability to return to the mediator's neutrality. In this sense, even a nonbinding arbitration award may render ineffective further mediation efforts thereafter. This, of course, is a contingent matter, dependent on the parties, their situation, and their perception of the mediator-arbitrator.

B. Settlement escrow[20]

Negotiations sometimes fail because the parties are nondisclosing. Each side might be willing to make a concession—factual, financial, what have you—but

[20] Robert H. Gertner & Geoffrey P. Miller, *Settlement Escrows*, 24 J. of Legal Stud. 87 (1995).

fears that it will appear weak or be taken, or that the other side will not reciprocate. If the parties are some distance apart, but fail to disclose, there will be no agreement. On the other hand, they are afraid to disclose, so they remain apart.

There is a useful device, called a settlement escrow, that parties can invoke in this situation. In the settlement escrow, the parties agree to bring in a neutral third party to act as a mediator. They each meet with the mediator in private and disclose their information—what they're willing to pay or receive, what facts they might concede, and so on. The mediator checks the information from each party to see whether the concessions cross or overlap, that is, whether they are better than each side's reservation point. If they do cross, the mediator announces there is a deal, and explains what it is. In the case of settlement prices—for example, the price as between buyer or seller, the settlement value of a lawsuit—if the prices cross, the mediator calculates the midpoint price, and the parties settle at that price. (This solves the fair division problem.) If they don't cross, the mediator simply announces that no deal was possible, and neither side learns what the other side was willing to do.

C. High-low agreements

A high-low agreement is another hybrid process possibly useful when negotiating parties have made final offers, yet remain somewhat apart because of some factual dispute. The parties can agree that, in order to avoid costly litigation, they will allow a neutral third party to decide the issue and make an award. Whichever settlement offer this award is closest to will be the eventual final award.

Suppose, for example, that A and B have a disagreement about a particular contract. A and B maintain a long-standing business relationship which in the past has been very profitable and, with the exception of this transaction, very positive. Both sides wish to continue their dealings after this dispute if at all possible. Both wish to avoid trial because of the time, costs, and the possible damage to future relations. Both are also incredibly stubborn and feel that their way of looking at the disagreement is the correct view, and that the other is mistaken. Each can also see that the offer the other side is making would be fair if the situation was how the other side saw it.

Let's assume that A offers B $200,000 to settle, but B demands $300,000. B feels that he is being fair because he thinks at trial he would certainly get $400,000. A thinks that he is being fair because at trial he is sure that B would get no more than $100,000. It would cost each side $100,000 to litigate this case (including both court costs and time lost).

A and B could agree to have C, either an expert in this area or a sample jury, come in and decide the issues. C would not be aware of the offers, or the amounts in question. If C gives an award closer to, or above $300,000, then B would get $300,000. If C was closer to, or below $200,000 (even if C gave B nothing) then B would get $200,000. The parties would have to decide ahead of time what to do if C gave $250,000 (the midpoint between the offers). A simple way of dealing with this is by deciding that the presumption would go against whomever would have had the burden of proof at trial. For example, if B had the burden of proof, then B would get $200,000, but if A had the burden of proof then B would get $300,000.

This process may seem mechanical, but it may be a way to get to a settlement when negotiation has failed. It has the advantage of med-arb in that it is sure to end in an agreement. It also has the advantage that the final award is, to a certain degree, based on how the parties value the case.

X. CHOOSING ALTERNATIVE PROCESSES

Negotiating parties, either by themselves or with the help of a mediator or other neutral advisor, determine whether and how to use one of these alternative processes, or some variant on them, to solve their particular negotiation difficulty. Most of the processes described address the issue of fact-finding, but they do it differently, with more or less formality, more or less relevance to parties' concerns, more or less expense, and possibly more or less accuracy and acceptability.

Skilled negotiators and mediators should be able to detach themselves from their immediate situation and find different creative approaches that maximize the settlement options. Nowhere is that more important than when negotiators hit a roadblock and feel they can move no further through traditional negotiation or mediation practices. When this happens, and the choice is between employing some ancillary process or abandoning the possibility of a negotiated agreement, it's important to identify exactly what it is that stymies further negotiation. If it is disagreement about facts or quasi facts, then neutral fact-finding or evaluation or possibly even a simple version of a mini-trial, may be a solution. If the case is complicated and in litigation, then a mini-trial or the even more elaborate summary jury trial might serve, albeit expensively.

Neutral evaluation, med-arb, settlement esrows, and even a mini-trial might also be useful in cases where negotiators have locked themselves into fixed positions and fail to see ways to move. These processes might also be helpful in situations where the negotiating parties are competing for gain and engaged in risky bargaining behavior, or where saving face or a recalcitrant constituency are factors that impede settlement. Getting an objective view or balanced presentations of competing views may prompt the parties to move (as may the potential threat of an arbitration decision) and find the solution and rationalization they need to reach an acceptable agreement. Whatever processes the participants do choose to utilize, however, it is important that they do so willingly and wholeheartedly. By the time that negotiators employ one of these processes, it may be the last chance the parties have to reach a negotiated agreement.

CHAPTER 15

COMPLEX NEGOTIATIONS AND MEDIATIONS

Many organizational and international negotiations are inherently complex. While increasing the number of issues or parties almost always increases negotiation complexity, there are additional reasons for the complexity of organizational and international negotiations. These negotiations involve collective actors having complex internal structures and decision-making processes that affect the negotiation process. In addition, international negotiations, public and private, often involve actors from substantially different cultures. National and ethnic culture deeply shapes how these actors understand situations, communicate, and characteristically negotiate. The following explores these complications.

I. DIFFUSE NEGOTIATIONS AND COMPLEX INTERDEPENDENCIES

When governments and large organizations negotiate, simple models of negotiation, which involve parties who know their reservation points, interests, and the values of trade-offs, remain relevant, but organizational processes and politics also become highly salient. All negotiation involves uncertainty and learning, and, whatever their initial plan, negotiators must adjust and make decisions as they learn from other sides in a negotiation. But organizations and nations deal with uncertainty, learn, and make decisions differently than do individuals.

Take, as an example, two large corporations contemplating a possible merger. Although we can think of the corporations as single, unified actors, they are actually collectivities of different personal and organizational interests. Among the groups and interests reflected in a corporation are corporate management, the board of directors, the shareholders, the employees, the customers, the suppliers, and the regulators. Each of these groups comprise multiple actors and may or may not act univocally. Corporate management consists of top executives, various division heads, and middle and front-line management. Amongst the employees, there may be several unions. Even if some or all employees are unorganized, there may be job specialties or different career tracks. Among the shareholders, there may be a few individuals who own significant blocks of stock, and on different corporate issues, there will be majority and minority shareholders.

Suppose now, in order to forestall problems and to determine whether to go forward with merger discussions and what to ask for, each corporation consults its various constituencies. If the latter are organized, at least some of the actors comprising them will negotiate among themselves to work out their subgroup's interests in the proposed merger and what its negotiating posture should be. Within any given constituency, for example, the employees, this can be a complex process in itself: the group may already be divided, even factionalized, and coalitions may develop.

Note as well that any intragroup negotiations are likely to be ongoing and fluid, rather than one-shot. This is because there are likely to be continuous flows of new information, and group members will have to adjust to these and reassess their positions. Furthermore, a single corporate subgroup is not the only actor: there are other corporate subgroups or constituencies, shareholders, for example, engaged in a similar process. Finally, while engaged in negotiations internal to itself, each subgroup may also be engaged in external negotiations with other subgroups or corporate representatives. There may be additional complications if coalitions arise within subgroups and they seek to strike deals with other subgroups or coalitions within other subgroups.

While I have used a corporation as an example, virtually the same things could be said about any complex organization. Governmental negotiations involving several agencies and multilateral negotiations between nations or nongovernmental organizations would fit the basic pattern. In the case of governments or governmental agencies, the public, or agency clientele, might also comprise an additional important constituency, just as a corporation's customers form a significant constituency for it.

In a simplified diagram (see Figure 15–1), we can visualize the internal communication and decision-making network of a complex organization as it prepares for and undertakes major external negotiations.

As the diagram illustrates, the external negotiations of a complex organization implicate a large communications and decision-making network involving many interconnected and mutually dependent negotiations and individual and group decision-making activities.[1] In this hypothetical situation, because all the

[1] Dean G. Pruitt, *Negotiation Between Organizations: A Branching Chain Model*, 10 Negotiation J. 217 (1994). Obviously, not every individual in the organization or in any group will be involved in all or

Figure 15–1
Organizational Negotiation as a Communications Network

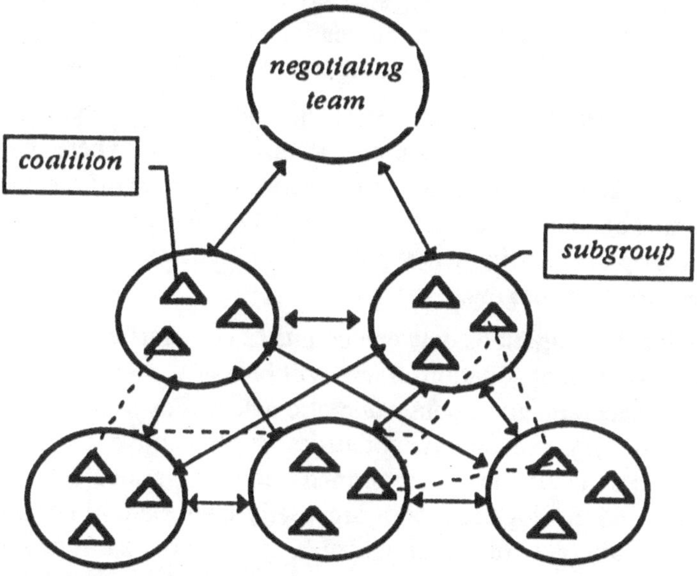

Arrows = group communications/negotiations
Dotted lines = negotiations between coalitions

subgroups belong to the same organization, the stakeholding groups are interdependent. In the democratic case, this means that they must negotiate with one another and that each stakeholding group's alternatives depend on what other groups do and what the organization as a whole determines to do.[2]

Not all of these groups individually may have a veto power over the negotiation, but some of them might, and some combination of them certainly will. Whatever subgroups comprise the critical set of stakeholders—and the configuration could change from issue to issue—the agreements they work out as between themselves will set the lowest common denominating position for the organization's negotiations. The more democratic the group, the lower the denominator, the more likely the negotiation will be highly complex, and the more likely the group's negotiating position will be strongly resistant to change.[3]

---

even many of these negotiations. Each coalition and each stakeholder group will operate, at least part of the time, through representatives who will act as negotiators and as communications nodes or relay points.

[2] Of course, in reality, not all groups would be equally interdependent.

[3] An interesting, culturally based example of this involves Japanese organizations and a consensual decision-making system known as *ringisei* (*ringi* means *circular*). In this system, initiatives can originate anywhere in any organization, often from below. A draft (*ringisho*) circulates among officials or employees, who appraise, discuss, and revise it. As the document works its way through various levels, any disagreement forces a rewriting. By the time the document reaches the highest organizational levels, it embodies an organizational consensus of opinion. Nathaniel B. Thayer & Stephen B. Weiss, *The Changing Logic of a Former*

As is perhaps evident, whether interorganizational negotiations can succeed depends as much, or more, on *what happens away from the table* as on what happens at the table. Negotiation success also depends critically on internal organizational structures, the communication connections and barriers between organizational subunits, and on intraorganizational decision-making processes.

As one can readily conceive, managing, and keeping open and responsive, such an internal network is a complex and difficult task. Where the negotiation aims to maximize the satisfaction of the various interests of the various stakeholders in the negotiation, problem-solving activities occur *throughout* the organization. This places an immense premium on accurate information flow and coordinated decision making.

International negotiations between countries comprise a variant on the basic model. In many such negotiations, there will be many interested parties on each side, both bureaucratic and nonbureaucratic actors. For example, in the United States, in major arms reduction negotiations, the Executive, the Departments of State, Defense, and Commerce, the Armed Services, various defense industries, and academic and ideological groups are vitally interested. Major trade negotiations involve many governmental agencies. In addition, trade negotiations will affect manufacturers, importers, exporters, wholesalers, retailers, employees, and consumers, and the respective groups that represent their interests.

Assuming similar organization in two countries, we can diagram the negotiation network complex as shown in Figure 15–2.[4]

In a negotiation involving a network such as appears in the diagram, negotiation "management" takes on a new meaning and a determinative importance.

> The chief negotiator or head of delegation normally mediates between the soft-line agencies (which tend to concede too easily) and the hard-line agencies (which may be unwilling to settle at any price), with the aim of building an interagency consensus behind a balanced negotiating position that is likely to lead to agreement without giving away too much. . . . [He] must also spend a great deal of time working behind the scenes to build and preserve the interagency consensus needed for progress in the external negotiation. In particular, he or she must manage the bureaucratic and domestic constituencies back in the national capital by keeping the stakeholder agencies fully informed of developments and gaining their concurrence in advance to proposed positions.[5]

Minor Power, in HANS BINNENDIJK, ED., U.S. FOREIGN SERVICE INSTITUTE, NATIONAL NEGOTIATING STYLES 60 (1987); RAYMOND COHEN, NEGOTIATING ACROSS CULTURES 102 (1991). At that point, "[l]eaders, seen as being above the detailed day-to-day management of affairs and playing a largely moral and representative role, are expected to have absolute confidence in subordinates and to approve the document [and negotiating position] without change." COHEN, *id.*

[4] The diagram is adapted from P. TERENCE HOPMANN, THE NEGOTIATION PROCESS AND THE RESOLUTION OF INTERNATIONAL CONFLICTS 165 (1996).

[5] Jonathan B. Tucker, *Interagency Bargaining and International Negotiation: Lessons from the Open Skies Treaty Talks,* 12 NEGOTIATION J. 275, 277 (1996).

Figure 15–2

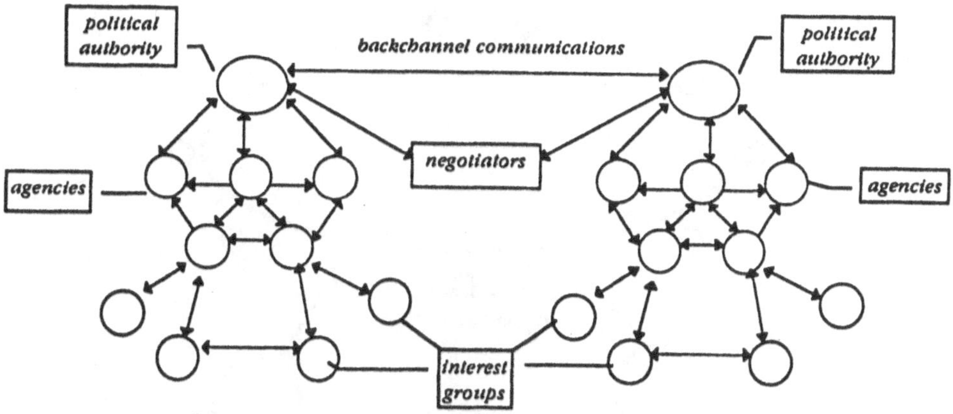

A different form of complex negotiation takes place when stakeholding groups are relatively independent, that is, when they themselves are not part of a larger negotiating entity. Consider, for example, a major public policy negotiation concerning management of a major river used for drinking water, irrigation, power, recreation, fishing, and treated effluent. The parties who would be most intensely interested in river water management would be communities using the river for drinking water, effluent, and recreation; farmers and interest groups representing them; electricity users and utilities; river users, including recreational and commercial fishermen; and environmentalists and environmental organizations. If each group sends a representative to the bargaining table, we can visualize the table as as shown in Figure 15–3.

Here different, independent organizations, each organized on the basis of a dominating interest, comprise stakeholding groups. Any interdependency the different organizations have comes from whatever concerns bring them to the negotiating table. While each stakeholding group will have its own internal politics, each represents a major interest. What holds the stakeholding group together is the overall interest its members seek to further: the policy predilections they share. The shareholder groups are thus distinct, and the boundaries between them are clear. The primary communications network resides at the negotiating table. Unlike the corporate example, stakeholder communications with other stakeholders occur through representatives. If there is other crosstalk or backchannel communication between the stakeholding organizations or their members, it is informal and happenstance. There is little information redundancy in the system and little ability to correct misinformation.

The diagram outlines the negotiation structure of complex negotiations such as public policy negotiations or mediations. It also describes the *gross* structure

Figure 15–3

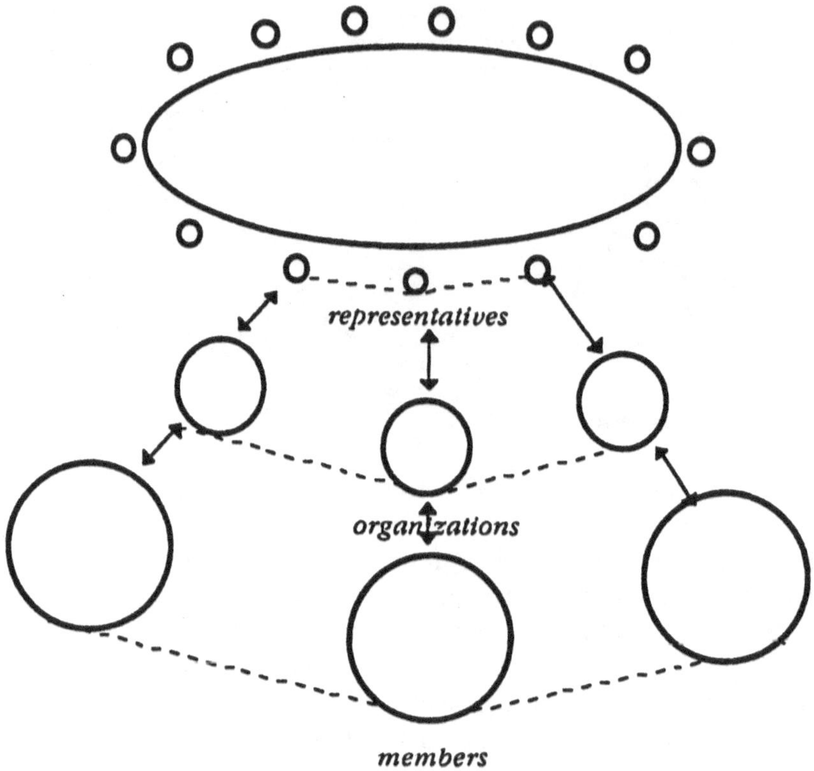

of large multilateral negotiations such as the Law of the Sea Treaty negotiations[6] or the Uruguay Round of the GATT.[7] We can refine our visualization of the latter, however, as shown in Figure 15–4.

In the model, information flows not only through official intermediaries, but through other interconnected communication paths as well; thus the system has some redundancy and some self-correcting ability. When issues are particularly difficult, however, communication and feedback alone will not serve. Concerned stakeholders make decisions, and this may entail meetings of the constituents of particular subgroups. What this means, however, is that there may be no clear distinction between "interorganizational negotiation and intraorganizational preparation for negotiation."[8]

---

[6] Official Text of the United Nations Convention on the Law of the Sea with Annexes and Index, The Law of the Sea 1–157 (1983). *See generally,* James K. Sebenius, Negotiating the Law of the Sea (1984).

[7] General Agreement on Tariffs and Trade, Protocol of Provision Application, 61 Stat. (5), (6), T.I.A.S. No. 1700, 55 U.N.T.S. 639.

[8] Pruitt, *supra* note 1, at 225.

Figure 15–4

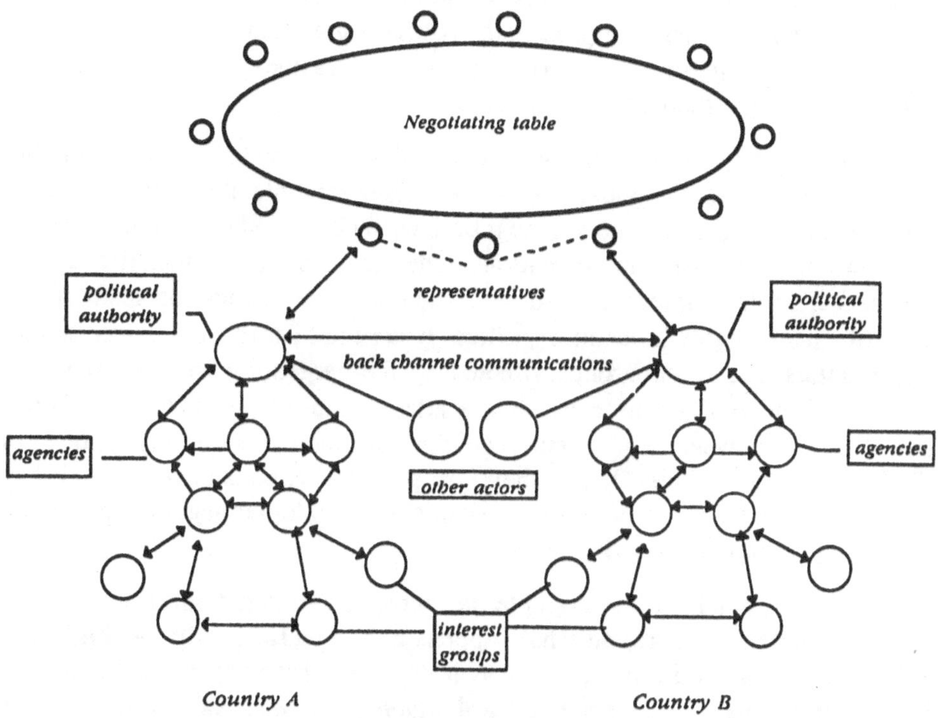

The model assumes full, ongoing consultation and participation of all affected stakeholder groups. It is easy, however, to conceive of variations that perhaps better reflect reality. Many organizations are not democratic: they have a clear decision-making hierarchy that may dictate to, rather than consult with, constituent groups. However, the complexity of the negotiation and the difficulty of managing and coordinating the communication so that it will lead to convergent decision making suggest a number of strategies pursuable separately or jointly.

The first is involving in the consultation and negotiation only those stakeholders whose assent is essential. In the corporate example, that might well be only the board of directors, top management, and a voting majority of the shareholders. In practice, this would require attaining the assent of only the critical coalitions within each essential stakeholder group.

A second strategy involves settling the organizational negotiating position, as much as possible, in advance of external negotiations. This creates efficiency and communication advantages because organizational actors need not react to specific negotiation proposals as they arise. On the other hand, this strategy may lead to rigidity and make the organization far less able to respond to new and unexpected proposals. To do so would require renegotiating the organizational consensus. As the number of actors making up the organization grows, this becomes increasingly difficult. One would expect that organizations using such a strategy would resist new proposals. To the degree that they could not, they might take a long time in responding to them, as they must work the new proposals through their internal bureaucracies.[9]

A final strategy involves using the external negotiation to limit, or restructure the results of, internal negotiations. In the merger example, the corporate negotiating team manages the merger negotiations with the other corporation. It is therefore the principal communications node for the entire organization, and, in this sense, controls information flows. The corporate negotiating team is thus in a critical and highly influential position. It can add to or reduce the information uncertainties that all subgroups affected by the bargaining will experience. It can control much of the information that subgroups use to evaluate their alternatives.[10] Its "inbetweenness" position confers information and framing power on the boundary role player. It can therefore play off its constituencies and their negotiators against those of the other side, play off internal negotiations against external negotiations and vice versa.

As in the organizational example, the prospects of negotiation success may depend as much, or more, on what happens intraorganizationally, within stakeholder groups, away from the table, as it does on what happens at the table. It is one thing to have representatives at the table who can speak for *and commit* their organizations. It is quite different when representatives must seek approval of decision makers within their own organization. That situation will also vary depending on who the decision maker is and on what its decision-making processes are. Consulting, and getting the approval of, an organization president is different from getting the approval of a majority of the members of a membership organization.

This all suggests that anyone who wants to manage complex negotiations to maximize their chances of success—for example, a facilitator, mediator, or a negotiator who takes the initiative in brokering a deal between numerous parties—must understand and utilize the communication and decision-making networks to which the negotiation connects. When the negotiation is interorganizational, this means understanding the internal structure of the organizations represented at the table and their internal communication and decision-making processes. Each entity at the table may have a different structure. Depending on its own internal "political" structure, each will have a different response to new proposals, and new information. To have a fair chance of success, the

---

[9] This is exactly what occurs in Japanese organizations that stress consensual decision making. *See* text accompanying note 48, Chapter 16, *infra*.

[10] JEFFREY PFEFFER, POWER IN ORGANIZATIONS 111–112, 119–120 (1981).

negotiation manager needs to understand who holds the decision-making authority within each entity, what its decision-making procedures are, and what particular concerns it might have about specific proposals.

In a large complex negotiation, this is a major management task requiring substantial staff. When the communication processes seem inadequate to support the negotiation—that is, will fail to provide accurate two-way or multi-channel information between organizational subgroups—the negotiation manager must help the organizations improve them. Furthermore, the negotiation manager must assist all parties at the table in understanding the possibilities available to, and the constraints imposed on, the organization representatives at the table. Understanding organizational decision-making processes would also permit the negotiation manager to frame matters in ways tailored to the individual needs of each party.

II. FACILITATING COMPLEX NEGOTIATIONS AND MEDIATIONS

A. Negotiating about negotiation: prenegotiation

There are times, particularly in complex situations, when parties don't know, or can't decide, whether to negotiate with other parties. They may not know whether other parties are willing to negotiate and fear that an overture on their part might signal weakness. Where the prospect is of a large multilateral negotiation, the number of parties and the complexity of issues may deter possible participants. They may fear that a negotiation between them might be unmanageable, or that it might touch on topics they do not wish to discuss. It could be that the potential issues are highly sensitive, or that trade-off complexities are so great that even to enter negotiations poses great risks. Further, parties may be unsure about who should participate in the negotiation. Finally, they may have concerns about their own constituencies—whether the constituencies will support or resist the negotiation and whether to involve them in decisions regarding it.

Common to these situations is the prospect that negotiation poses major uncertainties and risks. To reduce these, parties sometimes engage in what is called "prenegotiation." Prenegotiation is the process of "getting to the table," of holding exploratory or "diagnostic" discussions between parties aimed at determining whether, and about what, the parties can productively negotiate. One might say that prenegotiation involves a negotiation about whether, and how, to negotiate.[11]

---

[11] JANICE GROSS STEIN, ED., GETTING TO THE TABLE: THE PROCESSES OF INTERNATIONAL NEGOTIATION (1989).

Without committing themselves to negotiate, prenegotiation allows parties to communicate, to develop relationships and gain some trust, and jointly to define problems on which they might work. It also helps them to otherwise reduce the uncertainties and risks they perceive may be involved in negotiating with one another. If, during these discussions, a party determines that the negotiation option is attractive, it may commit itself to negotiate, at least on certain issues, and begin to define for itself the scope of the negotiation.[12] At some point, one of the parties may propose negotiation to the others. If they agree, the emphasis shifts to defining the negotiation. If they do not agree, no negotiation ensues, but neither do any of the losses that attend a failed negotiation.

Prenegotiation gives parties information, stimulates new learning, and enables negotiation by reducing the complexities, uncertainties, and risks associated with negotiation. It enables parties to set boundaries on negotiations, to determine who should participate, to set the agenda, and to manage internal politics, that is, to deal with their own constituencies and engage in coalition building.[13] Although it need not go so far, prenegotiation allows parties to see the shape of the final deal even before they commit themselves to negotiate. This is a possibility of great interest when there are many parties, complex issues and trade-offs, and constituencies or public audiences vitally interested in the outcome of a negotiation. "In the prenegotiation of the Uruguay Round [of the GATT], for example, agreement to negotiate came only at the end, after much of the structuring of trade-offs had taken place."[14]

Prenegotiation may be particularly useful for parties that must answer to various constituencies or, to put it another way, for parties for whom politics away from the table affect negotiation at the table.[15] Prenegotiation gives such parties options. If, during the prenegotiation, important opposing forces organize to block any deal, those engaged in the process may delay a commitment to negotiate. If necessary, they can withdraw or leave the prenegotiation process inconclusive. On the other hand, if forces organize in support of a negotiated agreement, a party may commit itself to negotiation. Once the negotiation process is underway, it may even be possible to use it to assist in managing constituencies.[16]

Aside from its evident use in negotiation between nations, prenegotiation makes sense in any complex negotiation where there are major uncertainties

---

[12] Janice Gross Stein, *Getting to the Table: The Triggers, Stages, Functions, and Consequences of Prenegotiation*, in STEIN, *supra* note 11, at 239, 249.

[13] *Id.* at 252–261.

[14] *Id.* at 251.

[15] Gilbert R. Winham, *The Prenegotiation Phase and the Uruguay Round*, in STEIN, *supra* note 11, at 44, 56.

[16] *See* text accompanying notes 9 and 10, *supra*.

and important constituencies that need satisfying. Corporate mergers come to mind as a possible case, as do complex public policy mediations. In the latter, for example, an environmental mediation over water flows, the need to manage the complexity of issues, parties, trade-offs and possible outcomes may be great. Indeed, such mediations often do not occur unless some of the parties, or the mediator and some parties, engage in prenegotiation.

Finally, one might use prenegotiation profitably even in situations of lesser issue or party complexity, but where the cultural norm for negotiation is relationship-based.[17] In fact, the practice in relationship-based cultures seems always to involve a kind of prenegotiation and discloses that the line between prenegotiation and negotiation is neither clear nor fixed.

B. Problem-solving workshops and third-party consultation

Problem-solving workshops, sometimes also referred to as third-party consultations, are a form of prenegotiation that conjoin human relations training with group problem solving.[18] Used in instances of severe or seemingly intractable conflict, such workshops aim at improving the perceptions of, and the relationships, communications, and trust between parties in conflict. Usually organized and facilitated by impartial third-party intermediaries—the consultants—"[t]he process is designed to create the conditions conducive to establishing and maintaining certain patterns of social interaction and to utilize the ongoing interactions themselves as raw materials for gaining greater understanding of the dynamics of the conflict."[19]

Problem-solving workshops attempt to create favorable interactions between parties in conflict and generate positive attitude change. The invited participants are usually "influential yet informal representatives of the parties in conflict," important members of the "decision-making elites."[20] The small work-group setting allows these participants to interact—under enforced ground rules assuring equality, respect, openness, and trust—to break down stereotyped perceptions of their respective groups and their conflict. The consultants assist the participants in working through realistic cooperative problem-solving tasks relating to their conflict and its actual context.[21]

---

[17] *See* Chapter 16, Section II(D), *infra*.

[18] Ronald J. Fisher, *Prenegotiation Problem-Solving Discussions: Enhancing the Potential for Successful Negotiation*, in Stein, *supra* note 11, at 206, 215.

[19] H.C. Kelman, & S.P. Cohen, *Resolution of International Conflict: An Interactional Approach*, in THE PSYCHOLOGY OF INTERGROUP RELATIONS 323, 340 (S. WORCHEL & W.G. AUSTIN, EDS.; 2nd ed. 1986) *quoted in* Fisher, *supra* note 18, at 212.

[20] Fisher, *supra* note 18, at 217.

[21] *Id.* at 214–215.

Problem-solving workshops seem to be successful in changing the perceptions and attitudes of participants. The hope is that, after the workshop, the participants will convince parties in power in their own group that ameliorating changes in the conflict posture are possible.

Although problem-solving workshops appear to be a form of mediation, such workshops focus primarily on attitude and relationship changing, in order to increase trust between parties, rather than on securing agreement on some issue. In this sense, one could say that problem-solving workshops aim at creating the conditions essential to prenegotiation, negotiation, and mediation.

III. USING INTERMEDIARIES

Intermediaries often help settle international disputes, and international mediation activities are extensive and often successful.[22] International mediation is a separate and specialized study in itself. Two uses of intermediaries in international and complex negotiations are of particular interest because they point to mediation possibilities not yet discussed. These involve using intermediaries as intercultural liaisons and buffers and mediators assuming the role of a bargaining principal.

A. Cross-cultural Intermediaries

When negotiating parties share a culture, they communicate within a framework of shared conventions and meanings.[23] When the parties are of significantly different cultures, however, they risk negotiation failure because they are likely to misunderstand one another. President Carter's mediation at Camp David between Anwar Sadat and Menachem Begin provides a good example of the usefulness of a cross-cultural intermediary.

> For all their idiosyncrasies, their [Sadat's and Begin's] leadership and negotiating styles were unmistakably rooted in their respective cultures. President Sadat of Egypt moved in a lofty realm of seeking "general principles and broad strategic concepts." The *rais* (leader, president) of a paternalist and authoritarian society, he was not subject to democratic controls and could disregard, if he wished, the advice of other members of his delegation. . . . Begin, on the other hand, was every inch the Talmudic scholar and Polish-Jewish lawyer, engrossed in nitpicking detail and special pleading. . . . As a democratically elected prime minister in the Western sense and leader of the majority party,

---

[22] Jacob Bercovitch & Allison Houston, *The Study of International Mediation: Theoretical Issues and Empirical Evidence*, in JACOB BERCOVITCH, ED., RESOLVING INTERNATIONAL CONFLICTS: THE THEORY AND PRACTICE OF MEDIATION 11, 12–13, 18 (1996).

[23] *See* Chapter 16, Cross-Cultural Negotiations and Mediations.

his authority in the Israeli delegation was that of a first among equals; he could neither ignore nor override the views of his colleagues or of the Israeli parliament.[24]

Carter solved the intercultural mediation problem by acting quite differently with the two men as he shuttled between them. Carter had a warm rapport with Sadat, and he and Sadat trusted each other. "[W]ith the Israelis he [Carter] displayed the energy, acumen, and drafting ingenuity of a high-powered lawyer; with President Sadat, he played the part of the political patron, protective and deeply caring but occasionally sternly authoritative, reminding his client of hard truths."[25]

B. Intermediaries as principals

In a typical negotiation, the mediator acts as a neutral, intervening to shape disputants' interactions with one another. The mediator is interested in getting the parties to agree. Whether they do so may affect the mediator's reputation, future mediation business prospects, and sense of skill and accomplishment. But the neutral has no substantive interests beyond these. In other words, while the mediator helps the parties bargain effectively, the mediator is not bargaining for himself.

There is another kind of intervention or "mediation," however, typical in international arenas and complex negotiations, in which the party intervening as an intermediary itself brings resources and interests to the table. While continuing to manage the negotiation, the intervenor also becomes a bargainer.[26] As bargainer, the intermediary cares about how a settlement between the parties will affect its own interests. Furthermore, it can shape the settlement between the parties by offering or denying benefits to them, by changing the payoffs between them, or by forming coalitions.

In this situation, an outside party, perceiving that a dispute between other parties affects its own substantive interests, intervenes by offering its services as an intermediary or "mediator." In reality, the intervention changes the basic negotiation from a two-party (or 'n' party) negotiation into a three-party (or 'n + 1' party) negotiation. The addition of the new party brings new interests to the table: those of the new party and those which the original disputants share with the new party. This changes the bargaining issues, creates different possible payoff and trade-off schedules, and changes the bargaining dynamic and the disputing parties' alternatives.

---

[24] Raymond Cohen, *Cultural Aspects of International Mediation*, in BERCOVITCH, *supra* note 22, at 107, 122.

[25] *Id.* at 123.

[26] THOMAS PRINCEN, INTERMEDIARIES IN INTERNATIONAL CONFLICT 23–26 (1995).

In some situations, a party initially acting as a neutral mediator may evolve its role into that of a principal mediator.[27] This can occur, of course, only when the mediator has both substantive interests in the dispute and resources to bring to the table. The clearest examples of this occur in international conflicts involving nations. When a major country, such as the United States or France, enters an international dispute as an intermediary, there is always a chance it will shift its role over time from that of "good offices"[28] or facilitator to that of a principal bargainer.

> What starts as mere good offices becomes an effort to build international pressure. A multilateral conference aimed at facilitating a rational, comprehensive solution to a regional problem ends in a limited, bilateral agreement sweetened with the intermediary's aid and guarantees. A fact-finding mission becomes a formal mediation process. A simple message-carrying effort leads to substantive proposal making. Because of the indeterminacy of the role . . . therefore, intermediary interventions are full of surprises.[29]

To the degree that the intermediary's role shifts from that of neutral to principal, or the disputing parties perceive that it will, however, the role shift simultaneously constrains the intermediary and opens new possibilities. As the intermediary becomes an interested bargainer, the original parties are less likely to share information freely, for the mediator is no longer a neutral. On the other hand, if the intermediary entered as a neutral and thereby gained information, it could use that information to guide its substantive intervention into the dispute.

It may seem improbable that disputing countries would be likely to look upon a third country, particularly a powerful country with global interests, as a

---

[27] *Id.* at 43.

[28] There are a range of different roles that a third party may assume in order to help interested parties resolve their conflict in international contexts. The terminology, however, is different. The least intrusive form of intervention is known as "good offices" or facilitation. This is where a "neutral" third party provides neutral ground on which the interested parties meet. Generally the third party does not bring anything to the negotiating table, and is not an active participant in the negotiating process. This sort of process is most helpful where the parties have deep ideological feelings about each other, and it would be a major loss of face to travel to the other's territory for a meeting.

On the other end of the spectrum, there is conciliation. This is a much more formal and ongoing process than good offices. In conciliation the parties establish a committee charged with the duties of making an impartial examination of the dispute and presenting information and possible solutions to the parties which will aid in the settlement of the dispute. These committees may be permanent, as in the case of some international treaties, or ad hoc, looking at one or only a few particular disputes. This is different from arbitration in that it is still a method aimed at facilitating a dialogue between the parties, and any recommendations are not binding on the parties.

Mediation lies somewhere between the two poles. The mediator may act like a facilitator or give good offices by merely guiding the parties in their dispute. Likewise, he may act like a conciliator and make proposals to the parties (although he is less likely to engage in independent fact-finding). It is important to note that a mediator's role changes as the situation develops.

For further discussion, *see* J.G. MERRILLS, INTERNATIONAL DISPUTE SETTLEMENT (1984).

[29] *Id.* at 220.

neutral. Indeed, it is often clear that countries taking on a "neutral" role are in some sense not impartial. The United States, for example, is clearly a patron of Israel. Of course, the United States also has important interests in Arab countries, and on some issues, Arab countries might view it as impartial or, at least, balanced. More important, however, the issue for disputing parties is not so much whether the intervenor is impartial as whether the intervention is likely to better their alternatives.[30] If the intermediary can influence the parties and brings to the table resources which they believe can advance their interests, the lack of intermediary neutrality is not an impediment to success.[31] If so, the parties are better off with the intervention than without it, regardless of whether the intervenor is impartial or not.

---

[30] *Id.* at 62.

[31] Jacob Bercovitch, *Understanding Mediation's Role in Preventive Diplomacy*, 12 NEGOTIATION J. 241, 252 (1996).

CHAPTER 16

CROSS-CULTURAL NEGOTIATIONS AND MEDIATIONS

Familiarity with a particular nationality's characteristic negotiating style is of obvious use to anyone who would negotiate with a member of that group. It is relatively well known, for example, that members of certain ethnic or nationality groups have characteristic bargaining styles. For example, the Arabs are shrewd, competitive bargainers.[1] The Russians, particularly under Soviet rule, had the reputation of being tough, hard-line, hard-bargainers.[2] The Chinese are viewed as given to using competitive bargaining ploys and tactics.[3] But the idea of different negotiating styles is inadequate to capture the often profound differences in negotiating behavior between parties from significantly different cultures, differences that can have an enormous substantive impact on negotiation.

I. CULTURE AS A NEGOTIATION BARRIER

Culture, used here to mean a shared way of life and a shared way of perceiving life, profoundly shapes negotiation interactions. Culture involves patterned and shared ways of thinking and reacting, usually unconscious. It is the frame that shapes how people perceive and interact with others and with their environment, and what meaning and value they assign to acts and interactions. In that sense, "culture constructs reality; different cultures construct reality differently;

[1] Robert C. Ciricillo, Adam Fremantle & Jeanne M. Hamburg, *International Negotiations: A Cultural Perspective*, in JAMES R. SILKENAT AND JEFFREY M. ARESTY, EDS., THE ABA GUIDE TO INTERNATIONAL BUSINESS NEGOTIATIONS 5, 13 (1994).

[2] RAYMOND F. SMITH, NEGOTIATING WITH THE SOVIETS (1989).

[3] LUCIAN PYE, CHINESE COMMERCIAL NEGOTIATING STYLE 70–74 (1982).

communication across cultures puts different constructions of reality against each other."[4]

When parties share a culture, they approach the world with the same, general interpretive frame. This does not mean that parties of the same culture interpret specific situations the same way nor that they will not have disputes. It does mean, however, that they will share a set of general background assumptions and behavioral approaches. When parties of different cultures interact, they perceive the interaction through different interpretive frames. Ethnicity and nationality, therefore, are important determinants of negotiating attitudes and behaviors.[5] When parties from different cultures negotiate, they may define situations differently and misinterpret or misunderstand negotiation conventions, moves, and signals.

Consider, for example, an important difference between Japanese and American culture. The Japanese communicate indirectly; for the Japanese, vagueness and ambiguity in communication is thought to be a virtue.[6] Americans, by contrast, prize directness and specificity. The potential for miscommunication between Japanese and American negotiators is therefore considerable. Although they might not show it, the Japanese are likely to view American directness and demands for detail as confrontational and offensive. Americans, on the other hand, are likely to view the Japanese as being evasive and noncommittal.

In this example, each party unreflectively interprets the other through its own cultural frame, taking its own culture as the norm and unconsciously assuming that all people understand matters in fundamentally similar ways. Because the parties are unaware of deep cultural and perceptual differences, they seriously misread the communication.

Negotiations between parties from significantly different cultures therefore entail serious risks of misperception and misunderstanding. There is more, however. When members of different cultures negotiate and bring different cultural negotiating norms to the table, they are "playing" different, and possibly conflicting, negotiation "games." This may make it very difficult for them to bargain together effectively.

Chinese from the People's Republic of China, for example, insist that others disclose their interests and priorities, but mask, and decline to reveal, their own.[7] One might wish to interest-bargain with the Chinese, but their cultural norms require them to keep the upper hand through nondisclosure. The best one could

---

[4] Raymond Cohen, *Cultural Aspects of International Mediation*, in JACOB BERCOVITCH, ED., RESOLVING INTERNATIONAL CONFLICTS: THE THEORY AND PRACTICE OF MEDIATION 122 (1996).

[5] Oded Shenkar and Simcha Ronen, *The Cultural Context of Negotiations: The Implications of Chinese Interpersonal Norms*, 23 J. OF APPLIED BEHAVIORAL SCI. 263, 264 (1987).

[6] ROBERT MARCH, THE JAPANESE NEGOTIATOR 15–16, 85–89 (1988).

[7] PYE, *supra* note 3, at 35.

do would be to guess at Chinese interests and priorities and attempt to problem solve on that basis.[8] At the same time, in self-disclosing, the bargainer puts himself at risk of competitive moves. It helps greatly to know that for the Chinese, this behavior is not a mere competitive ploy, but culturally based and reinforced behavior. If one is to negotiate with the Chinese, this is what one faces.

Obviously knowledge of, and experience with, the different culture is of great value in managing cross-cultural negotiations. In some cases, however, using bicultural intermediaries or mediators capable of operating effectively in the different cultures would serve even better. Such intermediaries could help parties interpret one another, buffer them from culturally inappropriate, face-injuring communication, and help them mesh different negotiation conventions.[9] Aside from these remedies, the best one can do is to attempt to develop intercultural communication competence, beginning with an understanding of how cultures may differ.

II. APPRECIATING CULTURAL DIFFERENCES: VARIABLES

There is an enormous variety among cultures; the differences between them both too great and too nuanced to allow developing a universally valid guidebook for cross-cultural negotiation sensitivity. There are, however, some variables that negotiators can consider to help them appreciate some of the major cultural differences and cross-cultural dissonances that may bear on negotiating behavior. As my aim is to sensitize rather than catalogue, I focus on cultures that strongly contrast with North American and Northern European cultures, and will limit discussion to variables which, taken together, seem to comprise an understandable gestalt.[10]

Obviously, this kind of discussion involves generalizations—not offered as gospel, but rather as a suggestive rendering for comparative purposes. Note also that the pictures drawn reflect current circumstances of cross-cultural interactions. As individuals from different cultures increasingly interact, they learn of their cultural differences and begin to adjust. Over time, with increasing globalization, parties from different cultures will develop greater intercultural communication competence.

---

[8] *Id.*

[9] Cohen, *supra* note 4, at 111–112.

[10] Two different, but similar, schemes for comparing different cultural communication and negotiating behavior may be found respectively in Christopher W. Moore, *"Have Process Will Travel"*: Reflections on Democratic Decision Making and Conflict Management Practice Abroad, FORUM 1, 6–9 (Winter, 1993); and DAVID A. VICTOR, INTERNATIONAL BUSINESS COMMUNICATION 14 (1992).

In any case, in discussing cultural differences that bear significantly on negotiation or conflict, I will use as variables cultural characteristics or attitudes regarding:

- individualism and collectivism;
- contexting;
- "face";
- relationships;
- power, status, and authority; and
- role of law.

A. Individualism and collectivism

The United States and many western countries have individualist cultures. Such cultures value individuals highly and are far less concerned with group membership or individual identification with a group.[11] According to one study, American individualism includes greater self-concern than group concern, more concern for one's own goals than for group goals, self-reliance, competitive behavior, and strong inclinations to decide on one's own rather than consult others.[12]

In contrast, many Asian cultures, particularly the Japanese and Chinese,[13] are collectivist in character. In such cultures, persons derive much of their own value from group membership. In particular, group aims, success, and harmony are more important than are those of the individual.[14] Collectivist cultures value group consensus and discourage individual initiative and "adventuring," except in certain well-defined areas. In such cultures,

> [w]ithin the family the authority of the father is unquestioned, and this model of superior-subordinate relations is replicated at all levels of society and politics. Roles are ascribed. Consequently, members of collectivistic societies accept hierarchy as part of the natural order of things and are strongly status conscious. Education fosters not individual autonomy, but respect for tradition

[11] VICTOR, *supra* note 10, at 102.

[12] Harry Triandis, Robert Bontempo, Marcelo J Villareal, Masaaki Asai, & Nydia Lucca, *Individualism and Collectivism: Cross-Cultural Perspectives on Self-Ingroup Relationships*, 54 J. OF PERSONALITY & SOC. PSYCHOL. 323, 331 (1988).

[13] *Id.* at 326.

[14] "Self-reliance for the collectivist cultures implies not being a burden on the ingroup, and competition [with others in the group] is unrelated to it. Competition in collectivist cultures is among ingroups, not among individuals. . . . [I]n collectivist cultures, groups achieve. People feel proud of their achievements and their success in personal competition in the individualist cultures and people feel proud of their group's achievement and the success of their groups in the collectivist cultures." *Id.* at 335.

> and authority. Truth reposes in the traditions of the group and is not to be uncovered by lone intellectual inquiry or the give-and-take of debate. . . . Actions likely to disrupt group harmony are to be shunned and those that promote it, highly valued. Confrontation is anathema. Conflict is resolved not by resort to formal processes of law, but by mechanisms of communal conciliation, concerned less with abstract principles of absolute justice than with the requirements of continuing harmony.[15]

Cultures that revere group harmony place a high premium on formality, politeness, limited overt expression, and restrained, moderate, nonemotional behavior.[16]

B. Contexting

Contexting[17] refers to the degree to which people of particular cultures read meaning into the contexts or circumstances of communication. A culture is said to be *low-context* when its members understand communications primarily on the basis of what is said. A culture is said to be *high-context* when its members take the context or circumstances of a communication heavily into account in interpreting, or assigning meaning to, the communication. Respective sayings from two different cultures illustrate the difference between low- and high-context cultures. "Say what you mean and mean what you say," is a low-context saying. "Those who know do not speak; those who speak do not know," is a high-context saying.

Communication and interaction styles differ substantially as between low- and high-context cultures: they are virtually the inverse of one another. Low-context cultures rely heavily on direct and clear verbal communication, tend to ignore nonverbal communication, interpret communications literally, concern themselves with detail, and find silence noncommunicative and anxiety producing.[18]

Persons in high-context cultures "read" the context on the basis of shared knowledge and experiences; what is hinted at, or not said, is as important, or perhaps even more important, than what is said. In this sense, high-contexters live in a social world crowded with unstated meaning. High-context cultures are thus far less literal and much more interpretive than low-context cultures, use indirection, and rely on inferential rather than explicit communication. This means that individuals in high-context cultures rely far less on verbal communication and more on nonverbal communication. They neither express nor seek

---

[15] Raymond Cohen, Negotiating Across Cultures 25 (1991).

[16] Shenkar & Ronen, *supra* note 5, at 268.

[17] Edward T. Hall, Beyond Culture (1976).

[18] Victor, *supra* note 10, at 153.

specificity and detail in communication, and respect silence, considering it both communicative and pregnant with meaning.[19]

In high-context cultures, individuals have to figure out meanings implied in communicative settings. They must therefore be highly sensitive to others and attuned to situational and communicative clues. As it is much easier to interpret others when one is familiar with them, in high-context cultures, knowledge of others and established relations with them are important predicates for effective communication and negotiation. The evidence supports this conclusion: business and negotiation success in high-context cultures depends on developing personal relationships based on trust and understanding.[20]

In a low-context culture, where communication is much more direct, explicit, and detailed, individuals need not be so sensitive to nuance and situational clues. As communications are treated literally, established relationships with, and knowledge of, others are less important.

Ranking cultures on a scale from low- to high-context, German, Scandinavian, and North American cultures rank as low-context, while Latin, Arabic, Japanese, and a number of other Asian cultures rank as high-context.[21] One would therefore expect that a German or United States citizen communicating with a Japanese or Thai citizen would be direct and forthright, while the latter would be indirect and circumspect. What each side in the communication views as a virtue—directness in the one case and indirectness in the other—the other side sees as a flaw or fault. The low-contexter's directness would offend the high-contexter: "[t]he common Western ideal of a persuasive communicator—someone who is highly skilled in argumentation, who overcomes objections with a verbal flair, who is an energetic extrovert—would be regarded by most Japanese as superficial, insincere, and more subtly, a little vulgar."[22] On the other hand, the high-contexter's indirectness would seem to be noncommittal, evasive, or even insincere to the low-contexter.

C. "Face"

North American and Northern European cultures are guilt-based, in the sense that they rely on an individual's sense of guilt at wrongdoing—the personal

---

[19] *Id.*

[20] *Id.* at 145.

[21] *Id.* at 143. There does not appear to be a direct correlation between a culture's ranking on the individualism/collectivism scale and its ranking on the contexting scale. For example, while the United States culture values individualism the most highly and is a low-context culture as well, England also ranks high in individualism, but has a considerably higher context culture than does the United States. Japan is a country of middling individualism, but ranks highest among the high-context cultures. *Id.* at 103, 143.

[22] March, *supra* note 6, at 15.

conscience—as a substantial mechanism of social control. By contrast, many group-oriented Asian cultures, and Southern European, Middle Eastern, and Latin American cultures are shame-based, that is, they tend to rely more heavily on shame, which results from a public or group condemnation, as a device for controlling individual behavior. In these latter cultures, much of what a person deems himself to be is bound up with group identity and standing within a group, and people greatly fear being shamed, or losing face, in public.[23]

Beyond this, there are also important differences between how low- and high-context cultures conceive of the self, differences that bear on how parties handle interactions with others and manage conflict. In low-context, individualistic cultures, maintaining congruity between the "authentic" self and the "social" self, between one's private self-image and public self-image, is important.[24] The basic norm is "be yourself," and maintaining freedom and autonomy is paramount.[25] By contrast, in high-context, collectivist cultures, a web of intersecting personal and social relationships defines who one is, defines one's very self.[26] Recognizing the interdependence of individuals, persons from such cultures concern themselves not only with maintaining their own "face," but also with maintaining that of others.[27] Furthermore, in these cultures, face also reflects "one's status hierarchy, role position, and power resources. The more one is in power, the more one knows how to bestow, maintain, honor, and destroy face."[28]

Persons in face-sensitive cultures go to great lengths to avoid giving, or receiving, a public affront. The basic communication strategy for individuals in such cultures involves politeness, indirectness, and nonconfrontation, takes closely into account the sensitivities and social standing of others, and tolerates considerable vagueness and subtlety in expression.[29] In a face-sensitive culture, directly telling someone in public that they were wrong or that they had made a mistake would comprise a considerable insult or constitute an occasion for an unbearable loss of face.[30]

---

[23] "The heavy use of shame as a social control mechanism from the time of early childhood tends to cause feeling [sic] of dependency and anxieties about self-esteem, which naturally enough produce self-consciousness about most social relationships" PYE, *supra* note 3, at 89.

[24] Stella Ting-Toomey, *Intercultural Conflict Styles, A Face-Negotiation Theory*, in YOUNG YUN KIM & WILLIAM B. GUDYKUNST, EDS., THEORIES IN INTERCULTURAL COMMUNICATION 213, 215 (1988).

[25] *Id.* at 229.

[26] *Id.*

[27] *Id.*

[28] *Id.* at 228.

[29] VICTOR, *supra* note 10, at 160.

[30] Some face-saving cultures go to such extraordinary lengths to avoid offending or disturbing others publicly that individuals may refuse to give anyone bad news or even to say no to a request. Leo J. Moser, *Cross-cultural Dimensions: U.S.-Japan*, in U.S. FOREIGN SERVICE INSTITUTE, TOWARD A BETTER UNDERSTANDING OF U.S.-JAPAN RELATIONS 21, 28 (1986). The Japanese are particularly famous for this.

> A Japanese may say "it is difficult" ("*muzukashii*") to convey a rejection or refusal or "it can't be helped" ("*sho go nai*") to tell the listener that he will not stop an event about to take place.

> From the HCC [high-context culture] perspective, dominating or confrontational conflict strategies are viewed as posing a direct threat to the other person's face without leaving room for further negotiations and maneuvers in the conflict process. From the LCC [low-context culture] perspective, the obliging or the roundabout way of handling conflict in the HCC system poses a direct insult to the face of the negotiators in the LCC conflict situation. While the LCC members would view the indirect way of handling conflict as a cowardly act, the HCC members would view the direct way of handling conflict as lacking in good taste.[31]

For negotiators or mediators, the appreciation of cultural differences regarding face is plain. When dealing with parties from face-sensitive cultures, one must be careful to avoid offending through bluntness or directness and to avoid publicly questioning the other's honor, honesty, integrity, or course of conduct in any way. One must also learn to read polite and vague expressions, even lack of communication feedback, as efforts to avoid giving offense or creating bad feelings. Finally, one must learn to give face, to help others navigate social interactions safely, with their dignity and public stature intact.

D. Relationships

In the problem-solving model of negotiation, relationships comprise a possible interest among other interests. High-context cultures place great value on developing close, personal relationships and view a sound relationship between parties as the foundation of the negotiation. One might say that such cultures view relationship as the primary interest in any negotiation. Thus this view is but a variant of the problem-solving model. However, this statement misses something of fundamental importance.

In relationship-based cultures, a good relationship is the foundation for all subsequent interactions. Where no relationship exists and parties consider dealing with one another, the principal aim of meetings is to develop a relationship, not the negotiation of a deal. The assumption is that if there is a good relationship, everything else can be worked out. In this sense, *relationships,* rather than particular agreements, *are binding*. An established relationship becomes the precondition for continued dealings, and developing a relationship is a kind of prenegotiation. Once there is a relationship, negotiations become episodes rather than the aim of the relationship.[32]

A Japanese may use the phrase, " I will seriously consider it" ("*kento shi-masu*") and "I will do my best" ("*zensho shimasu*") when he isn't sure how he wants to respond. Nathaniel B. Thayer & Stephen B. Weiss, *The Changing Logic of a Former Minor Power*, in HANS BINNENDIJK, ED., U.S. FOREIGN SERVICE INSTITUTE, NATIONAL NEGOTIATING STYLES 48 (1987).

[31] Ting-Toomey, *supra* note 24, at 229.

[32] COHEN, *supra* note 15, at 31.

Considered as a type of preliminary negotiation, developing a relationship involves a different dynamic than other kinds of bargaining. Indeed, it is probably mistaken to view it as a type of ordinary bargaining. Instead, it involves the creation of deep, knowledge-based trust,[33] reciprocal obligation, and partnership for mutual benefit. Such relationships involve genuine, personal, moral commitments rather than legalistic and contractual obligations. For example, "Japanese businessmen strive to move toward a family-type relationship with their partners, whether foreign or Japanese. In Japan, an important aspect of such relationships is the degree to which 'dependency' (*amae*) can be developed."[34]

The Chinese appear to take a similar view. The Chinese Confucian tradition emphasizes cultivating and managing interpersonal relations (*guanxi*), enveloping individuals in a web of relationships and mutual obligations.[35] Chinese "prefer to do business with individuals and/or firms that they consider 'known quantities.' . . . Once a sense of mutual attraction (*bici ganqing*) has been established, it must be carefully nurtured and developed."[36] The Chinese consider that the partner who indicates a willingness to be helpful has taken on a *guanxi* commitment.[37] In a *guanxi* relationship, however, the advantage often goes to the weaker partner, for the superior is deeply obligated to help it.[38] Consequently, the driving purpose behind much of Chinese negotiating tactics is the goal of creating a relationship, characterized as friendship, in which the other partner will feel strong and not precisely limited bonds of obligation toward the Chinese.[39]

Developing this kind of relationship, as opposed to negotiating the terms of a contract, takes a great deal of time and mutual exploration. Parties contemplating entering such a relationship will likely undertake considerable research and intelligence work regarding one another. They will also be careful and cautious in making a commitment until they have concluded that the other party is a trustworthy and desirable partner.

Once the parties establish a relationship, however, much follows. Complete openness, trust, and fair-dealing as between themselves in all matters affecting the relationship are expected. Because the relationship has such value, the parties would expect both to understand and be understood, to accommodate and to be accommodated, when either party has difficulty in meeting the terms of a specific commitment, e.g., a production contract. Indeed, in general, they would not act

---

[33] *See* Chapter 6, Compromise Negotiation, Section III(C).

[34] Ciricillo et al., *supra* note 1, at 12.

[35] Richard H. Solomon, Chinese Political Negotiating Behavior 17 (1995).

[36] Shenkar & Ronen, *supra* note 5, at 271.

[37] Pye, *supra* note 3, at 89.

[38] *Id.*

[39] *Id.*

legalistically with regard to one another, preferring to stand on, and protect, the relationship rather than stand on and enforce legal rights and obligations.

While great benefits may flow from creating a relationship of mutual trust, understanding, and obligation, there are costs as well, and the "obligation" part of the relationship bears emphasizing. Entering such a relationship is not the same as simply securing an advantageous deal. Having a good relationship does not, by any means, exclude making competitive moves to make gains. Parties can use the relationship in an emotional way to extract concessions. For example, one can make demands of "friends" that one cannot make of others, pressure friends to grant favors and make compromises or concessions for the sake of the friendship or relationship. This certainly seems to be one aspect of Chinese *guanxi*[40] and the Japanese *amae* relationship.[41] Indeed the Chinese seem particularly adept at using the relationship in just this way.

> Businessmen . . . report that the Chinese sometimes put pressure on them when discussing the final concrete arrangements by suggesting that they have broken the spirit of friendship in which the business relationship was originally established. The ploy, of course, allows the Chinese to play the role of the innocent and aggrieved party while adopting an aggressive and prickly manner, designed to intimidate the other party into becoming more yielding on the substantive details of the negotiations.[42]

As the focus of relationship-based negotiation is the relationship rather than specific issues in a proposed deal, it is very easy to see how extreme misunderstandings might arise when members of other cultures attempt to negotiate with members of a culture that values relationships greatly. The relationship-based negotiator would take time to develop knowledge of the other party, focus on relationship issues, and work on knowledge-based trust. A competitor or problem solver would attempt to focus on particular problems, issues, and details, and develop only the information necessary to handle them. Insofar as trust was an issue, he would be satisfied with calculus-based trust, that is, be satisfied with deals in which the calculated benefits outweighed the calculated costs or losses. The parties would "miss" and misunderstand each other because they targeted quite different objects. Even if the parties managed to negotiate an agreement, serious misunderstandings could arise later on when the parties interpreted the nature of their arrangement differently, that is, where one party believed it had established a relationship and the other party thought there was just a specific agreement.

---

[40] SOLOMON, *supra* note 35, at 87.

[41] MARCH, *supra* note 6, at 134. "*Japanese quickly come to resent those who refuse to accede to requests to help in times of trouble.*" *Id.* at 98 (emphasis in original).

[42] PYE, *supra* note 3, at 43.

E. Power, status, and authority

The United States and many Western European countries have rather individualistic cultures that value relative equality, individual achievement, personal freedom, and majority rule. The United States is extreme in this regard and attempts to ignore status and authority distinctions between persons. These are not, by any means, universal values. Many societies are hierarchical, inegalitarian and strongly stratified. In them, rather strict norms of interaction operate between persons of dominant and subordinate status. In these societies, negotiating parties know the status and authority of those with whom they negotiate. Some would find it demeaning, or would refuse, to negotiate with a person of subordinate status. In this connection, it is also important to consider the status and roles of women in particular societies. Although Western societies attempt to draw few distinctions between men and women with regard to most opportunities in life, this is not the case in many traditional societies.

Beyond these rather obvious matters, there is a deeper question of how different societies conceptualize power and authority. Western European cultures typically associate power with decision making and conceive of power as vested in particular positions or offices, rather than as a personal possession of any particular individual. This conception is tied to the idea of limited authority. In the West, limiting the authority of particular offices limits the officeholder's ability to abuse the powers the office confers.

Asian conceptions of power and authority are different. Asians believe that authority is necessary and desirable, do not share the West's distrust of authority and power, and are less concerned with limiting them.[43] Furthermore, Asians view power as personal rather than as attached to offices.[44] "This view manifests itself in various forms, all associated with a central patron or set of patrons, each of whom has his or her own set of client-subordinates. The workplace is itself transformed . . . since the social organization that results links subordinates to their patrons . . . by intense bonds of obligation."[45]

In rather sharp contrast to Western notions, Asians also conceive of the possession of power as relieving, or sparing, the powerholder from accountability for decision making.[46] This conception of power fits well with the group orientation of Asian cultures, and maintains social stability and order. Those

---

[43] *Id.* at 34.

[44] VICTOR, *supra* note 10, at 172–173.

[45] *Id.* at 175.

[46] "In Chinese political culture, . . . in the ranks of the powerful, proof of importance lies precisely in being shielded from accountability." PYE, *supra* note 3, at 16.

below protect those above from criticism and defer to the assumed, intuited, or actual wishes of powerful patrons, rather than question them.

> Japan is a society where . . . the exercise of power plays a great part in influencing behavior while persuasive argumentation is less important. Powerful people command and exercise influence because the consequences of failing to do what a powerful person requires are feared as being devastating, even to the loss of one's social status and social acceptance, and perhaps even of one's livelihood.[47]

Group orientation and this particular conception of authority play out in negotiation in interesting ways. The Japanese, for example, always seek to develop and maintain a group consensus for any decision, negotiation decisions included. Japanese negotiators work as a team, but often the power person in the negotiation "will not be someone directly involved in the discussions, but rather a person on the sideline listening quietly."[48]

The inclusive nature of the Japanese decision-making process, while creating group cohesion, often creates negotiation difficulties as well.

> Japanese negotiating teams are usually not vested with sweeping powers to negotiate within their mandate. Instead, they are required to report back to the head office in minute detail each day, and request instructions on how to proceed the next day. Not infrequently what the team has agreed to during negotiations is unacceptable to the home office, or is impossible to build a consensus around, with the result that it later must be renegotiated. Often, it takes the head office time to reach a consensus on how to proceed, making the negotiating team appear to be stalling.[49]

In China, the need of negotiating officials to protect themselves from all possible criticism makes "Chinese negotiators exceptionally meticulous, astute, and tough, people who have extraordinary endurance and the ability to negotiate seemingly forever."[50] The same need, however, impels Chinese negotiators to refer many negotiation issues to their superiors, leading to substantial delay and frustration in negotiation.[51] By contrast, Korean organizations have centralized and autocratic power structures, and Korean executives often ignore their subordinates' views and opinions and reject terms they have negotiated.[52]

---

[47] March, *supra* note 6, at 22.

[48] Yasuharu Nagashima, *International Business Negotiations in Japan*, in James R. Silkenat & Jeffrey M. Aresty, The ABA Guide to international Business Negotiations 150, 155 (1994).

[49] *Id.* at 154.

[50] Pye, *supra* note 3, at 17.

[51] *Id.* at 17–18.

[52] Kyu Wha Lee, *International Business Negotiations in Korea*, in James R. Silkenat & Jeffrey M. Aresty, eds., The ABA Guide to International Business Negotiations 157, 159 (1994).

F. Role of law

In some cultures, predominantly European and North American, the rule of law plays a powerful role. These cultures are considered legalistic because they highly value law, legal rules, and the written word and consequently resort to legal proceedings and courts to resolve many disputes. The United States is probably the most extreme in this regard. American lawyers, for example, are famous, or infamous, for the length and extreme detail of their legal documents, a practice reflecting a deep impulse to attempt to anticipate and bring under some legal rule every possible contingency. There are other cultures, however, particularly Asian cultures, which place far less value on the rule of law as a regulatory and social ordering force and on legal proceedings and courts as appropriate fora for the resolution of disputes.

These rather disparate views of the role of law deeply affect the manner and aims of negotiation as between members of the respective cultural groups. Americans and, to a lesser extent, Europeans concern themselves with legal details and the specific terms and language of agreements. An operative assumption is that a party may violate the agreement and that there will have to be some kind of legal action in a court to resolve disputes. This assumption also has the consequence that many business negotiations involving Americans—and, to a considerably lesser extent, Europeans—are lawyer-laden. That is, legal considerations play a major role in deal-making, and lawyers act as business advisors and are often involved in negotiations.

Asian cultures simply do not see matters this way. Relatively homogeneous, certainly when compared to the United States or other immigrant societies, they emphasize group harmony, consensus, and face-saving. They also rely far more heavily on cultural and group norms and interpersonal relationships to regulate behavior than they do on law, legal rules and obligations, and the written word.

> The fundamental Japanese approach to contracts is to emphasize the relationship being created, instead of the document being drawn up. . . . [T]he written document . . . is only a tangible acknowledgment of a relationship between two or more parties rather than a precise instrument that defines the relationship. . . . Most Japanese assume that rights and duties under the contract, even when written down, are provisional and tentative rather than absolute. Instead of trying to spell out all possible contingencies and provisions for enforcement in inflexible terms, the Japanese prefer to handle problems as they arise, often recognizing the doctrine of "changed circumstances" (*jijo henko*).[53]

For such a culture, a concern about agreement breakdown suggests a lack

[53] MARCH, *supra* note 6, at 111–112.

of good faith and trust.[54] Involving lawyers in negotiations also signals mistrust, for it indicates the party will quickly resort to law, a move viewed as highly undesirable.

Koreans also prefer simple agreements, view contractual arrangements as fluid, and expect to work out problems as they arise rather than in advance.[55] In a somewhat similar way, Chinese from the People's Republic of China begin negotiations by focusing on broad goals and principles to which they seek the other side's agreement. In carrying out any agreement, the Chinese will proceed on the basis of these broad goals and principles rather than on the basis of the detailed terms of a written contract.[56]

In addition to understanding the distinctive views that different cultures take about the role of law, lawyers, and written agreements in their societies, it is important to realize that some countries do not have effective legal systems. In them, resort to law to enforce agreements or resolve disputes is not a realistic option. The People's Republic of China once abolished the country's legal system and its lawyers. Although it is now re-establishing its legal system, partly in response to international investment demands, that system, in contrast with those in the United States and Western Europe, is weak. The countries which made up the former Soviet Union, Russia chief among them, also presently have weak legal systems.

Finally, there are some countries in the world in which the legal system is either completely under the control of an authoritarian government, or corrupt, or both. In such systems, rule of law does not have much meaning. Parties from these countries know this and would think it ludicrous to have legalistic concerns. Negotiation and dispute resolution with such parties must be conducted outside the frameworks of law and an effectively functioning legal system, at least insofar as the issue is one of legal enforcement in their countries.

---

[54] *Id.* at 17.

[55] Lee, *supra* note 52.

[56] Ciricillo et al., *supra* note 1, at 12; Stanley B. Lubman, *Negotiations in China: Observations of a Lawyer,* in ROBERT A. KAPP, ED., COMMUNICATING WITH CHINA 59, 57 (1983).

BIBLIOGRAPHY

Abstruse, Robert M. and Joseph D. Harbaugh, Interviewing, Counseling, and Negotiating (Little, Brown and Co., 1990).

Alexander, Janet Cooper, *Do the Merits Matter? A Study of Settlements in Securities Class Actions*, 43 Stanford Law Review 497 (1991).

American Bar Association, Model Code of Professional Responsibility.

Ancona, Deborah G., Raymond A. Friedman, and Deborah M. Kolb, *The Group and What Happens on the Way to "Yes,"* 7 Negotiation Journal 155 (1991).

Applbaum, Arthur Isak, *Knowledge and Negotiation: Learning Under Conflict, Bargaining Under Uncertainty* (Unpublished Ph.D. dissertation, Harvard University, 1987).

Argyle, Michael, Cooperation: The Basis of Sociability (Routledge, 1991).

Arrow, Kenneth J., Robert H. Mnookin, Lee Ross, Amos Tversky, and Robert B. Wilson, Barriers to Conflict Resolution (W.W. Norton & Company, 1995).

Axelrod, Robert, The Evolution of Cooperation (New York: Basic Books, 1994).

Bacharach, Samuel B. and Edward J. Lawler, Bargaining: Power, Tactics, and Outcomes (Jossey-Bass, 1981).

Bacharach, Samuel B. and Edward J. Lawler, Power and Politics in Organizations (Jossey-Bass, 1980).

Baron, Jonathan, Thinking and Deciding, 2d. ed. (Cambridge University Press, 1988).

Bazerman, Max H. and John S. Carroll, *Negotiator Cognition*, in L.L. Cummings and Barry M. Staw, eds., Information and Cognition in Organizations 127–168 (JAI Press, Inc., 1990).

Bazerman, Max H. and Roy J. Lewicki, eds., Negotiating in Organizations (Sage, 1983).

Bazerman, Max H., Roy J. Lewicki, and Blair H. Sheppard, eds., Research on Negotiation in Organizations, 3 vols., (JAI Press, Inc., 1986).

Bazerman, Max H., Elizabeth A. Mannix, and Leigh L. Thompson, *Groups as Mixed-Motive Negotiations*, in Edward J. Lawler and Barry Markovsky, eds., Advances in Group Processes: Theory and Research, vol. 5 (JAI Press, Inc., 1988).

Bazerman, Max H. and Margaret A. Neale, *Negotiator Rationality and Negotiator Cognition: The Interactive Roles of Prescriptive and Descriptive Research*, in H. Peyton Young, ed., Negotiation Analysis (University of Michigan Press, 1991).

Bendahmane, E.P., and Moser, L.J., eds., Toward a Better Understanding of U.S.-Japan Relations 21 (U.S. Foreign Service Institute, 1986).

Bercovitch, Jacob, *Understanding Mediation's Role in Preventive Diplomacy*, 12 Negotiation Journal 241 (1996).

Bercovitch, Jacob, ed., Resolving International Conflicts (Lynne Reiner Publishers, 1996).

Binnendijk, Hans, ed., National Negotiating Styles (U.S. Foreign Service Institute, 1987).

Blake, Robert R. and Jane S. Mouton, Group Dynamics: Key to Decision-Making (Houston: Gulf Publishing, 1961).

Blake, Robert R. and Jane S. Mouton, Solving Costly Organizational Conflicts (Jossey-Bass, 1985).

Blaker, Michael, Japanese International Negotiating Style (Columbia University Press, 1977).

Bok, Sissela, Lying: Moral Choice in Public and Private Life (Vintage Books, 1978).

Bowyer, J. Barton, Cheating (St. Martin's Press, 1982).

Bradford, Leland P., Making Meetings Work: A Guide for Leaders and Group Members (University Associates, 1976).

Brams, Steven J., Negotiation Games (Routledge, 1990).

Brams, Steven J. and Alan Taylor, Fair Division (Cambridge University Press, 1996).

Brazil, Wayne D., Effective Approaches to Settlement (NJ: Prentice-Hall, 1988).

Brockner, Joel and Jeffrey Z. Rubin, Entrapment in Escalating Conflicts (Springer-Verlag, 1985).

Brooks, Earl and George S. Odiorne, Managing by Negotiations (Van Nostrand Reinhold Company, 1984).

Bunker, Barbara Benedict, Jeffrey Rubin, and associates, eds., Conflict, Cooperation, and Justice (Jossey-Bass, 1995).

Burton, John, Conflict: Resolution and Prevention (St. Martin's Press, 1990).

Caplow, Theodore, Two Against One (Englewood Cliffs, NJ: Prentice-Hall, 1968).

Carnevale, Peter J.D., Rodney G. Lim, and Mary E. McLaughlin, *Contingent Mediator Behavior and Its Effectiveness*, in Kenneth Kressel and Dean G. Pruitt, eds., Mediation Research: The Process and Effectiveness of Third-Party Intervention (Jossey-Bass, 1989).

Carpenter, Susan L. and W.J.D. Kennedy, Managing Public Disputes (Jossey-Bass, 1988).

Cartwright, Dorwin and Alvin Zander, eds., Group Dynamics, 3d ed. (Harper & Row, 1968).

Cialdini, Robert B., Influence (Morrow, 1984).

Ciricillo, Robert C., Adam Fremantle, and Jeanne M. Hamburg, *International Negotiations: A Cultural Perspective*, in James R. Silkenat and Jeffrey M. Aresty, eds., The ABA Guide to International Business Negotiations 5 (1994).

Cohen, Herb, You Can Negotiate Anything (L. Stuart, 1980).

Cohen, Raymond, *Cultural Aspects of International Mediation*, in Jacob Bercovitch, ed., Resolving International Conflicts 107 (1996).

Cohen, Raymond, Negotiating Across Cultures (United States Institute of Peace Press, 1991).

Condlin, Robert J., *"Cases on Both Sides": Patterns of Argument in Legal Dispute-Negotiation*, 44 Maryland Law Review 65 (1985).

Cooter, Robert, Stephen Marks, and Robert Mnookin, *Bargaining in the Shadow of the Law: A Testable Model of Strategic Behavior*, 11 Journal of Legal Studies 225 (1982).

Costantino, Cathy A. and Christina Sickles Merchant, Designing Conflict Management Systems (Jossey-Bass, 1996).

Dawes, Robyn M., Rational Choice in an Uncertain World (Harcourt, Brace, Jovanovich, 1988).

Deutsch, Morton, The Resolution of Conflict (Yale University Press, 1973).

Edwards, Harry T. and James J. White, The Lawyer as a Negotiator: Problems, Readings, and Materials (St. Paul: West, 1977).

Eisenberg, Theodore, *Testing the Selection Effect: A New Theoretical Framework with Empirical Tests*, 19 Journal of Legal Studies 337 (1990).

Fisher, Glen, Mindsets: The Role of Culture and Perception in International Relations (Intercultural Press, 1988).

Fisher, Roger, Elizabeth Kopelman, and Andrea Kupfer Schneider, Beyond Machiavelli (Harvard University Press, 1994).

Fisher, Roger and Scott Brown, Getting Together (Penguin, 1989).

Fisher, Roger and William L. Ury, Getting to Yes (Penguin, 1983).

Fisher, Roger, ed., International Conflict and Behavioral Science: The Craigville Papers (Basic Books, 1964).

Fisher, Ronald J., *Prenegotiation Problem-Solving Discussions: Enhancing the Potential for Successful Negotiation*, in Janice Gross Stein, ed., Getting to the Table: The Processes of International Negotiation 206 (1989).

Fisher, Ronald J., The Social Psychology of Intergroup and International Conflict Resolution (Springer-Verlag, 1990).

Folberg, Jay and Alison Taylor, Mediation (Jossey-Bass, 1984).

Follett, Mary Parker, Dynamic Administration: The Collected Papers of Mary Parker Follett, 2d ed. (Hippocrene Books, 1982).

Galanter, Marc, *Why the "Haves" Come Out Ahead: Speculations on the Limits of Legal Change*, 9 Law and Society Review 95 (1974).

Gamson, William A., *A Theory of Coalition Formation*, 26 American Sociological Review 373 (1961).

Gifford, Donald G., Legal Negotiation (West, 1989).

Gilovich, Thomas, How We Know What Isn't So (Free Press, 1991).

Goldberg, Stephen B., Eric D. Green, and Frank E.A. Sander, Dispute Resolution (Little, Brown, and Co., 1985).

Goldman, Alvin L., Settling For More (BNA Books, 1991).

Goodman, Gerald and Glenn Esterly, The Talk Book (Rodale Press, 1988).

Gottlieb, Marvin and William Healy, Making Deals: The Business of Negotiating (New York Institute of Finance, 1990).

Green, Eric D., *The Growth of the Mini-Trial*, 9 Litigation Journal 12 (1982).

Gross, Samuel R. and Kent D. Syverud, *Getting to No: A Study of Settlement Negotiations and the Selection of Cases for Trial*, 90 Michigan Law Review 319 (1991).

Guernsey, Thomas F., *Truthfulness in Negotiation*, 17 University of Richmond Law Review 99 (1982).

Gulliver, P.H., Disputes and Negotiations (Academic Press, 1979).

Hackman, J. Richard, ed., Groups That Work (Jossey-Bass, 1990).

Hall, Edward T., Beyond Culture (1976).

Henry, John F., *Mini-Trials*, 1 Negotiation Journal 13 (1985).

Holler, Manfred J., Coalitions and Collective Action (Physica-Verlag, 1984).

Hopmann, P. Terence, The Negotiation Process and the Resolution of International Conflicts (Johns Hopkins University Press, 1996).

Jandt, Fred E., Win-Win Negotiating (John Wiley and Sons, 1985).

Kagel, Sam and Kathy Kelly, The Anatomy of Mediation (BNA Books, 1989).

Kahan, James P. and Amnon Rapoport, Theories of Coalition Formation (Lawrence Erlbaum Associates, Inc., 1984).

Kahneman, Daniel and Amos Tversky, *Conflict Resolution: A Cognitive Perspective*, in Kenneth J. Arrow, Robert H. Mnookin, Lee Ross, Amos Tversky, and Robert B. Wilson, eds., Barriers to Conflict Resolution (W.W. Norton and Co., 1995).

Kahneman, Daniel and Amos Tversky, *Prospect Theory: An Analysis of Decision Under Risk*, 47 Econometrica 263 (1979).

Kahneman, Daniel, Paul Slovic, and Amos Tversky, eds., Judgment Under Uncertainty: Heuristics and Biases (Cambridge University Press, 1982).

Kapp, Robert A., ed., Communicating with China (Intercultural Press, 1983).

Keeney, Ralph L. and Howard Raiffa, *Structuring and Analyzing Values for Multiple-Issue Negotiations*, in H. Peyton Young, ed., Negotiation Analysis (University of Michigan Press, 1991).

Keeney, Ralph, Values Focused Thinking (Cambridge, Mass.: Harvard University Press, 1992).

Kelly, Michael, *This Year's Model*, The New Yorker Magazine (June 17, 1996).

Kepner, Charles H. and Benjamin B. Tregoe, The New Rational Manager (Princeton Research Press, 1981).

Kim, Young Yun and Gudykunst, William B., eds., Theories in Intercultural Communication (Sage Publications, 1988).

Kolb, Deborah M., The Mediators, (Cambridge, Mass.: MIT Press, 1983).

Kolb, Deborah M. and Jean M. Bartunek, eds., Hidden Conflict in Organizations (Sage Publications, 1992).

Komorita, S.S. and Jerome M. Chertkoff, *A Bargaining Theory of Coalition Formation*, 80 Psychological Review 149 (1973).

Kreisberg, Louis, International Conflict Resolution (Yale University Press, 1992).

Kressel, Kenneth, Dean G. Pruitt, and associates, eds., Mediation Research: The Process and Effectiveness of Third-Party Intervention (Jossey-Bass, 1989).

Kritzer, Herbert M., The Justice Broker (Oxford University Press, 1990).

Kritzer, Herbert M., Let's Make a Deal (University of Wisconsin Press, 1991).

Lambros, Thomas D., *The Federal Rules of Civil Procedure: A New Adversarial Model for a New Era*, University of Pittsburgh Law Review 789 (1989).

Lax, David A. and James K. Sebenius, *Thinking Coalitionally: Party Arithmetic, Process Opportunism, and Strategic Sequencing*, in H. Peyton Young, ed., Negotiation Analysis (University of Michigan Press, 1991).

Lax, David A. and James K. Sebenius, The Manager as Negotiator (Free Press, 1986).

Lebow, Richard Ned, The Art of Bargaining (Johns Hopkins University Press, 1996).

Lee, Kyu Wha, *International Business Negotiations in Korea,* in James R. Silkenat and Jeffrey M. Aresty, eds., The ABA Guide to International Business Negotiations 157 (1994).

Lewicki, Roy J. and Joseph A. Litterer, Negotiation (R.D. Irwin, 1985).

Lubman, Stanley B., *Negotiations in China: Observations of a Lawyer*, in Robert A. Kapp, ed., Communicating with China 57 (1983).

Maggiolo, Walter A., Techniques of Mediation (Oceana Publications, 1985).

March, James G. and Herbert A. Simon, Organizations (Wiley, 1958).

March, Robert M., The Japanese Negotiator (Tokyo: Kodansha International, 1988).

Mather, Lynn and Barbara Yngvesson, *Language, Audience, and the Transformation of Disputes*, 15 Law and Society Review 775 (1981).

Mautner-Markhof, Frances, ed., Processes of International Negotiations (Westview Press, 1989).

McKean, Kevin, *Decisions*, Discover Magazine (June, 1985).

McMillan, John, Games, Strategies, and Managers (Oxford University Press, 1992).

Menkel-Meadow, Carrie, *Toward Another View of Legal Negotiation: The Structure of Problem Solving*, 31 UCLA Law Review 754 (1984).

Moore, Christopher W., *"Have Process Will Travel": Reflections on Democratic Decision Making and Conflict Management Practice Abroad*, Forum 1 (Winter, 1993).

Moore, Christopher W., The Mediation Process, 2d ed. (Jossey-Bass, 1996).

Moser, Leo J., *Cross-cultural Dimensions: U.S.-Japan*, in E.P. Bendahmane and L.J. Moser, eds., Toward a Better Understanding of U.S.-Japan Relations 21 (U.S. Foreign Service Institute, 1986).

Nagashima, Yasuharu, *International Business Negotiations in Japan,* in James R. Silkenat and Jeffrey M. Aresty, eds., The ABA Guide to International Business Negotiations 150 (1994).

Neale, Margaret A. and Max H. Bazerman, *The Effects of Framing and Negotiator Overconfidence on Bargaining Behaviors and Outcomes,* 28 Academy of Management Journal 34 (1985).

Nisbett, Richard and Lee Ross, Human Inference, Strategies and Shortcomings of Social Judgment (Prentice-Hall, 1980).

Perschbacher, Rex R., *Regulating Lawyers' Negotiations*, 27 Arizona Law Review 75 (1985).

Pfeffer, Jeffrey, Power in Organizations (Marshfield, Mass.: Pitman, 1981).

Priest, George L. and Benjamin Klein, *The Selection of Disputes for Litigation,* 13 Journal of Legal Studies 1 (1984).

Princen, Thomas, Intermediaries in International Conflict (Princeton University Press, 1995).

Pruitt, Dean G., *Negotiation Between Organizations: A Branching Chain Model,* 10 Negotiation Journal 217 (1994).

Pruitt, Dean G., Negotiation Behavior (Academic Press, 1981).

Pruitt, Dean G. and Jeffery Z. Rubin, Social Conflict (Random House, 1986).

Pruitt, Dean G. and Peter J. Carnevale, Negotiation in Social Conflict (Brooks/Cole Publishing Co., 1993).

Pye, Lucian W., Chinese Negotiating Style (Quorum Books, 1992).

Pye, Lucian, Chinese Commercial Negotiating Style (Oelgeschlager, Gunn & Hain, Publishers, Inc., 1982).

Raiffa, Howard, The Art and Science of Negotiation (Harvard University Press, 1982).

Riskin, Leonard, *Mediation and Lawyers*, 43 Ohio State Law Journal 29 (1982).

Rogers, Nancy H. and Craig A. McEwen, Mediation: Law, Policy, and Practice (Lawyers Cooperative and San Francisco: Bancroft-Whitney, 1989).

Rubin, Jeffery Z. and Bert Brown, Social Psychology in Bargaining and Negotiation (Academic Press, 1975).

Sander, Frank E.A. and Stephen B. Goldberg, *Fitting the Forum to the Fuss,* 10 Negotiation Journal 49 (1994).

Schelling, Thomas, The Strategy of Conflict (Harvard University Press, 1960).

Sebenius, James K., Negotiating the Law of the Sea (Harvard University Press, 1984).

Shaw, Marvin E., Group Dynamics (McGraw-Hill, 1971).

Shenkar, Oded and Simcha Ronen, *The Cultural Context of Negotiations: The Implications of Chinese Interpersonal Norms*, 23 Journal of Applied Behavioral Science 263 (1987).

Sheppard, Blair H., Max H. Bazerman, and Roy J. Lewicki, Research on Negotiation in Organizations, 2 vols. (JAI Press, Inc., 1990).

Sibley, Susan S. and Sally E. Merry, *Mediator Settlement Strategies*, 8 Law and Policy 7 (1986).

Silkenat, James R. and Jeffrey M. Aresty, eds., The ABA Guide to International Business Negotiations (American Bar Association, 1994).

Singer, Linda R., Settling Disputes, 2d. ed. (Westview Press, 1990).

Smith, Raymond F., Negotiating with the Soviets (Indiana University Press, 1989).

Solomon, Richard H., Chinese Political Negotiating Behavior (Rand, 1995).

Stein, Janice Gross, ed., Getting to the Table: The Processes of International Negotiation (Johns Hopkins University Press, 1989).

Stein, Janice Gross, *Getting to the Table: The Triggers, Stages, Functions, and Consequences of Prenegotiation*, in Janice Gross Stein, ed., Getting to the Table: The Processes of International Negotiation 239 (1989)

Stewart, Edward C., American Cultural Patterns: A Cross-Cultural Perspective (Intercultural Press, 1972).

Susskind, Lawrence and Jeffrey Cruikshank, Breaking the Impasse (Basic Books, 1987).

Tedeschi, James T., Barry R. Schlenker, and Thomas V. Bonoma, Conflict, Power and Games: The Experimental Study of Interpersonal Relations (Aldine, 1973).

Thayer, Nathaniel B. and Stephen B. Weiss, *The Changing Logic of a Former Minor Power*, in Hans Binnendijk, ed., National Negotiating Styles (U.S. Foreign Service Institute, 1987)

Thibaut, John W. and Harold H. Kelly, The Social Psychology of Groups (Transaction, Inc., 1986).

Ting-Toomey, Stella, *Intercultural Conflict Styles, A Face-Negotiation Theory*, in Young Yun Kim and William B. Gudykunst, eds., Theories in Intercultural Communication 213 (1988).

Triandis, Harry, Robert Bontempo, Marcelo J. Villareal, Masaaki Asai, and Nydia Lucca, *Individualism and Collectivism: Cross-Cultural Perspectives on Self-Ingroup Relationships*, 54 Journal of Personality and Social Psychology 323 (1988).

Tucker, Jonathan B., *Interagency Bargaining and International Negotiation: Lessons from the Open Skies Treaty Talks*, 12 Negotiation Journal 275 (1996).

Tversky, Amos and Daniel Kahneman, *Judgment Under Uncertainty: Heuristics and Biases*, 185 Science 1124 (1974).

Tversky, Amos and Daniel Kahneman, *The Framing of Decisions and the Psychology of Choice*, 211 Science 453 (1981).

Ury, William L., Jeanne M. Brett, and Stephen B. Goldberg, Getting Disputes Resolved (Jossey-Bass, 1988).

Victor, David A., International Business Communication (Harper Collins, 1992).

von Winterfeldt, Detlof and Ward Edwards, Decision Analysis and Behavioral Research (Cambridge University Press, 1986).

Wall, James A., Negotiation: Theory and Practice (Scott, Foresman, 1985).

Walton, Richard E. and Robert B. McKersie, A Behavioral Theory of Labor Negotiations (McGraw Hill, 1965).

Wenke, Robert A., The Art of Negotiation for Lawyers (Richter Publications, 1985).

Wetlaufer, Gerald B., *The Ethics of Lying in Negotiations*, 75 Iowa Law Review 1219 (1990).

White, James J., *Machiavelli and the Bar: Ethical Limitations on Lying in Negotiation*, 1980 American Bar Foundation Research Journal 926 (1980).

Winham, Gilbert R., *The Prenegotiation Phase and the Uruguay Round*, in Janice Gross Stein, ed., Getting to the Table: The Processes of International Negotiation 44 (1989).

Winham, Gilbert R., International Trade and the Tokyo Round Negotiation (Princeton University Press, 1986).

Wolfram, Charles W., Modern Legal Ethics (West, 1986).

Yergin, Daniel, The Prize (Simon and Schuster, 1991).

Young, H. Peyton, ed., Negotiation Analysis (University of Michigan Press, 1991).

Zander, Alvin F., Making Groups Effective (Jossey-Bass, 1982).

Zander, Alvin F., The Purposes of Groups and Organizations (Jossey-Bass, 1985).

Zartman, I. William and Maureen R. Berman, The Practical Negotiator (Yale University Press, 1982).

Zimmerman, Mark R., How to Do Business With the Japanese (Random House, 1985).

INDEX

www.ingramcontent.com/pod-product-compliance
Lightning Source LLC
LaVergne TN
LVHW090311210926
848480LV00001B/213